HORACE *ODES* I

Horace *Odes* I

Carpe Diem

DAVID WEST

CLARENDON PRESS · OXFORD
1995

OXFORD
UNIVERSITY PRESS

Great Clarendon Street, Oxford OX2 6DP

Oxford University Press is a department of the University of Oxford.
It furthers the University's objective of excellence in research, scholarship,
and education by publishing worldwide in

Oxford New York

Athens Auckland Bangkok Bogotá Buenos Aires Calcutta
Cape Town Chennai Dar es Salaam Delhi Florence Hong Kong Istanbul
Karachi Kuala Lumpur Madrid Melbourne Mexico City Mumbai
Nairobi Paris São Paulo Singapore Taipei Tokyo Toronto Warsaw

with associated companies in Berlin Ibadan

Oxford is a registered trade mark of Oxford University Press
in the UK and in certain other countries

Published in the United States
by Oxford University Press Inc., New York

British Library Cataloguing in Publication Data

Data available

Library of Congress Cataloging in Publication Data

Carpe diem: Horace Odes I / [edited, translated,
and with an introduction by] David West.
Includes bibliographical references.
1. Horace—Translations into English.
2. Laudatory poetry, Latin—Translations into English.
3. Odes—Translations into English.   4. Rome—Poetry.
I. West, David Alexander.   II. Title.
PA6395.W4   1995   8749.01—dc20   94-44514
ISBN 0-19-872160-9
ISBN 0-19-872161-7 (pbk.)

3 5 7 9 10 8 6 4

Printed in Great Britain on acid-free paper by
Bookcraft (Bath) Ltd., Midsomer Norton

Acknowledgement

I am deeply grateful to Rosemary Burton, who has read several drafts of everything in this book and made innumerable corrections and suggestions.

Contents

Introduction

THE PURPOSE

Horace is one of the world's greatest lyric poets, but not one of the most accessible. I would like this book to do three things: to help non-Latinists who like poetry to enjoy Horace; to stimulate young people who have to study the poems; and to add to the scholarly debate by putting forward my own views, which seem on occasion to go against present-day orthodoxies. For me Horace is a profound poet of love, religion, and friendship, with a powerful sense of humour and love of fantasy, a master of tone and pace and shape. The book tries to demonstrate this by translating the poems and adding brief comments to explain how they work.

DEBTS

Those who wish to go more deeply should start with the great commentaries by Nisbet and Hubbard (1970) and Syndikus (1972). These have won new understanding for us by their immense learning and sound sense, and I have repeatedly pillaged them without acknowledgement. After working through them and the works they refer to, students could make a beginning on the vast amount of writing on the *Odes* by consulting the works referred to ode by ode in the more recent commentaries by Quinn and Romano. Their next step would be to use the annual entries in *L'Année philologique* and the bibliography by Kissel. This book does not pretend to provide a systematic bibliography, but where my thefts are glaring or the countercase is important, I give a bare name of the author in the text and full reference in the List of Works at the end.

THE TRADITION

Horace's advice to young writers was to study the Greek models by day and by night (*Ars Poetica* 268–9) and he had certainly done that himself.

There was a political background to this strategy. In Horace's lifetime the Romans had clearly emerged as the rulers of the Mediterranean world, but they knew that in art, architecture, literature, music, philosophy, scholarship, and science, they were far behind the Greeks. After Octavian's victory over Antony and Cleopatra at Actium in 31 BC, Octavian set himself to build the greatest city the world had seen and create a civilization to rival or surpass what the Greeks had achieved. In the 20s Virgil, for instance, was writing an epic which was expected to be greater than Homer's *Iliad* (so Propertius, 2. 34. 66), and Horace was writing odes which he dared to hope (in 1. 1. 35–6) would add a Roman name to the canon of the nine great lyric poets of Greece.

The thirty-eight poems in this first book are all inspired by his predecessors, of whom the most important were Alcaeus, who wrote his poems of love and war and wine in Lesbos at the beginning of the sixth century BC, and the Boeotian Pindar (518–438 BC) whose odes celebrating victories in the great games of Greece seemed to Horace to attain a sublimity beyond the trajectory of any other poet (*Odes* 4. 2. 1–32). Horace showed his reverence by imitating Pindar in points of style and in tackling Pindaric themes: politics, religion, mythology, ethics. Callimachus (*c.*305–*c.*240 BC) cataloguer of the great Library of the Ptolemies at Alexandria, was an influence for his wit, scepticism, originality, and distaste for pretentiousness. Horace showed also that he was more than a match for the skill and sophistication of the poets preserved for us in the *Palatine Anthology* of Greek epigrams. His *Odes* used all that earlier poetry, and everything he used he made his own. Samples of the writings of these Greek poets and discussions of Horace's treatment of them can be found under their names in the Brief Notes on Ancient Authors at the end of this book.

THE LIFE

How was a political system which evolved to meet the needs of a market town to cope with the demands of a world empire? How could its annually elected magistrates gain military experience and learn to deal with the temptations and responsibilities of conquest? How were they to reward their victorious troops if they had to return to private life after their year in office? Such problems as these led to the Civil Wars which filled more than the first half of Horace's life.

He was born in 65 BC, two years before Octavian. When Julius Caesar was assassinated on the Ides of March 44 BC, Horace was studying in Athens. Brutus, the leading conspirator, withdrew there, and when he raised an army Horace received a commission as a *tribunus militum*, roughly brigadier rank. Brutus and Cassius were defeated at Philippi in 42 BC by the armies of Antony and Octavian, who was Caesar's great-nephew and adopted son and heir, and Horace returned to Rome to find employment in the treasury, as a *scriba quaestorius*. Early in the 30s he was introduced to Maecenas, who was one of Octavian's principal advisers. While working on his first book of *Satires* in the 30s he received from Maecenas an estate in the Sabine hills north-east of Rome. By the year 31 and the decisive victory at Actium, Horace had started work on the *Odes*. The following year saw the publication of the *Epodes* and the second book of *Satires*. In 29 Octavian came back to Rome to celebrate a triple triumph. In 28 he took the name Augustus and dedicated the great temple of Apollo next to his home on the Palatine Hill. The first three books of *Odes* all came out together in 23 and were followed by the first book of the *Epistles* in 20, the second book piecemeal in 18–14. Horace was asked to compose the *Carmen Saeculare* to be performed at the Secular Games of 17, and his final work was the fourth book of the *Odes* in 13. According to the short biography by Suetonius, Maecenas died in 8 BC and in his will, which left all his property to Augustus, there was a clause 'Be mindful of Horatius Flaccus as though he were myself', *Horati Flacci ut mei memor esto*. Horace died fifty-nine days after his friend, and was buried on the furthest part of the Esquiline Hill next to Maecenas' tomb.

THE SOUND

Sound is part of the essence of poetry but even with the help of Allen's *Vox Latina* we cannot recapture the sound of Latin, let alone the sound of Horace's verse. Nevertheless the closer we can come to it, the nearer we come to the essence of the poetry. Beginners could do worse than pretend they are speaking Italian, but with -c- and -g- always hard.

Horatian metres are easy. Vowels are treated as long (–) or short (◡) and if readers know the metrical plan (see Appendix on Metre), they will find it fits the words of the poem snugly and without any problems. For example the first two lines in the book run – – –◡◡– –◡◡– ◡~ (the last syllable being either long or short) and that is the perfect template for:

Maece	nas atavis	edite re	gibus
o et	praesidi et	dulce decus	meum.

The quantities offer a repetitive pattern and to read by quantity alone would be as fatal to Latin as it would be to read by stress alone in English:

> Shall Í compáre thee tó a súmmer's dáy?
> Thou árt more lóvely ánd more témperáte.

This is rank doggerel. In English the iambic rhythm is an expectation against which we hear principally the sense of the utterance as we interpret it, perhaps:

> Sháll I compáre thee to a súmmer's dáy?
> Thou art more lóvely and more témperate.

In Latin we hear a triple counterpoint. Against the fixed pattern of the quantities there play the stresses on the individual words, on the second last syllable if it is long, as in *Maecénas*, and on the third last syllable if the second last is short, as in *átavis*. So the stresses run:

> Maecénas átavis édite régibus
> ó et praesídi et dúlce décus méum

and we hear the emphasis borne by the symmetry of the last three words of the first line and by the different symmetry of the last three words of the second. Against these two elements there runs the third, the sense of the utterance as we understand it.

The metrical patterns are given in the Appendix on Metres. Obvious refinements to listen for are the cadence in the short fourth line of Sapphic stanzas, and the ritardando in the third line of the Alcaics followed by the release in the fourth.

Beginners would be well advised to avoid the dactylic metres. Here a long syllable is taken to be equal to two shorts. The standard foot is therefore either a dactyl $-\smile\smile$ or a spondee $--$. The result is that the long lines in 1. 7, for instance, cannot be read without some knowledge of the quantities of Latin syllables. In effect lines 1, 3, 5, and 7 run:

```
 --    -⌣⌣   --    -⌣⌣   -⌣⌣   --
-⌣⌣    --    --    -⌣⌣   -⌣⌣   --
-⌣⌣   -⌣⌣    --    --    -⌣⌣   -⌣
-⌣⌣    --    --    --    -⌣⌣   -⌣
```

The dactylic rhythm is reasserted at the end of each verse but the first four feet all offer a choice.

Elision offers another complication. A word ending with a vowel or -m- loses its final syllable in scansion if it is followed by a word beginning with a vowel or -h-. Hence *praesidi{um} et* in the second line above. But Latin loves exceptions. The rule can be ignored, for obvious reasons, with exclamations. So not {*o*} *et* as one syllable, but *o et* spoken as two syllables.

A good next step for a beginner would be to study the much more substantial account in Goold's Catullus and then the metrical section of Nisbet and Hubbard's introduction.

THE TEXT

The text printed is the Oxford Classical Text by E. C. Wickham in its second edition by H. W. Garrod (1912) with variations as follows:

1.13 dimoveas]demoveas
2.39 Mauri]Marsi
6.19 cantamus vacui, sive quid urimur]cantamus, vacui sive quid urimur,
7.27 auspice: Teucri]auspice Teucro
8.2   hoc deos vere]te deos oro
8.6   equitet]equitat
8.7   temperet]temperat
9.18 campus]Campus
12.31 †quia]quom
13.6 manent]manet
15.20 cultus]crinis
15.22 gentis]genti
17.9 Haediliae]haediliae
20.5 care]clare
21.8 Cragi]Gragi
23.5 veris]vepris
23.6 adventus]ad ventum
25.20 Hebro]Euro
26.9 Piplei]Pimplei
31.11 culullis]culillis
31.18 at]et
32.1 poscimur.]poscimus

Odes Book 1

I

MAECENAS atavis edite regibus,
o et praesidium et dulce decus meum,
sunt quos curriculo pulverem Olympicum
collegisse iuvat, metaque fervidis

evitata rotis, palmaque nobilis   5
terrarum dominos evehit ad deos;
hunc, si mobilium turba Quiritium
certat tergeminis tollere honoribus;

illum, si proprio condidit horreo
quidquid de Libycis verritur areis.   10
gaudentem patrios findere sarculo
agros Attalicis condicionibus

numquam demoveas ut trabe Cypria
Myrtoum pavidus nauta secet mare.
luctantem Icariis fluctibus Africum   15
mercator metuens otium et oppidi

laudat rura sui; mox reficit ratis
quassas, indocilis pauperiem pati.
est qui nec veteris pocula Massici
nec partem solido demere de die   20

spernit, nunc viridi membra sub arbuto
stratus, nunc ad aquae lene caput sacrae.
multos castra iuvant et lituo tubae
permixtus sonitus bellaque matribus

detestata. manet sub Iove frigido   25
venator tenerae coniugis immemor,
seu visa est catulis cerva fidelibus,
seu rupit teretes Marsus aper plagas.

me doctarum hederae praemia frontium
dis miscent superis, me gelidum nemus   30
nympharumque leves cum Satyris chori
secernunt populo, si neque tibias

2

I

Maecenas, sprung from an ancient line of kings,
my stronghold, my pride, and my delight,
there are some who enjoy collecting Olympic dust
on their chariot, and if they graze the turning-post

with scorching wheels and win the palm of glory,   5
they are lords of the earth and rise to the gods;
one man is pleased if the fickle mob of Roman citizens
competes to lift him up to triple honours;

another, if he stores away in his own granary
all the sweepings from the threshing-floors of Libya;   10
the man who delights to cleave his ancestral fields
with the mattock, you could never move, not with the legacy

of Attalus, to become a frightened sailor
and cut the Myrtoan Sea with Cyprian timbers;
the merchant, afraid of the African gale brawling   15
with Icarian waves, praises leisure and the countryside

round his own home town, but soon rebuilds his shattered
ships—he cannot learn to endure poverty;
there is a man who sees no objection to drinking
old Massic wine or taking time out of the day,   20

stretched out sometimes under the green arbutus,
sometimes by a gently welling spring of sacred water;
some enjoy the camp, the sound of the trumpet merged
in the bugle, the wars that mothers

abhor; staying out under a cold sky,   25
the huntsman forgets his tender wife
if his faithful dogs catch sight of a hind
or a Marsian boar bursts the delicate nets;

as for me, it is ivy, the reward of learned brows,
that puts me among the gods above. As for me,   30
the cold grove and the light-footed choruses of nymphs
with Satyrs set me apart from the people

3

Odes 1. 1

Euterpe cohibet nec Polyhymnia
Lesboum refugit tendere barbiton.
   quodsi me lyricis vatibus inseres,   35
   sublimi feriam sidera vertice.

H ow serious is Horace? The heart of this poem (lines 3–33) is a
survey of nine different ways of life. Without a single word of open
disapproval or of mockery, Horace succeeds in making all of them,
including his own, seem slightly ridiculous. He has a battery of devices
at his disposal. First, he exaggerates. Olympic victors are not quite lords
of the earth (6); no grain merchant could pack *all* the grain winnowed on
the threshing-floors of Libya into a single granary, let alone everything
so winnowed, *quidquid verritur* (10); nobody is going to offer an Italian
peasant a legacy on the terms of that bequeathed to the Roman people
by Attalus III, who gave the glorious Pergamene Empire to the Roman
people in 133 BC. Second, he pounces on strangely vivid details to char-
acterize the different lives. The charioteer is a dust collector; the sparks
fly from his iron-shod wheels as he scrapes the turning-post; the peasant
would never cut the sea with a beam (*trabs*, a wooden beam, a ship); the
wild boar plunges through the fine nets set for small game. Third, he
mischievously suggests the absurdity of human behaviour by describing
different ambitions in similar terms. *Plus ça change, plus c'est la même
chose.* The palm raises the charioteer; the people lift the politician; the
people, too, compete like both of them (*certat*, 8); charioteers, it goes
without saying, move quickly but the people, these Quirites, sons of
Romulus, are also mobile (in line 7 'fickle' translates *mobilium*). The
Italian peasant splitting clods and rocks with the day-long, overhead
swing of a heavy mattock would not wish to be a sailor cleaving the sea.
The storm-tossed merchant praises leisure and the drinker enjoys it. The
soldier is linked with the man engaged in hunting, which Horace else-
where calls Roman campaigning, *Romana militia* (*Satires* 2. 2. 10–11),
by allusions to domestic affections, of mothers, of a wife and faithful
dogs. Fourth, after insinuating that one human ambition is like another,
he keeps a sense of the absurd running through the poem by pointing out
differences. The grain merchant stores what Libyans grow; the peasant
tills his native soil. He is surrounded by three lives all demanding move-
ment; nothing will move him. And Horace has fun shaping the geo-
graphical terms from Italy to Cyprus and to the Myrtoan Sea between
Greece and the Cyclades, then from the Icarian Sea off Asia Minor
swept by winds from Africa back to an Italian country town and its

if Euterpe lets me play her pipes, and Polyhymnia
does not withhold the lyre of Lesbos.
But if you enrol me among the lyric bards   35
my soaring head will strike the stars.

hinterland. Then after these first four strenuous activities we leave the
wild sea and come to a solitary, idle drinker lying by a gentle spring, fol-
lowed by a soldier enjoying a more strident music. When the huntsman
under the *cold* sky forgets his *tender* wife, in this chain of contrasts it
may not be absurd to suggest that *frigido* is in some sense an opposite of
tenerae.

So Horace has gently mocked eight different ambitions of men. Now,
typically, he ends with himself. German scholars call it the *Ich-Schluss*.
How serious is Horace about poetry? He certainly deploys the same
devices in his own case. He exaggerates when he says that he mingles
with the gods. He picks on amusing details when he visualizes nymphs
with satyrs. (The nymphs are nimble-footed because in that company
they have to be.) He uses the same terms for his own aspirations as he
used for the aspiration of others. He may win a crown of ivy as the cha-
rioteer wins the palm and each is raised to the gods, Horace even to the
stars. He glories in the cold grove of the Muses and the huntsman waits
under a chilly sky.

Is the poem, therefore, little more than a sheepish apology for
Horace's own enthusiasm and is Horace little more than a harmless
humorist? Surely not. The first clue lies in the form:

> Some glory in their birth, some in their skill,
> Some in their wealth, some in their body's force
>
> .   .   .   .
>
> But these particulars are not my measure;
> All these I better in one general best
>
> (Shakespeare, *Sonnet* 65).

This is a common form in classical Greek and Latin literature. Scholars
call it the 'priamel', an invented word meaning simply 'preamble'.
Sappho (fragment 16) gives a compact example:

> Some say that an army of horsemen
> is the most beautiful thing upon the black earth,
> others an army of foot-soldiers or a fleet of ships,
>   but for me it is whatever one loves.

5

Odes 1. 1

The expectation in the priamel is that the last item is preferred. Horace teases us by means of the details we have just noted but the expectation stands despite the gentle self-mockery.

OLYMPA

PINDAR

The second clue to this poem is Pindar. When Horace begins a collection of lyric poems in Rome with talk of chariot-races in the Olympic arena, this is a clear signal that he is aware of the composer of the Olympian Odes. When, by ring composition, he talks about being enrolled among the lyric bards, this is a reference to the canon of nine Greek lyric poets of whom the first and greatest was Pindar, 'the ruler of the lyric cohort', *regnator lyricae cohortis*, (Statius, *Silvae* 4. 7. 5). At line 34 he announces his debt to Sappho and Alcaeus, the poets of Lesbos, but he has already called on Pindar by implication in talking of the pipes of the Muse Euterpe. Monodic (solo) lyric poets accompany themselves on the lyre, but no poet can sing and blow a pipe at the same time. The pipe here is the mark of choral lyric and therefore a statement of Pindaric intent. Horace will attempt to write poetry which, in so far as the language and the age permit, will be able to stand beside all the great lyric poetry of Greece.

LYRIC

Horace is deeply serious, but not solemn. Rome had never seen a collection of poems like these three books which came out in 23 BC and Horace is too fly a bird to start with lofty claims for his achievement. 'There is a man who does not despise draughts of old Massic' he says at line 18 in a nice understatement. We might be tempted to put a name to that man. We should certainly be wise to remember the understatement and the smile.

In Horace the tone is often elusive. Perhaps the nearest thing in English is the parody by Kipling in 'A Diversity of Creatures':

> There are whose study is of smells,
>   Who to attentive schools rehearse
> How something mixed with something else
>   Makes something worse.

Odes 1. 1

Some cultivate in broths impure
  The clients of our body; these,
Increasing without Venus, cure
  Or cause disease.

Others the heated wheel extol,
  And all its offspring, whose concern
Is how to make it farthest roll
  and fastest turn.

Me, much incurious if the hour
  present, or to be paid for, brings
Me to Brundisium by the power
  Of wheels or wings,

Me, in whose breast no flame has burned
  Life long, save that by Pindar lit,
Such lore leaves cold; nor have I turned
  Aside for it,

More than when, sunk in thought profound
  of what the unaltered Gods require,
My steward (friend but slave) brings round
  Logs for my fire.

Here too is the priamel with variation, in the opening word of each
occupation ('There are whose . ∴. Some . . . Others . . .'). Here too we
hear the technical perfection of the verse and enjoy the humour carried
in the grave poetic diction. Here, too, when we come to Pindar and the
love of poetry, the tone modulates. In Kipling it modulates towards an
acceptance of the unalterable laws of life and an appreciation of its
pleasures. This is not the turn taken by Horace at the end of Odes 1. 1,
but it is profoundly Horatian, even to the triple *me*.

II

IAM satis terris nivis atque dirae
grandinis misit Pater et rubente
dextera sacras iaculatus arces
    terruit urbem,

terruit gentis, grave ne rediret   5
saeculum Pyrrhae nova monstra questae,
omne cum Proteus pecus egit altos
    visere montis,

piscium et summa genus haesit ulmo
nota quae sedes fuerat columbis,   10
et superiecto pavidae natarunt
    aequore dammae.

vidimus flavum Tiberim retortis
litore Etrusco violenter undis
ire deiectum monumenta regis   15
    templaque Vestae,

Iliae dum se nimium querenti
iactat ultorem, vagus et sinistra
labitur ripa Iove non probante u-
    xorius amnis.   20

audiet civis acuisse ferrum
quo graves Persae melius perirent,
audiet pugnas vitio parentum
    rara iuventus.

quem vocet divum populus ruentis   25
imperi rebus? prece qua fatigent
virgines sanctae minus audientem
    carmina Vestam?

cui dabit partis scelus expiandi
Iuppiter? tendem venias precamur   30
nube candentis umeros amictus,
    augur Apollo;

Already Father Jupiter has sent enough fierce hail
and snow and his red right arm has struck
his holy citadel and brought
    fear to the city

and fear to the nations. The cruel age of Pyrrha seemed   5
to be returning, when she bewailed strange sights
and Proteus drove his herds to visit
    the high mountains,

shoals of fishes stuck in the tops
of elms where once the doves had nested   10
and deer swam in terror in seas thrown down
    upon the earth.

We have seen yellow Tiber wrench his waves back
from the Tuscan shore and rush
to hurl down king Numa's memorials   15
    and Vesta's temple,

to show himself the avenger of Ilia's loud grievances.
Leaving his course, without the blessing
of Jupiter, the doting husband flooded
    the left bank.   20

Young men will hear that fellow citizens sharpened swords
that should rather have slain Persians. They will hear—
what few there are, thanks to the sins of their fathers—
    of the battles that were fought.

What god can the people call upon to shore up   25
their crumbling empire? What prayer can the Virgins
din into the ears of Vesta who does not hear
    their chanting?

To whom will Jupiter give the task of expiating
our crime? Come at long last, we pray,   30
your white shoulders veiled in cloud,
    augur Apollo;

9

q hic φιλοψγώδγ:

sive tu mavis, Erycina ridens,
quam Iocus circum volat et Cupido;
sive neglectum genus et nepotes   35
   respicis auctor,

heu nimis longo satiate ludo,
quem iuvat clamor galeaeque leves
acer et Marsi peditis cruentum
   vultus in hostem;   40

sive mutata iuvenem figura
ales in terris imitaris almae
filius Maiae patiens vocari
   Caesaris ultor:

subj s

serus in caelum redeas diuque   45
laetus intersis populo Quirini,
neve te nostris vitiis iniquum
   ocior aura

tollat; hic magnos potius triumphos,
hic ames dici pater atque princeps,   50
neu sinas Medos equitare inultos
   te duce, Caesar.

emphatic:

This is a difficult poem and first-time readers are earnestly advised not to worry about it until they have read a little more Horace. He starts by describing portents—snow, hail, and the lightning of Jupiter striking the Capitol, on whose two summits stood the Citadel and Jupiter's own temple. So severe are these signs that they make Romans and the peoples of the earth afraid that there is going to be another Flood. Here Horace indulges his taste for the surreal. Proteus is a sea-god and his flocks are seals. When they go to visit the mountains, we are bound to remember the standard ancient practice of transhumance whereby herdsmen took their livestock up to the hills for summer grazing. Although fish are the least sticky of animals, the tribe of fishes stick in an elm. The point here is that in antiquity birds were often caught by smearing mistletoe paste, birdlime, on the branches of a bush or tree. Post a decoy owl, and the birds of daylight will come to mob it and Papageno, as on the pot in the Shefton Museum in the University of Newcastle, then fills his bag. Finally, deer thrive in the hills but in 11–12 they are swimming in a level sea which

or you, smiling Venus of Eryx, come if you prefer,
with Jest and Cupid hovering round you;
or, if you take thought for the race you founded   35
    and your neglected descendants,

come, god of war, sated with your sport,
exulting in the battle cry, in polished helmets
and the face of the Marsian foot soldier showing no pity
    for his bleeding enemy;   40

or if you, winged son of bountiful Maia,
have changed shape and are imitating
a young man on the earth, accepting the name
    of Caesar's avenger,

do not return too soon to the sky. For long years   45
be pleased to stay with the people of Romulus,
and may no breeze come and snatch you up too soon,
    angered by our sins.

Here rather celebrate your triumphs.
Here delight to be hailed as Father and Princeps   50
and do not allow the Medes to ride unavenged
    while you, Caesar, are our leader.

has been *thrown down* on their natural terrain. Focalization is a fashionable tool of literary criticism. Here the focalizers are the bewildered deer.

Now Horace adds a fourth portent—the flooding of the Tiber. There are four characters in this drama—Jupiter, Vesta, Ilia (who was ravished by Mars the god of war, gave birth to Romulus and Remus, and was then thrown into the Tiber), and Tiber himself, the god of the river, who married Ilia. Now we know why she was complaining and why her husband was bent on revenge, whipping out of the bend to the north-west and rushing over the low ground of the Forum Boarium towards the temple of Vesta, presumably because he felt that the virgin goddess should have done more to protect his wife, her priestess. We know also why the husband's reaction is said to be fierce and why Jupiter interposed his veto. This was no time for the destruction of Rome. The refoundation by Augustus was yet to come.

All this is explained in lines 21–4. Such portents signified civil war and

Rome had had enough of civil war. If we could date this flooding of the Tiber, we would know the dramatic date of the poem. The last stanza tells us that it is after Actium in 31 BC when Octavian took over from Antony the responsibility for the Medes, that is the Parthians, and around 29 when Augustus celebrated his triple triumph. Dio Cassius regularly mentions floods of the Tiber and the only one between 54 and 23 was on 16/17 January 27 BC on the night after Octavian took the name Augustus and three days after he gave up his extraordinary powers and caused consternation by proposing to return to private life (Dio Cassius, 53. 4–8, 20). At this same time (*Res Gestae* 7) he was formally hailed as Leader of the Senate, *Princeps Senatus* (cf. line 50). This all works quite well for the ode. The wars have ended, Augustus is being acclaimed, and the Tiber floods. 'We have had enough of portents of war,' says Horace fervently and topically. 'Stay with us, Augustus, as Princeps and lead us in wars against our foreign enemies.'

But prophets and portents speak with double tongues. This poem is heavily indebted to the most famous poem of the most famous poet of the day, to Virgil's Georgics, even to the deification of the young Augustus, *iuvenis* (*Georgics* 1. 500, cf. line 41 of our ode). This passage of the *Georgics* contains also a long list of portents observed after the assassination of Julius Caesar including lightning (488) and the flooding of a river, the river Po (*contorquens*, *Georgics* 1. 481 cf. *retortis* line 13 of our ode). There are other reasons for connecting Horace's portents with the death of Caesar. First the Regia (15) was the seat of the Chief Priest, the Pontifex Maximus, and Julius Caesar was Pontifex Maximus; second, the Pontifex Maximus appointed and controlled the Vestal Virgins; third, this particular Vestal Virgin was Ilia, a Julian, of the family of Ilus/Iulus, who gave his name to the Julian family. Ilia had therefore good reason to be interested in the fate of her fellow-Julian, Julius Caesar, and to persuade her husband to give warning of danger to Rome. This Ilia, raped by Mars, mother of Romulus and Remus, is part of the antiquarian authentication of the Julian family, part of the propaganda of Julius Caesar and his adoptive son, Augustus, and is so celebrated by Virgil at Aeneid 1. 273–7 and 6. 777–9; fourth, the end of his ode (44) connects with the beginning by alluding to the assassination and Augustus' revenge. Horace's portents are not so numerous or so violent as Virgil's. That also makes sense. Horace's anxiety at or near January 27 BC is a panegyric posture. He would have been foolish to invest this situation with the horror felt at the assassination of Julius Caesar. It therefore seems that the primary application of these portents was to the floods of January

27 BC, but as here presented they would be bound to stir the minds of contemporary Roman readers to think of the portents which preceded the death of Caesar and a round of civil war—'let it not be the same again'. On this analysis this is a sweeping poetic view of twenty years of history from the assassination of Julius Caesar in 44 BC through the Civil Wars to the establishment of the Augustan settlement.

The second half of this poem is in the form of a kletic hymn, whereby a god is summoned and a prayer is offered. A regular feature of such hymns (see on 1. 32) is that the god is addressed by several different titles: 'Whether you wish to be called A, or (*sive*) B, or (*sive*) C, or (*sive*) whatever . . . we pray that . . .'. Horace here applies the formula not to four different titles of one god, but to four different gods: 'Come, Apollo, or you, Venus, if (*sive*) you prefer, or you, Mars, if (*sive*) you have a thought for . . .' (and now there comes the sleight of syntax) or if you, Mercury, are imitating Octavian, do not be in haste to return to the sky.' There is a calculated blur in Horace's logic and it is a little crude to say simply, as some scholars do, that he is claiming that Octavian is the god Mercury in human form.

But despite the subtleties we may still wonder if this is contemptible sycophancy on the part of Horace. Let others judge, but they should remember that Augustus was offering peace and prosperity after a hundred years of violence and disorder. He had been swift to claim divinity for Julius and as early as 42 BC had been known as *Divi Filius*, 'the Son of the Deified Julius'. After Actium he had been away from Rome for nearly two years, till August 29 BC, and while Rome waited for his return, there could have been no certainty about the manner of regime he would impose. When he did come back his name was inserted in the hymn of the Salii, the priests of Mars (*Res Gestae* 10). Planned before Actium and well on in its construction by this time was his colossal Mausoleum, so called because it was grossly out of scale with any comparable building in Rome and could be likened only to the tomb of the Carian dynast Mausolus. Hellenistic kings were deified. Was this what Augustus was going to require when he returned?

Virgil is again helpful. He opens the first *Georgic* (published in the early 20s) by addressing a dozen gods or groups of gods who take an interest in farming. He then wonders what divine function to ascribe to Augustus when he leaves the earth, and advances about eight possibilities in land, sea, and sky. For Romans who did not know what to expect from the returning Augustus, for poets who were clients of Maecenas, one of his two chief ministers, the early 20s posed this problem and it would not go away in a few months. Was Augustus going to yield to the example of the dynasties of the Greek East and allow himself to be hailed as a god? The answer was not simple and in

4 Sat. 1.6.58 - optimu V.

III

o ship, you kot

SIC te diva potens Cypri,
sic fratres Helenae, lucida sidera,
    ventorumque regat pater
obstrictis aliis praeter Iapyga,

    navis, quae tibi creditum   5
debes Vergilium, finibus Atticis
    reddas incolumem precor,
et serves animae dimidium meae.

    illi robur et aes triplex
circa pectus erat, qui fragilem truci   10
    commisit pelago ratem
primus, nec timuit praecipitem Africum   lit, xiv.5

    decertantem Aquilonibus
nec tristis Hyadas nec rabiem Noti,
    quo non arbiter Hadriae   15
maior, tollere seu ponere vult freta.
        (seu)

    quem mortis timuit gradum,
qui siccis oculis monstra natantia,
    qui vidit mare turbidum et
infamis scopulos Acroceraunia?   20

    nequiquam deus abscidit
prudens Oceano dissociabili
    terras, si tamen impiae
non tangenda rates transiliunt vada.

14

the beginning when Augustus was feeling his way to an ideology of
power, Virgil and Horace were both feeling their way to a grammar of
panegyric.

III

    May the goddess who rules over Cyprus,
may Helen's brothers, those shining stars,
      and the father of the winds, shutting them all up
except the northwester Iapyx, govern your sailing,

    O ship, to whom Virgil has been entrusted   5
and who has that debt to pay, only deliver him safe,
      I pray you, to the boundaries of Attica,
and preserve half of my soul.

    Oak and triple bronze
were round the breast of the man who first committed   10
      a fragile ship to the truculent sea.
He was not afraid of the swooping sou'wester

    battling it out with the winds of the north,
nor the weeping Hyades, nor the madness of the south wind,
      the supreme judge of the Adriatic   15
whether his will is to raise or lay the seas.

    He did not fear the approaching step of death
but looked with dry eyes on monsters swimming,
      on boiling ocean and on
the ill-famed Acroceraunian rocks.   20

    In vain in his wise foresight did God cut off
the lands of the earth by means of the dividing sea
      if impious ships yet leap
across waters which they should not touch.

audax omnia perpeti   25
gens humana ruit per vetitum nefas.
        audax Iapeti genus
ignem fraude mala gentibus intulit.

        post ignem aetheria domo
subductum macies et nova febrium   30
        terris incubuit cohors,
semotique prius tarda necessitas

        leti corripuit gradum.
expertus vacuum Daedalus aera
        pennis non homini datis: 35
perrupit Acheronta Herculeus labor.

        nil mortalibus ardui est:
caelum ipsum petimus stultitia neque
        per nostrum patimur scelus
iracunda Iovem ponere fulmina.   40

'I do not understand this poem at all,' said the German professor. 'It must be humorous.' There are perhaps some glints of wit and humour. But these are only fleeting. The prevailing tone is severe and humour will never solve the difficulties of this poem.

Some have suggested that since Prometheus, son of Iapetus (27), Daedalus, and Hercules are normally seen as benign or admirable figures, the poem is celebrating the courage of man in the face of the sternness of his destiny, in other words it is 'a study of man's tragic heroism'. This will not do either. The whole thrust from line 21, the crucial mid-point of the poem, is a condemnation of man's impiety through excessive ambition.

The most popular approach is simply to say that it is a bad poem, trite, insincere, ill-constructed. This is a very long shot. Horace is a great poet. He starts this dazzling collection, like nothing else in classical literature, with a poem of gratitude towards his patron, follows it with a poem in praise of the most powerful man in the known world, and now proceeds with a poem of affection for his friend, the most famous poet of the age, who was known to be writing an epic in praise of Augustus. Horace clearly thought 1. 3 deserved this place in the collection and he is a bet-

Boldly enduring everything   25
the human race rushes through forbidden sin.
    Boldly the offspring of Iapetus brought down fire
by wicked deceit to the peoples of the earth.

    After the theft of fire from its home
in the heavens, wasting disease and a cohort   30
    of new fevers fell upon the lands
and the slow necessity of death, once so remote,

    speeded its step.
Daedalus ventured upon the empty air
    with wings not meant for man.   35
The labour of Hercules burst through Acheron.

    For men no height is too steep:
in our stupidity we try to scale the very heavens
    and by our wickedness we do not allow
Jupiter to lay down his angry thunderbolts.   40

ter judge of these things than his critics. This poem says something
Horace wants to say.

It has to be read in context. In 1. 1. 8–9 we noted a satirical reference
to the fickleness of the Roman electorate and to the political ambitions
which had brought down the Republic. The second poem, apparently
written in the early 20s, deplores the Civil Wars and praises Octavian.
Our present poem talks of Jupiter's punishment of man for his ambi-
tions. From 1. 2. 21–4 and from Virgil's *Georgics*, we know that this pun-
ishment was the Civil Wars. This explanation fits the sudden transition
from the mythological past to the present tense and the first-person pro-
noun in the last stanza. '*We* attempt in our folly to scale the heavens. *We*
by our sin make it impossible for Jupiter to lay aside the lightning of his
wrath.' The sin is the ambition of Romans and the lightning is the Civil
Wars.

After Actium clemency was part of Augustan policy. This was a time
not for recrimination but for reconciliation. This may even explain the
choice of benefactors of mankind, Prometheus, Daedalus, and Hercules,
as *exempla*. Octavian would not have wished Romans who had fought
against him to be compared to the sinners of mythology or the villains of

previous Roman history. The indictment is therefore general, almost philosophical in tone. But the lightning of Jupiter in the last word of the poem is not only philosophical. Another motif of the Augustan presentation of the battle of Actium was to compare it to the attempt of the Giants to scale heaven (as in *Odes* 3. 4) and it was the lightning of Jupiter which hurled down the Giants (that is the forces of Antony and Cleopatra) at *Odes* 3. 4. 74.

The imagery and the ideology are therefore Virgilian and also Augustan (as argued by Traill). The poem is a unity, its argument moving skilfully from Virgil's voyage to the daring of the first sailor, and then to the daring of men who do not accept their human limitations and hence to an oblique condemnation of the struggle for power which had destroyed the Republic. With all of this Virgil would have agreed.

Throughout the imagery is vivid, powerful, and quirky, as one expects from Horace. In line 2 Castor and Pollux are the constellation Gemini and they are called shining because they descend as blue luminescences now known as St Elmo's fire, which play around the masts of ships to signal the end of a storm. In the second stanza there is a strange four-point commercial metaphor to let the ship know its obligations. In line 9 we should remember that Roman ships could be made of oak and that

3ʳ Archilochean

IV

SOLVITVR acris hiems grata vice veris et Favoni,
    trahuntque siccas machinae carinas,
ac neque iam stabulis gaudet pecus aut arator igni,
    nec prata canis albicant pruinis.

iam Cytherea choros ducit Venus imminente Luna,   5
    iunctaeque Nymphis Gratiae decentes
alterno terram quatiunt pede, dum gravis Cyclopum
    Vulcanus ardens visit officinas.

nunc decet aut viridi nitidum caput impedire myrto
    aut flore terrae quem ferunt solutae;   10
nunc et in umbrosis Fauno decet immolare lucis,
    seu poscat agna sive malit haedo.

their triremes were clad with bronze armour. In the next stanza the Hyades are gloomy, *tristis*, because they are the rainy stars, and we are made to wonder what manner of arbiter suffers from rabies. We then find a typically surrealistic play by which dry eyes see monsters swimming, and seas swelling, then look up to the peaks which Virgil will pass on his way down the coast of Greece, Acroceraunia, 5,300 feet high and 2 miles from the shore (in Greek *akra* are peaks and *keraunos* is the thunderbolt and off Acroceraunia, according to Suetonius, *Life of Augustus* 17. 3, Octavian's ship lost its rigging and broke its rudder in a storm after Actium). And so on with the cohort of fevers on the attack, the speeding-up of the sluggish step of Death, the mystery of how a flier is supported in *empty* air, the no-nonsense violence of Hercules with the verb *perrupit* coming first in its clause, the pun in *ardui* which means 'difficulty' but also plays with the steep descents and ascents made by Prometheus, who brought down fire, Daedalus, the first man to fly, and Hercules, who descended into the Underworld and rose to Olympus from his funeral pyre.

After two millennia this is not the most accessible of Horace's poems, but he chose it for this place and it does what he wanted it to do.

---

change of season — death
coming — city

IV

Harsh winter is melting away in the welcome change to spring and zephyrs,
    winches are pulling down dry-bottomed ships,
the cattle no longer like the steading, the ploughman does not hug the fire
    and meadows are not white with hoar-frost.

Venus of Cythera leads on the dance beneath a hanging moon,   5
    and the lovely Graces, linking arms with Nymphs,
shake the ground with alternate feet while burning Vulcan
    visits the grim foundries of the Cyclopes.

Now is the time to oil the hair and bind the head with green myrtle
    or flowers born of the earth now freed from frost;   10
now too it is time to sacrifice to Faunus in shady groves
    whether he asks a lamb or prefers a kid.

19

pallida Mors aequo pulsat pede pauperum tabernas
    regumque turris. o beate Sesti,
vitae summa brevis spem nos vetat incohare longam.   15
    iam te premet nox fabulaeque Manes

et domus exilis Plutonia; quo simul mearis,
    nec regna vini sortiere talis,
nec tenerum Lycidan mirabere, quo calet iuventus
    nunc omnis et mox virgines tepebunt.   20

Julius Caesar was assassinated in 44 BC by conspirators led by Brutus. In the war that ensued Lucius Sestius (line 14) served under Brutus, providing him at one point with some splendid ships (*navigia luculenta*, Cic. *Att*. 16. 4. 4), which may or may not have been his own. He was proscribed by Antony, Octavian, and Lepidus but was amnestied after the defeat and death of Brutus at Philippi in 42 BC. In the years that followed he remained true to the memory of Brutus, keeping statues of him in his house and composing eulogies in his praise. In 23 BC when Augustus gave up the consulship, Sestius was appointed to take his place. This was a striking and no doubt calculated act of magnanimity by Augustus, and he was praised for resigning the consulship *and* for choosing Sestius to replace him according to Dio Cassius, 53. 32. It is no coincidence that the fourth poem in this volume of Augustan poetry published in this same year is addressed to a man whom Augustus had so conspicuously favoured.

There may be some slight difficulty in the run of the sense at line 13, as shown by the note in the margin of W. S. Landor's Horace: '*Pallida mors* has nothing to do with the above.' But Horace is simply dramatizing a familiar and irresistible argument: 'The seasons come and go. We, on the other hand, die once and for all. Let us therefore enjoy our lives.' After the joys of spring when Venus leads the dance and her cripple, ardent, and frequently cuckolded husband goes to inspect, *visit*, his foundries with a view to the springtime demand for thunderbolts, after the feasting in line 9 (at a convivial dinner, a Roman would wear garlands and anoint his head with fragrant unguents), after the lovemaking (myrtle is the plant of Venus), after the ritual killing of a lamb or kid to honour the god of the countryside on his festival which was celebrated in Rome on the morning of 13 February before the Parentalia, the festi-

Pale death kicks with impartial foot at the hovels of the poor
    and the towers of kings. O fortunate Sestius,
the brief sum of life does not allow us to start on long hopes.   15
    You will soon be kept close by Night and the fabled shades

and Pluto's meagre house. When you go there
    you will no longer cast lots to rule the wine
nor admire tender Lycidas whom all the young men
    now burn for, and for whom the girls will soon be warm.   20

val of the dead, began at midday—suddenly, at the very mid-point of the poem, there comes a kicking at the door. Death does not give a gentle tap, but follows the practice of Roman comedy and uses the foot. This is certainly sudden, but the connection is so familiar that it is impossible to understand how Landor failed to see it.

Beatus (line 14) includes good fortune, the blessing of the gods, and wealth. L. Sestius was without doubt wealthy and recent discoveries discussed by Will suggest where the wealth came from. For generations his family had owned a pottery which produced distinctive long-necked amphorae, of which hundreds were found in the Grand Congloué underwater excavation. Seventy per cent of the total of Sestius amphorae have been found near Cosa, a town 85 miles north-west of Rome on the coast of Etruria. At some stage in the first century BC the business diversified and bricks have been found in and around Rome with the name of this same L. Sestius stamped upon them. These have also been discovered at Sette Finestre, a turreted villa, where Sestius' father had connections. Thousands of these bricks are stamped with the letters OF, meaning *officina*, factory.

The sceptic will hold that all this information is irrelevant to our ode, but believers will remember that many of Horace's poems are tooled to the interests and character of their addressees—these are *ad hominem* poems. At line 2 we will imagine commerce resuming in the springtime and Sestius' cargo ships being winched down into the sea at Cosa and loaded up with Sestius amphorae. Where Vulcan pays a visit to his foundry, *officina* (8), we will think of other furnaces, there in the famous *officina* of Sestius. The towers of kings in line 14 will remind us of the villa of Sette Finestre with its ring of turreted walls, particularly because *reges*, kings, is often used not of kings but of wealthy men. We will savour the contrast between the expansive luxury of the Cosan villa of the Sestii and the cramped quarters of the tomb (*premet*, 16) furnished by the sparse provisions (*exilis*, 17) of the king of the Underworld.

We may even ask if Sestius indulged in homosexual love affairs. After all, Horace implies that he admires a Lycidas. Nisbet and Hubbard believe that 'the homosexual implication has no bearing on Sestius's actual behaviour, but is a conventional motif derived from Greek erotic poetry.' On the other hand Nisbet and Hubbard know that 'the practice was widespread ... and at least where slave boys were concerned

3ʳ ʰˢˡᵖ ᴶ

Lɪꞯᴜɪᴅ ꜱᴠᴇʀʏᴡʜᴇʀᴇ

V

QVIS multa gracilis te puer in rosa
perfusus liquidis urget odoribus
    grato, Pyrrha, sub antro?
        cui flavam religas comam,

simplex munditiis? heu quotiens fidem   5
mutatosque deos flebit et aspera
    nigris aequora ventis
        emirabitur insolens,

qui nunc te fruitur credulus aurea,
qui semper vacuam, semper amabilem   10
    sperat, nescius aurae
        fallacis! miseri, quibus

intemptata nites. me tabula sacer
votiva paries indicat uvida
    suspendisse potenti   15
        vestimenta maris deo.

When Greeks or Italians retired, they might dedicate the tools of their trade in the temple of the appropriate god. The fisherman might hang up his nets, the gladiator a wooden spear, the courtesan her mirror. Saved from shipwreck, they might offer up the clothes they had been washed ashore in. In the sixth book of the *Palatine Anthology* there provoked little censure.' At the moment we shall leave the question there, asking only why young men are hot, *calet*, whereas young women will be warm, *tepebunt*. Is it because the beauty of Lycidas is also subject to the depredations of time and will not excite the girls as much as now it excites the men? Or is Horace mischievously suggesting that young men tend to be passionate, but young girls are more restrained? Or is it more innocent? The young men are hot now and soon the girls will be warming up (as Lycidas grows to manhood and they begin to take an interest).

V

What slim youngster soaked in perfumes
is hugging you now, Pyrrha, on a bed of roses
   deep in your lovely cave? For whom
     are you tying up your blonde hair?

You're so elegant and so simple. Many's the time   5
he'll weep at your faithlessness and the changing gods
   and be amazed at seas
     roughened by black winds,

but now in all innocence he enjoys your golden beauty
and imagines you always available, always lovable,   10
   not knowing that breezes are treacherous—
     I pity poor devils with no experience of you

and dazzled by your radiance. As for me,
the votive tablet on the temple wall announces
   that I have dedicated my dripping wet clothes   15
     to the god who rules the sea.

are scores of poems which accompanied such votive offerings or purported to. This ode of Horace's transcends them all.

It juggles the metaphorical and the literal. On the literal side, the young man who loves Pyrrha knows nothing of broken promises, changes of fortune, and violent rages, but he will soon find out. At the moment he is lost in admiration, enjoying her golden beauty and imagining in his innocence that she will always be amiable and always at his beck and call (*vacuam* literally means 'empty'). No wonder Horace pities those who are infatuated by her radiant beauty and have no experience of the other side of her character. On the metaphorical side, we see the Mediterranean calm broken by sudden storms, and the landlubber admiring the view of the vast and empty ocean, golden at dawn or sunset, and thinking it is set fair, not knowing that a breeze can become a squall. But all this is to look at the poem like an accountant at a balance sheet. The metaphor and the literal are not in two columns. Readers of poetry have to learn to read accounts but, since we all start with a different capital of experience, we do not all have to arrive at the same bottom line.

Horace is fashioning a persona. He is plump—Augustus teases him about it in a letter in the Suetonian *Life of Horace*. He is middle-aged, no longer a great lover, but watching the young and the rich and the slim and the passionate loving and winning, being betrayed and bullied, weeping and wailing and beating their mistresses. This life does not appeal to him. The greatest possible misunderstanding of this poem is to think of it as a farewell to love. It is a farewell to Pyrrha, to love fouled up with tantrums and silliness and misery.

This is a contemporary issue. It was also an issue in Horace's day, dealt with some thirty years before by the sublimest of the Roman poets. At the end of the fourth book of *De Rerum Natura* Lucretius had vigorously argued the Epicurean viewpoint that infatuation is folly. The wise man will enjoy women but not allow them to disturb the true pleasure which comes from tranquillity of spirit. Horace was at times attracted by some aspects of Epicurean philosophy.

But there's more to this than philosophy. Elegiac poetry was in full swing. Gallus had long since carved his mistress's name on trees in lonely woods. Tibullus had wept over Delia and Propertius over Cynthia. This is a programme poem, the first love poem in a collection which includes some of the greatest ever written. Horace is saying goodbye to Pyrrha (if there ever was a Pyrrha in his life) and the kind of love she has to offer. He is also informing his readers and his patrons Maecenas and Augustus (no doubt to their relief) that he will not be writing elegiac poetry.

All this is only clearing the ground. One of the pleasures in Horace is the music and some of that can be sensed in the shape of this poem. A long question ('What youngster . . . is making hot love to you these days?') is followed by a shorter one ('Who are you tying up your hair for these days?') and then a huge central sentence where Horace imagines in all its detail what this youngster will go through and ends with the pitying exclamation in four words of Latin in lines 12–13, *miseri quibus intemptata nites*, his whole fantasy being half the poem and straddling three stanzas. Horace remembers the experience only too well.

The effect of a poem depends upon the order of events and the effect of a Latin poem depends upon Latin word-order. This was famously expressed by Nietzsche as translated by Wilkinson (1945):

To this day I have got from no poet the same artistic delight as from the very first a Horatian ode gave me. In certain languages what is here achieved is not even to be thought of. This mosaic of words, in which every word by sound, by position and by meaning, spreads its influence to right and left and over the whole; the minimum in compass and number of symbols, the maximum achieved in the effectiveness of these symbols, all that is Roman, and believe me, of excellence unsurpassed.

In English 'Dog bites man' does not mean the same as 'Man bites dog'. In Latin the logic is carried not by the order of the words, but by their endings. *Canis hominem mordet* denotes the same action as *hominem mordet canis* or *mordet hominem canis*. What is different is the nuance, the emphasis. So, for instance, the last of these three formulations is high drama. To savour how the Latin works in this ode, the non-Latinist might well study the version by John Milton, translated not into English, but into English words, painful to read and therefore a great lie, but a fascinating attempt to put Latin through the hoops of another language:

> What slender youth bedew'd with liquid odours
> Courts thee on roses in some pleasant cave,
>   Pyrrha, for whom bind'st thou
>   in wreaths thy golden hair,
>
> Plain in thy neatness? O how oft shall he
> On faith and changed Gods complain: and seas
>   Rough with black winds and storms
>   unwonted shall admire:
>
> Who now enjoys thee, credulous, all-gold,
> Who always vacant, always amiable
>   Hopes thee; of flattering gales
>   unmindfull. Hapless they

To whom thou untry'd seem'st fair. Me in my vow'd
Picture the sacred wall declares t'have hung
My dank and dripping weeds
To the stern God of Sea.

This is as close as a translation could come without becoming a crib, and the price is high. The untranslatable *simplex munditiis* is not so demure and Puritan as 'plain in thy neatness'. 'Faith' is word for word but the wrong word. And how could we tell without the Latin whether the storms were unwonted, and Pyrrha credulous and unmindful? These are avoidable accidents, but there is no alchemy in Milton or any other English, to catch the effect of Pyrrha between *gracilis* and *puer* and the pair of them between *multa* and *rosa*. This is only one of such effects throughout the poem in the long run of nouns each with its single adjec-

2° Asclep

Sat. 1. 10. & Ecl. IX,

VI

whateva

Scriberis Vario fortis et hostium
victor Maeonii carminis alite,
quam rem cumque ferox navibus aut equis
    miles te duce gesserit:

nos, Agrippa, neque haec dicere nec gravem   5
Pelidae stomachum cedere nescii
nec cursus duplicis per mare Vlixei
    nec saevam Pelopis domum

powerful but now a cliche

conamur, tenues grandia, dum pudor
imbellisque lyrae Musa potens vetat   10
laudes egregii Caesaris et tuas
    culpa deterere ingeni.

quis Martem tunica tectum adamantina
digne scripserit aut pulvere Troico
nigrum Merionen aut ope Palladis   15
    Tydiden superis parem?

tive and almost every adjective subtly separated from its noun. Scholars call this separation hyperbaton and it is a vital part of the untranslatable essence of the Latin.

And then there is the metre: in Milton all iambics (sounding 'thou'ntry'd' in two syllables in line 13); in Horace a variegated texture, where the fixed quantities in each line of the Latin are in expressive counterpoint with the free rhythms of the word accents. Take the repeated *semper* in line 10. In Milton's iambics the second 'always' is metrically identical to the first, but in Latin poetry a short vowel before two consonants is scanned as long and therefore *semper* before *vacuam* is two long syllables whereas before *amabilem* it is a long followed by a short. Not only that, but the different seating in the metre gives the two words two different verse accents—*cui sempér vacuam sémper amabilem sperat*. Who would be a translator?

VI

Varius, the eagle of Homeric song, will write
of your valour and victories over your enemies,
all the feats of soldiers, formidable on ship or horseback,
    fighting under your command.

We do not attempt, Agrippa, to speak of these things   5
nor of the bad temper of the son of Peleus who did not know
how to yield, nor the voyages of Ulixes the double-dealer
    nor the savage house of Pelops.

We are too slight for these large themes. Modesty
and the Muse who commands the unwarlike lyre forbid us   10
to diminish the praise of glorious Caesar and yourself
    by the shortcomings of our talent.

Who could write worthily of Mars girt in adamantine tunic,
or Meriones, black with the dust of Troy,
or the son of Tydeus, with the help of Pallas Athene   15
    the equal of the gods?

nos convivia, nos proelia virginum
sectis in iuvenes unguibus acrium
cantamus, vacui sive quid urimur,
 non praeter solitum leves.   20

The historian will note that M. Vipsanius Agrippa was the naval and
military genius whose victories in half a dozen crucial land and sea
battles between 42 and 31 BC made Octavian master of the world. So the
first poem was addressed to Maecenas, the second indirectly to
Augustus, the third to the poet laureate Virgil, the fourth to a
Republican now conspicuously rehabilitated by Augustus, the fifth to
Pyrrha. In the sixth now, Horace declines to write a patriotic epic but
praises the greatest soldier of the age, and includes a compliment to
Augustus at the centre-point of the poem. The Pyrrha poem demon-
strates that he is a poet of love. The Agrippa poem ends by saying so.

For the student of literature, the interest is twofold. When a poet has
to disappoint the expectations of a patron, the standard tactic is to plead
incapacity and suggest the name of a fellow poet who could do it better.
This courteous refusal, the *recusatio*, is common in Greek and Latin lit-
erature in eras when the balance of interest is passing from the state to
the individual. In Greek Callimachus (*c.*305–*c.*240 BC) leads the way, as
in fragment 1. 71–5:

> Mine not to thunder; that is Zeus's job.
> When first I laid my writing tablet on my knees,
>   Apollo, God of Lycia, spoke to me:
> 'Dear poet,' he said, 'do keep your sacrifices fat,
>   but give me, please, a nice slim Muse.'

The retreat is comprehensive: from the patriotic to the personal, from
the sublime to the colloquial, seriousness to wit, the grand to the plain,
from the central myths towards the byways where sexual deviation lurks,
from the long poem to the short, from the business of war to the plea-
sures of peace, from the anonymous and self-effacing poet to mutual-
admiration societies of sophisticated young men hoping to become
immortal by virtue of their originality. This is a rough profile of the New
Poets of Rome in the generation of Catullus, living in the second quar-
ter of the first century BC. Horace came after them and was influenced,
but he was a very different poet.

Some of these trends, however, appear in the *recusatio* which is 1. 6.

We sing of drinking parties, of battles fought
by fierce virgins with nails cut sharp to wound young men.
We sing, whether fancy free or a little moved,
    cheerfully, after our fashion.   20

There are flickers of wit (where, for example Horace's powerful Muse issues her refusal, *potens . . . vetat*, but her power is only over the unwarlike lyre). There are the contrast between the sublime and the slender caught in two words in line 9, *tenues grandia*, the modest plea of incapacity, and the suggestion that Horace's friend Varius could do what is required.

A third approach to this poem might be by those who like the company of Horace. They will notice that Agrippa is spoken of in the language of the military communiqué whereas Varius is treated to a sublime poetic metaphor. In the second stanza they will see the parodies of the opening lines of the *Iliad* and the *Odyssey*:

> Sing, O goddess, of the *wrath* of Achilles, son of Peleus

and

> Tell me, O Muse, of a man *of many resources*

Stomachum, being a colloquial word for anger, sounds absurd in the Horace alongside the epic patronymic 'son of Peleus', and the double-dealing of Ulixes (Odysseus) is a parody of *polutropos*. This does not mean that Horace is mocking Homer or making fun of Agrippa. The butt of his humour is himself—'This is the sort of mess I'd make of it if I tried to write an epic.' He is certainly not making fun of his dear friend Varius. This is shown by line 8, an allusion to a tragic theme, which therefore appears to have nothing to do with the argument. But when Augustus returned in triumph in 29 BC to Rome he was in time for the performance of Varius' famous tragedy *Thyestes* and Thyestes was the son of Pelops. Horace mentions the theme of this play quite plainly without any of the irony which we hear in the references to the *Iliad* and the *Odyssey*. This ode is a tribute not only to Agrippa, but also to Varius and to Octavian who rewarded Varius for his tragedy with a gift of a million sesterces.

The gentle self-mockery continues in the third stanza. Horace's Muse is powerful, *potens*, and she issues her refusal, *vetat*. She knows her strength and her limitations. If Horace wrote about Augustus and

Agrippa, he would be spoiling their splendour by overpolishing (*deterere*, to rub away).

Having made a botch of epic diction in stanza 2, it is all part of the fun when Horace now shows his mastery of it in stanza 4, with the clank of the alliteration in 13, the climax in 15–16 where a man becomes the equal of a god and the vivid picture of Meriones black with Trojan dust in 14–15. An important question now arises. Why Meriones, a second-rank hero, when Horace could have chosen from a score of more distinguished figures? The answer may be that Meriones, the squire of Idomeneus in the *Iliad*, is elsewhere associated with Diomede, the son of Tydeus, notably in *Odes* 1. 15. 26–8 and in Euripides' *Iphigenia in Aulis* 199–200, where we read of Diomede and then, 'beside him Meriones', *para de Merionen*. Of all the leading Greek heroes in the *Iliad* Diomede has perhaps the least conspicuous character defects. So, when the last two lines of the third stanza on the difficulty of praising Agrippa

VII

LAVDABVNT alii claram Rhodon aut Mytilenen
    aut Epheson bimarisve Corinthi
moenia vel Baccho Thebas vel Apolline Delphos
    insignis aut Thessala Tempe:

sunt quibus unum opus est intactae Palladis urbem   5
    carmine perpetuo celebrare et
undique decerptam fronti praeponere olivam:
    plurimus in Iunonis honorem

aptum dicet equis Argos ditisque Mycenas:
    me nec tam patiens Lacedaemon   10
nec tam Larisae percussit campus opimae,
    quam domus Albuneae resonantis

et praeceps Anio ac Tiburni lucus et uda
    mobilibus pomaria rivis.
albus ut obscuro deterget nubila caelo   15
    saepe Notus neque parturit imbris

and Augustus are followed by the last two lines of the next stanza asking who could praise Meriones and Diomede 'equal to the gods', Horace is setting Diomede and his henchman alongside the great contemporary Roman hero Augustus and his faithful henchman Agrippa. Agrippa, who bore the brunt of all Augustus' battles and lived only to serve his master, is the Roman Meriones.

In the last stanza the battles and 'the sharp girls with nails cut against young men', *virginum sectis in iuvenes unguibus acrium*, make a feeble comparison with the armies led by Agrippa, as Horace well knows. He is telling us that he is going to write love poetry but there has been so much play going on that we know that his œuvre is not going to be as limited as he here pretends for the purposes of this poem. We have been trained to be wary. His love poetry may not be quite so cool and limited as he claims.

VII

Others will praise bright Rhodes or Mytilene or Ephesus
    or the walls of Corinth with its two seas,
Thebes famous for Bacchus or Delphi for Apollo
    or Thessalian Tempe;

there are those whose one task is to celebrate the city   5
    of chaste Pallas in unbroken song
and to sport on their brows a crown of olive plucked wherever
    they can find it; in honour of Juno many a one

will speak of wealthy Mycenae and Argos good for horses.
    As for me, I am not so struck   10
by much-enduring Lacedaemon or the fat plain of rich Larisa
    as by Albunea's sounding home

and the plunging Anio, by the grove of Tiburnus and its orchards
    soaked by swiftly flowing water.
The bright south wind will often wipe the clouds from the dark sky. 15
    It is not always pregnant with rain.

31

perpetuo, sic tu sapiens finire memento
　　tristitiam vitaeque labores
molli, Plance, mero, seu te fulgentia signis
　　castra tenent seu densa tenebit　　　　　　　20

Tiburis umbra tui. Teucer Salamina patremque
　　cum fugeret, tamen uda Lyaeo
tempora populea fertur vinxisse corona,
　　sic tristis adfatus amicos:

'quo nos cumque feret melior fortuna parente,　　25
　　ibimus, o socii comitesque.
nil desperandum Teucro duce et auspice Teucro
　　certus enim promisit Apollo

ambiguam tellure nova Salamina futuram.
　　o fortes peioraque passi　　　　　　　　　　30
mecum saepe viri, nunc vino pellite curas;
　　cras ingens iterabimus aequor.'

This is one of the odes which may remind the reader of Stephen Leacock's Lord Ronald who 'flung himself upon his horse . . . and rode madly off in all directions'. The essence of the argument runs:

1–14: Others will praise Greek cities; I prefer Tibur.
15–21: The sky is not always rainy, Plancus. Whether at war or in Tibur, drown your sorrows in wine.
21–32: Teucer, exiled by his father, ordered his men to do the same.

Pindar displays similar sudden changes of topic, and Pindar's poems hang together by means of the strong thread of underlying argument and cunning links between the topics. So it is in this ode of Horace's, where the links between the first two topics are not provided until the end of the second picks up the end of the first. It is line 21 before we hear that Plancus, the addressee of the poem, has anything to do with the place Horace loves.

The opening of the poem takes the form of the priamel, which we have already met in *Odes* 1. 1, and the catalogue of Greek cities is more interesting than may appear at first sight. The brightness of Rhodes refers to its fame and the dazzling white of its marble buildings. Rhodes,

So you too, Plancus, would be wise to remember to put an end
   to sadness and the labours of life
with mellow wine unwatered, whether you are in camp among
   the gleaming standards or whether some day you will be   20

in the deep shade of your beloved Tibur. When Teucer was on the run
   from Salamis and his father, they say that nevertheless,
awash with wine, he bound his brow in a crown of poplar leaves
   and spoke these words to his grieving friends:

'Fortune, allies and comrades, is kinder than a father.   25
   Wherever she takes us, there we shall go. Do not despair
while Teucer takes the auspices and Teucer is your leader.
   Apollo does not err and he has promised

that in a new land there would be a second Salamis.
   You are brave men and have often suffered worse   30
with me. Drive away your cares away with wine. Tomorrow
   we shall set out again upon the broad sea.

Mitylene, and Ephesus are three of the wealthy Greek cities which Romans would have visited while engaged in political or military duties in Asia Minor, and Plancus was in that area with Antony from 41 to 32, including a term as governor of Asia in the early 40s. Corinth, which had been plundered and destroyed by the Romans in 146 BC, was set on terraces above the sea. The visiting Roman would climb the Acrocorinth (1,886 feet high) and look down on a circuit of about 7½ miles of city walls, the longest in Greece. On one side he would see Kenchreai, the port of Corinth on the Saronic Gulf, and on the other a double wall stretching about a mile and a half to Lechaion, her port on the Corinthian Gulf. All this fallen splendour was now a Roman colony, resettled by Julius Caesar in 44 BC as Colonia Laus Iulia Corinthus.

In 5–8 the focus shifts to Athens and to literature and the tone becomes sardonic. The *one* task of these poets is to celebrate the city and there is mischief afoot when Horace talks of their unbroken song, *perpetuo carmine*. This is a technical term translated from the first fragment of Callimachus *Aetia*, and serves to associate these poets with the writers of long, old-fashioned epics. It also feelingly refers to the hearers' fears that the readings are going to go on for ever. The olive they so ostentatiously wear (*praeponere*) is the emblem of Athens. And they pluck it 'anywhere and everywhere', *undique* (7), meaning that their writings are derivative, being made up of imitations culled from the whole body of Greek poetry.

'Unbroken song' has put the reader in mind of epic, and it is to epic that Horace now turns in the third stanza. These cities are the homes of the leaders of the Greek expedition to Troy in the *Iliad*—Argos the home of Diomede, Mycenae of Agamemnon, Lacedaemon (Sparta) of Menelaus, Larisa of Achilles—and each is provided with a translated version of its stock Homeric epithet. Horace, of course, is not deriding Homer, but poking fun at long epics on Greek mythological themes and at writings in praise of Greek cities. This is not simply a contest of cities. It is also literary polemic.

So much for Greece. We now turn to Italy and see immediately why Horace mentioned Apollo, Bacchus, Pallas Athene, and Ephesus which was famous for its temple of Artemis, the great goddess 'whom all Asia and the world worshippeth' (Acts 19: 27–8). Against these shrines of Olympian gods Horace sets the local cults of Tibur, 25 miles east of Rome in the Sabine hills. The Sibyl Albunea has her cave perhaps by the great falls of the Anio, and nearby the hero Tiburnus, one of the founders of Tibur, has his sacred grove (*lucus*) and presumably his shrine. In the first part of this poem Horace is disparaging some Greek poetry, but the message is not entirely literary. His is also setting Italian divinities above the Olympian gods and an Italian town above the hallowed place-names of Greece. One aspect of the Augustan settlement is the desire to reproduce the glories of Greece and to excel them. Horace's poetry is part of that endeavour.

With a cunning transition from the abundant waters of Tibur to the rain-laden south wind, Horace now offers advice to Plancus. Lucius Munatius Plancus was born sometime between 90 and 85 BC. From 54 BC he served under Caesar in Gaul, Spain, and Africa, founding the cities of Lyons and Augst as the Roman colonies of Lugudunum and Raurica. If Caesar found him useful, he was useful. In 43 BC he joined Antony and Lepidus who promptly proscribed his brother or perhaps cousin. In 42 he celebrated a triumph. For the next decade he served Antony in Egypt and the East, being governor first of Asia and then of Syria in 35 BC. In 32, objecting to Cleopatra's participation in the campaign which was to lead to Actium, he went over to Octavian and returned to Rome. In 27 he proposed the name Augustus for Octavian and in the year after these odes appeared he held the censorship, a senior and obviously respected member of the Augustan establishment.

These bare facts challenge the modern reader to fit the poem to the life, and many theories have been advanced. I once argued (1967: 115–17) for the view put forward by Kumaniecki that Teucer's return from Troy to Salamis with the news of his brother's death alluded to Plancus' alleged involvement in the death of his relative. Horace seemed to be implying that Plancus, like Teucer, was innocent, but was blamed. But in 23 BC that episode was twenty years in the past. And I am now much more keenly aware of the Augustan intent in the poetry of Horace. From an Augustan point of view, and that is what counted in 23 BC, the key episode in Plancus' history was his decision to abandon Antony. With this in mind we should surely ask how this ode could be imagined to fit that stage in his life.

If we posit that the *dramatic* date of this ode could be those critical days when Plancus was deciding to change sides, how would the poem be read? The advice in lines 17–18 to be sensible and put an end to gloom would be apposite, and the reference to the labours of life would be even more pointed as being addressed to a man who had been abroad at war and at work for more than twenty years and was now probably nearer 60 than 50 years of age. The striking play of tenses in line 21, 'whether you are in the camp or *will be* in your home at Tibur' (*tenent . . . tenebit*), could be read as a hint that it was perfectly reasonable for a man of that age not to go on campaigning with Antony and Cleopatra but to retire to his home in Italy. The mention of shade which we notice as a subtle link with the grove and the orchards of Tibur of lines 13–14, is also a hint at retirement. The advice to Plancus in line 18 to give up 'the labours of life' also chimes well with this interpretation.

The advice is now supported by a mythological parallel, in the language of Pindaric criticism paraenesis supported by exemplum. In line 21 Teucer is exiled from Salamis by his father (literally 'is fleeing from his father and from Salamis'); Plancus is leaving Antony and Egypt. Teucer and his friends are gloomy (*tristis* picks up *tristitiam* from line 18); in these circumstances Plancus will not have travelled alone and he will have had friends and dependants waiting in Italy. In those days they would not have been cheerful. Both men are going to follow Fortune, which is likely to be kinder than Teucer's father Telamon, and if the exemplum reflects suggestively upon Plancus' situation, there is here a glance at Antony. When we read that there is no need for despair while Teucer is leader, it is easy to transpose this to Plancus who had also had a distinguished military career. Teucer wears the poplar which is an emblem of Hercules and Hercules is the god of Tibur, whose effigy appears on a coin minted by this same Plancus (described by Sydenham, 169). The advice fits Teucer's situation perfectly, as he addresses his comrades before they are forced to set to sea when they thought they had returned home. It also hints that Plancus and his comrades had assumed that they would always be in the service of Antony. Here a feature which is entirely in place in the exemplum has to be massaged a little to make it apply to the facts—Plancus was only the follower of Antony, not his son. Similarly, in line 28 Teucer has received a promise from Apollo who does not err although his utterance may be baffling, as it is in line 29; so Plancus, for his part, is trusting in the clemency of Augustus. Teucer founds a new Salamis on the island of Cyprus; Plancus, from the viewpoint of 23 BC, has found a new life as a senior statesman in the Augustan settlement.

All this is speculation. It only suggests how the poem might be read if it were applied to this critical, 'Augustan' watershed in the life of Plancus. The question of the application of the poem to the life cannot be answered with certainty. But so much of this poetry is *ad hominem*, aimed directly or indirectly at the addressee, so much of it relates to the decade before its publication in 23 BC, and so much of it bears an Augustan message, including every poem of the first seven except the love poem 1. 5, that it is a question that has to be asked and this answer does correspond to the fact that the important thing about Plancus in

VIII

LYDIA, dic, per omnis
te deos oro, Sybarin cur properes amando
    perdere, cur apricum
oderit campum, patiens pulveris atque solis.

cur neque militaris   5
inter aequalis equitat, Gallica nec lupatis
    temperat ora frenis?
cur timet flavum Tiberim tangere? cur olivum

Augustan propaganda is that he came over from Antony to Octavian, was rehabilitated, and now he is, like Sestius in 1. 4, an embodiment of the Augustan policies of *clementia* and *concordia*.

For many readers this poem has seemed to have a powerful universal application. The best testimony is the end of Tennyson's *Ulysses*. 'The young Tennyson', writes Martindale, 'had learned the odes by heart and thoroughly internalized what they stood for.' Accordingly, he attaches some of the substance and tone of the end of 1. 7 to a more familiar figure than Plancus:

> for my purpose holds
> To sail beyond the sunset, and the baths
> Of all the western stars, until I die.
> It may be that the gulfs will wash us down:
> It may be we shall touch the Happy Isles,
> And see the great Achilles, whom we knew.
> Though much is taken, much abides; and though
> We are not now the strength which in old days
> Moved earth and heaven, that which we are, we are;
> One equal temper of heroic hearts,
> Made weak by time and fate, but strong in will
> to strive, to seek, to find, and not to yield.

VIII

Tell me, Lydia, by all the gods I beg you,
why you are in such a hurry to destroy Sybaris with your love.
    Why does he dislike the sunny Campus?
He never used to complain about dust or heat.

    Why is he not on horseback   5
and training for war with his young friends? Why is he not
    disciplining Gallic mouths
with the jagged bit? Why is he afraid to put his toe in the Tiber?

sanguine viperino
cautius vitat neque iam livida gestat armis   10
    bracchia, saepe disco,
saepe trans finem iaculo nobilis expedito?

quid latet, ut marinae
filium dicunt Thetidis sub lacrimosa Troiae
    funera, ne virilis   15
cultus in caedem et Lycias proriperet catervas?

This is a fun poem. Some scholars have seen in it a pacifist protest against the military imperialism of the Augustan regime, but the detail tells against them, even the syntax, a string of eight pained questions when there is never any doubt about the answers, coming to a climax in the lofty epic comparison filling the final stanza as the young rascal is compared to the greatest of the Greek epic warriors.

The shocked tone of the opening address to Lydia gives us the lead with its solemn adjuration in formulaic word-order, 'by all (you) gods I beg' and the suggestion that she is hurrying to corrupt Sybaris when she is obviously not in a hurry at all. From now on part of the fun is to contrast what Horace tells us the boy is *not* doing with what we can easily imagine he *is* doing. Instead of training on the Campus Martius with his old friends, he is staying indoors, beautifully toileted no doubt, growing pale like a lady, dealing in tenderness instead of disciplining Gallic horses by tugging spiked metal bits into their soft rear gums. There is no swimming in the formidable current of the Tiber but presumably he enjoys the pleasures of the bath. He does not rub olive oil into his body for such sports as wrestling but almost certainly his head is anointed with the aromatic oils a Roman male would apply for the banquet. His arms are soft now, no longer bruised with wrestling or fencing, and his old skills are no longer practised. This is all cheerful and teasing.

The epic ending clinches it. A typical epic touch and a touch of parody is that the name of Achilles is never mentioned. We have already met this lofty *antonomasia* with the unnamed Venus, Mars, and Mercury at the end of the second ode. Our poem ends in tears, deaths, slaughter, and enemy armies but is still not serious because Horace tells us Thetis dressed her young son as a girl and hid him amongst the women on the island of Lemnos in order to save him from being caught up in the Trojan War, yet we know that the motives of Lydia were rather different, and that Sybaris is no Achilles.

a bit too physical for R

Why does he avoid athletes' oil
like vipers' blood and why are his arms no longer bruised   10
   with weapons, this champion of the discus,
champion of the javelin, so often throwing beyond the mark?

   Why does he hide as the son
of the sea-goddess Thetis hid, so they say, before the tears and deaths
   at Troy in case man's clothes   15
should send him off to the killing and the Lycian cohorts?

And who was Sybaris? A Roman citizen obviously, training for mili-
tary service in a way that would have warmed the heart of Augustus. But
Sybaris is a Greek name, a pseudonym chosen to suggest that he is
enjoying the notoriously self-indulgent life of the most luxurious of all
the rich Greek cities in the south of Italy. This, of course, is not to sug-
gest there was a young Roman of the day who would have answered to
the name. This is a poem written for fun. It does not necessarily describe
anything Horace had seen. It must certainly have made sense in con-
temporary social conditions. It may be based on fact. It may depart from
it. We shall never know. And it doesn't matter.

This theoretical question is looked at here because it has bedevilled
writing on Latin poetry for many decades. Is it life or is it poetic inven-
tion? Is it Latin or is it taken over from the Greek literary tradition?
These are fatuous questions. In the first place, poetry is not a clinical
description of an experience. A poem starts from experience (and that
may include the poet's experience of literature) but as it comes into exis-
tence it is shaped by the complex dynamics of composition. What a poet
writes about himself may be true and it may be false. Without direct evi-
dence from outside the poem we can never know. The common argu-
ment 'literary therefore not true' is invalid. The only sound judgement
reads: 'There are literary parallels. Therefore it may be false and it may
be true.' Literature certainly imitates literature, but as Griffin has
demonstrated with an avalanche of evidence, literature and life also imi-
tate each other. In the second place, Rome in the age of Horace was a
Hellenistic city, interpenetrated by all forms of Greek culture. To ask
whether a poem or part of a poem is Hellenistic or Augustan is a waste
of time. The Augustan includes the Hellenistic (see West, 1967: 138–9;
Lyne, 192–200; and Griffin).

IX

VIDES ut alta stet nive candidum
Soracte, nec iam sustineant onus
　　silvae laborantes, geluque
　　　　flumina constiterint acuto.

dissolve frigus ligna super foco　　　　　　　　　5
large reponens atque benignius
　　deprome quadrimum Sabina,
　　　　o Thaliarche, merum diota:

permitte divis cetera, qui simul
stravere ventos aequore fervido　　　　　　　　10
　　deproeliantis, nec cupressi
　　　　nec veteres agitantur orni.

quid sit futurum cras fuge quaerere et
quem Fors dierum cumque dabit lucro
　　appone, nec dulcis amores　　　　　　　　　15
　　　　sperne puer neque tu choreas,

donec virenti canities abest
morosa. nunc et Campus et areae
　　lenesque sub noctem susurri
　　　　composita repetantur hora,　　　　　　20

nunc et latentis proditor intimo
gratus puellae risus ab angulo
　　pignusque dereptum lacertis
　　　　aut digito male pertinaci.

In a dramatic monologue we read the words of a character speaking and we take pleasure in piecing the story together from the scraps of evidence we overhear. Horace often uses the form. In 1. 5 he is addressing Pyrrha and as we read we gradually come to understand their story and their characters. In 1. 27 he is addressing a party of drunk young men and we know a good deal about the speaker and the listeners before the end of the poem. Here in 1. 9 the first word, *vides*, 'you see', tells us we are reading a dramatic monologue.

40

IX

You see Soracte standing white and deep
with snow, the woods in trouble, hardly able
   to carry their burden and the rivers
     halted by sharp ice.

Thaw out the cold. Pile up the logs   5
on the hearth and be more generous, Thaliarchus,
   as you draw the four-year-old Sabine
     from its two-eared cask.

Leave everything else to the gods. As soon as
they still the winds battling it out   10
   on the boiling sea, the cypresses stop waving
     and the old ash trees.

Don't ask what will happen tomorrow.
Whatever day Fortune gives you, enter it
   as profit, and don't look down on love   15
     and dancing while you're still a lad,

while the gloomy grey keeps away from the green.
Now is the time for the Campus and the squares
   and soft sighs at the time arranged
     as darkness falls.   20

Now is the time for the lovely laugh from the secret corner
giving away the girl in her hiding-place,
   and for the token snatched from her arm
     or feebly resisting finger.

If Horace and his addressee can see the snow on Mount Soracte, twenty miles to the north of Rome, they could in theory be in the city on the top of the Gianicolo, but the second stanza tells us that they are not going for a bracing winter walk but sitting indoors drinking by a log fire. If they can see Soracte from indoors, the deduction Horace is inviting us to make is that they are in a house near the mountain. This is confirmed by the log fire, a country pleasure, and by another country pleasure, the Sabine wine. Four years is young for one of the great wines of Italy but

41

if Horace has kept this Sabine for four years it is something out of the ordinary, a *riserva* (see on 1. 20. 1). Soracte is on the borders of the Sabine country. The rivers will not include the Tiber—if the Tiber had frozen over during Horace's lifetime we would know about it—but the shallow streams at the bottom of every other valley in mountain areas. In the second stanza Horace is asking his companion to keep the fire stoked up and to pour the wine. The poet of the dramatic monologue is giving us evidence and the obvious (but not necessary) deduction is that the companion is a slave. The word *benignius*, 'more generously' is then an affectionate tease. The master is telling the slave not to spare the master's wine. The joke is continued in the next line when the slave is called Thaliarchus, Greek for 'lord of the feast', and the four-year-old wine is in a two-handled jar, a *diota*, a striking Greek word which occurs nowhere else in surviving Latin literature. Horace is perhaps hinting that here in this Italian landscape with Italian wine he is enjoying a symposium, a Greek drinking-party, as lyric poets had done from Alcaeus onwards and is therefore once again claiming his place as a Roman among the great lyric poets of Greece. Indeed we have already had the hint, since the opening of the poem is like fragment 338 of Alcaeus:

> Zeus is sending rain and from heaven there is
> a great storm and the streams of water are frozen
>
> .   .   .   .
>
> Down with the storm. Stoke up the fire,
> mix the honey-sweet wine
> without sparing and round your head
> put a band of soft wool.

From the rigours of winter and the need for wine we move easily to moral reflection: 'When the winds stop blowing on the sea, the trees stop shaking.' Scholars have said that this destroys the picture. They do not see how in the first stanza we can have a still day in the hills with soft snow filigreeing the branches and now be in a storm at sea with branches tossing in the wind. This is a failure to understand the Latin and it has bedevilled the understanding of this poem. When the verb in an adverbial clause of time is in the perfect tense, *stravere* (10) and the verb in the principal clause is in the present, *agitantur* (11), we are being given a general law, not a particular description (compare 1. 12. 27–9). Horace and Thaliarchus are looking out at the snow. Horace says sententiously, 'When winds stop blowing, trees stop shaking', meaning of course that unpleasant things do not last for ever. This could be said of a plague of

42

locusts or a broken ankle or a professor with tenure. It does not mean that the wind is blowing. Horace has also been attacked for the weather at the end of the poem, where he advises Thaliarchus to enjoy out-of-door pursuits, and scholars envisage him flirting with girls in three feet of snow. But *nunc . . . repetantur* clearly does not refer to this winter evening in the country. Horace is advising Thaliarchus at his stage in life to turn his thoughts to such pleasures. 'Now is the time for the pleasures of the city', meaning obviously 'while you are still young' (lines 17–18), 'from now on, in the months that lie ahead'. There is no chronological or meteorological discrepancy.

There have also been attempts to split the poem historically by arguing that the sympotic opening which recalls the early Greek lyrics of Lesbos in the sixth century BC is inconsistent with the Hellenistic street-scenes at the end. The poem would then be a literary construct with no resemblance to real life, not only a succession of inconsistent images but also a blend of different cultures and literary genres. This again is wrong. There was a time and place where all these social practices occurred together—in and around Rome in the lifetime of Horace. Rome, as we argued at the end of the previous ode, was a Hellenistic city.

The subtlest pleasure of dramatic monologue lies in the observation of character. Do we know anything else about Thaliarchus? Here is a youngster (*puer* in line 16) to whom the middle-aged Horace is speaking affectionately as he asks him to pour the wine more generously. This is a symposium in the Greek manner and in Greek sympotic poems the boy who pours the wine is often the beloved. Indeed the very name Thaliarchus occurs on a fifth-century Athenian vase as a *kalos* name, the name of a beautiful boy. The details are in Nisbet and Hubbard, who, however, append a stern warning: 'But this by itself is not sufficient justification for suggesting a sentimental implication.' The name Thaliarchus is, however, only one of the hints in the text and the expectations of the symposiastic genre are already pointing us in this direction.

The poem now leaps into life. Why is Horace comforting Thaliarchus? Why is Horace advising him to enjoy the love of girls? Edmunds points to the importance of Alcaeus, whose homosexual love poems are praised by Horace at 1. 32. 11. Here in lines 13–14 of this Alcaean poem the lover-poet seems to be consoling his beloved for the onset of puberty when he will no longer be attractive to men. 'Time passes,' says Horace in line 17, always ready to exploit his age; 'look at my grey hairs. But don't be disconsolate and don't ask what the future will bring. You are only moving from one form of love to another. Your days of love with me in the country are over' (and 1. 17 will show us how Horace enjoyed love in the country), 'but you will now find a life in the city with dancing, with young men's activities in the Campus Martius; with the social life of the piazza and the flirtatious manœuvres of young girls, so unlike the sedate affections of 40-year-olds like myself.' It is typical of Horace that he has helped us to understand this ode by showing us a beloved boy who was precisely at this stage of life at the end of 1. 4. Thaliarchus is to Horace as Lycidas is to Sestius. Horace often provides progressive practice in how to read Horatian odes. Just so, for example, the first two odes alerted us to the Augustan implications of the third and Horace has helped us with *Campus* in line 18 by describing in the previous ode the camaraderie of the Campus Martius.

This is not to say that Horace had a love affair with a Thaliarchus, or indeed with any young man, slave or free. This is not a case history and poets are not on oath. As we read *Odes* 1. 9 we enter a world known by Horace and adjusted for his poem. There is nothing impossible or even implausible about it. The fact that it features in earlier poetry does not mean that it could not have occurred in Horace's Rome. Griffin and MacMullen show abundantly that Roman men made love to their slaves, female and male, and that life imitates poetry and poetry imitates life. Roman poets represented these activities in their poetry, sometimes movingly, as in 4. 1. 29–40, published in 13 BC, Horace's fifty-second year:

> me nec femina nec puer
> iam nec spes animi credula mutui
> nec certare iuvat mero
> nec vincire novis tempora floribus.
>
> sed cur, Ligurine, cur
> manat rara meas lacrima per genas?
> cur facunda parum decoro
> inter verba cadit lingua silentio?
>
> nocturnis ego somniis
> iam captum teneo, iam volucrem sequor
> te per gramina Martii
> campi, te per aquas, dure, volubilis.

I no longer take pleasure in woman or boy,
nor in the trusting hope that love will be returned
    nor in competing at drinking-bouts
nor in binding my head with fresh flowers.

But why, Ligurinus, why
does the stray tear trickle down my cheeks?
    Why in the middle of eloquent words
does my tongue become shamefully silent?

At night in my dreams sometimes
I catch you and hold you, sometimes I pursue you
    over the grass of the Campus Martius
or in the flowing river and you do not pity me.

Our poem 1. 9 ends with an effect which is pure Latin. In 1. 5 we saw how in English the logic is carried by the word-order, while Latin is free to convey emphasis and nuance and to suggest relationships by juxtaposition and by separation, which we have called hyperbaton on 1. 5. So here the events of the first two lines of the last stanza occur in this order:

Now also	of *hiding*	*betraying*	(from) *intimate*
lovely	(of) girl	laugh	from corner.

The three words *latentis proditor intimo* establish a triple mystery which is resolved in the next line in three stages as we learn that the person hiding is a girl, the betrayer is her laugh, and what is intimate is the corner. This makes glancing points which are beyond any device of English:

Now is the time for the lovely laugh from the secret corner
giving the girl away in her hiding-place.

X

MERCVRI, facunde nepos Atlantis,
qui feros cultus hominum recentum
voce formasti catus et decorae
    more palaestrae,

te canam, magni Iovis et deorum   5
nuntium curvaeque lyrae parentem,
callidum quidquid placuit iocoso
    condere furto.

te, boves olim nisi reddidisses
per dolum amotas, puerum minaci   10
voce dum terret, viduus pharetra
    risit Apollo.

quin et Atridas duce te superbos
Ilio dives Priamus relicto
Thessalosque ignis et iniqua Troiae   15
    castra fefellit.

tu pias laetis animas reponis
sedibus virgaque levem coerces
aurea turbam, superis deorum
    gratus et imis.   20

This is one of Horace's most genial and most cunning poems. The geniality comes in different forms in each stanza: in the first the praise of civilization including the beauty of Greek athletics; in the second the music and playful thieving; in the third the mischief of a baby god and the laughter of the victim, his own brother; in the fourth the meeting of Priam and Achilles in Homer's *Iliad* 24 and the successful escort of an old man through the ranks of his enemies to ransom the dead body of his son Hector; in the fifth the joyful seats of the blessed and the pleasure given by Mercury to all the gods. The ingenuity of Mercury features in each stanza until the last (in lines 3, 7, 10, and 16 of the Latin), but Horace exercises his own ingenuity in the details which link the five stanzas of the poem.

    The gift of speech, of eloquence, is celebrated in the first stanza and

X

Mercury, eloquent grandson of Atlas,
who cunningly moulded the brutish ways of early man
with the gift of speech and the beauty
    of the wrestling school,

of you shall I sing, messenger of mighty Jupiter   5
and the gods, father of the curved lyre,
ingenious concealer of whatever in your mischief
    you decide to steal.

Once when you were a baby and Apollo was booming
his terrifying threats if you did not return   10
the cattle you had driven away, he suddenly missed his quiver
    and burst out laughing.

Again, you were the guide when Priam left Troy
laden with riches, and the haughty sons of Atreus,
the Thessalian watch-fires and the camp of Troy's enemies   15
    were all deceived.

You guide the souls of the righteous
to their blessed seats and with golden staff you herd
the unsubstantial shades, dear to the gods above
    and the gods below.   20

extended to music and poetry in the second as Horace reminds us that
one of the first acts of this clever god was to kill a tortoise and string its
shell with sheep-gut to make the first lyre. The lyre takes us to poetry
and the story takes us to the Homeric *Hymn to Hermes* 20 ff. No lover of
Greek poetry can read the next stanza, on the meeting of Priam and
Achilles, without his mind being filled with recollections of the last book
of Homer's *Iliad*. Nor was Horace speaking without a smile when he
started that second stanza by saying 'You I shall sing of', *te canam*, to the
god who made music possible. Poetry and music are therefore one link-
ing item in the ode. Thieving is another. Horace mentions thieving and
the concealment of what is stolen at the end of the second stanza and
exemplifies it in the third. The story goes that Mercury drove Apollo's
cattle backwards into a cave, and the Latin word *amotas* does not only

mean 'driven away', but is also a technical legal term meaning 'expropri-
ated'. Dishonesty reappears in the fourth stanza, where the escort
Mercury provided for Priam is described as a deceitful trick (*fefellit*, 'he
cheated'). This time the deception is part of a service which Mercury
performed in obedience to Jupiter in his role as messenger of the gods, a
reminder of lines 5–6. And what Mercury does is to cheat the cruel ways
of men which he had been moulding at the beginning of the poem. The
last stanza gives another example of Mercury's work as an escort, this
time in a different field. The poem has moved from boyhood to death
but in every stanza there are traces of Horace's sense of the divine in
poetry. We may even hear a distant music in lines 19–20 where Horace
says that Mercury is welcome, *gratus*, to the gods above, since the last
stanza of 1. 32 explains how the tortoiseshell is welcome, *grata*, at the
banquets of highest Jupiter.

The music of Horace's verse is lost for ever because we do not know
how it was spoken. But in this metre there is a trick we can use to catch
a fragment of its rhythm. The Sapphic stanza consists of three long lines
and one short. Here in this poem the five-syllable cadence of the final
lines of the Latin carries five vivid effects, the surprise of the wrestling-
ground, the shock of divine thieving, then of divine laughter, the wit
whereby Mercury's escort duty is classed as an act of deceit, and finally
the indescribable close. For us this is just a technical detail. For the
ancient listener it would have been part of the complex emotional move-
ment of the poem from the sacral formality of the opening, through
humour and the evocation of one of the most moving parts of the *Iliad*
to the joy of the righteous and the gleam of gold at the end.

This poem begins with a string of features which occur in many
ancient kletic hymns (see on 1. 32): the name of the god in the vocative
case, followed by his parentage and an adjective clause which recounts
some of his achievements. Another standard feature, which we have
already noticed at the end of 1. 2, is the use of the second person *tu*. This
is part of the cement of our poem, occurring as it does in the Latin of the
first line of each stanza after the first. Many of these features are to be
found also in the one surviving stanza of Alcaeus' hymn to Hermes (frag-
ment 308):

Odes 1. 10

Hail, ruler of Cyllene, for my spirit moves me to hymn
your praises, whom Maia bore on the very peak
of the mountain, having lain with the son of Cronus,
    Lord of all.

Horace's poem therefore owes a great debt to tradition and it would be foolish to read it as a statement of simple faith. As Fraenkel says (p. 164): 'Horace, the son of an ageing civilisation, the pupil of refined and sceptical philosophers, did not write for people who would credit him with belief . . .' in such stories. Scholars have therefore called the poem 'a study', 'a simple poetic exercise'. This fails to do it justice. Fraenkel has a truer sense when he writes: 'What inspired him was not a personal religion of his own . . . but beliefs of a remote past, ennobled and perpetuated in works of poetry and in monuments of art.' But even that does not go far enough. Horace makes it quite plain in the first book of his *Epistles* that he hugely enjoyed making fun of 'refined and sceptical philosophers'. The same book, as well as many of the *Satires* shows us a Horace who repeatedly parades the inconsistency of his own views, sometimes writing as a Stoic, at other times as an Epicurean, sometimes as a sceptic, at other times as a believer in the Olympian gods. Accordingly these different approaches may be seen as the musings of a poet exploring the problems of existence in different ways at different times. Perhaps Horace shares with many artists the gift of total, temporary belief.

Perhaps too, like many others of us, Horace made gods in the likeness of the world as he saw it. In this ode, for instance, we see a god who embodied eloquence and civilization including the beauty of the palaestra, music and poetry, ingenuity, rascality and laughter, the relief of men in anguish, a universe where men die, where gods enjoy the company of gods, and the righteous are rewarded (in lines 17–18). Of course Horace is a sceptic, sometimes. But he seems here to be writing as a believer, of a god whom he loves, a god who is the eternal form of things he enjoys and things he accepts. If this were so, the ode would be an expression of that spirituality which finds the divine in the particulars of daily life. Such beliefs are not contemptible or inconsistent with the persona he adopts elsewhere and, taken straight, they go to make a wonderful poem.

Tv ne quaesieris, scire nefas, quem mihi, quem tibi
finem di dederint, Leuconoe, nec Babylonios
temptaris numeros. ut melius, quidquid erit, pati,
seu pluris hiemes seu tribuit Iuppiter ultimam,

quae nunc oppositis debilitat pumicibus mare   5
Tyrrhenum:: sapias, vina liques, et spatio brevi
spem longam reseces. dum loquimur, fugerit invida
aetas: carpe diem, quam minimum credula postero.

O nce again, as in 1. 9, bad weather leads to advice not to enquire
about the future, but instead to see to the wine and once again, if
we were right about 1. 9, Horace turns to thoughts of love.

Are we then to agree that Horace's thinking is trite and repetitive, that
'Horace's locutions far outnumber his ideas'? This is what comes from
judging a poem by its paraphrase. Poetry begins where paraphrase ends.
The purpose of this note will be to point to some of the things in this
poem which slip through the wide mesh of that prosaic net.

This ode, like 1. 9, is a dramatic monologue. As such it provides, in
driblets, evidence which encourages us to make deductions about the char-
acters and situation of Horace and Leuconoe. If Horace starts by telling
her not to ask, this is because she has been asking. If she is concerned about
his death, and her own, she loves him, and the Latin (which would have
been written without commas) is warmer than the English, *quem mihi
quem tibi finem*. Horace replies as the cool rationalist who is sceptical of the
elaborate calculations of Babylonian astrology and takes the common-
sense view that the best thing is to accept what comes, whether it be death
tomorrow or some more years of life. Then after the plain common sense
he speaks in terms of winter storms at sea, thus setting the endless opposi-
tion of sea and land against the shortness of human life, the vast energy of
elemental forces against the impotence of human beings.

But we expect the waves to batter on the shore. Horace cheats our
expectations by making the pumice wear out the sea. Pumice is the con-
gealed form of the lava that pours from volcanic eruptions. Since the
only part of the mainland of Italy where volcanic rock lies along the
shore is the Bay of Naples, unless Horace is laying a false clue, the hint

XI

Don't you ask, Leuconoe—the gods do not wish it to be known—
what end they have given to me or to you, and don't meddle with
Babylonian calculations. How much better to accept whatever comes,
whether Jupiter gives us other winters or whether this is our last

now wearying the Tyrrhenian Sea on the pumice stones   5
opposing it. Be wise, strain the wine and cut back long hope
into a small space. While we speak, envious time will have
flown past. Harvest the day and leave as little as possible for tomorrow.

is that Horace and Leuconoe are indoors on a wild winter's day in a villa
on the shore of the Bay of Naples. If that were so the obvious guess for
Horace's contemporary readers is that the poem was written during a
visit to Herculaneum, perhaps to the villa of Philodemus, Epicurean
poet, and teacher and friend of other Augustan poets (see Gigante and
d'Arms for Philodemus and his villa). Commentators and translators
think of the sea crashing against a barrier of rocks but nowadays the
steep shore of the Bay of Naples at Herculaneum is not composed of
huge obsidian blocks. Rather it is deep in small, roundish pebbles of
pumice, porous because of the escape of gas or steam as the lava cooled.
If this was true of the coastline below Herculaneum before the eruption
of AD 79 (and excavation may soon be able to tell us), Horace is not
thinking of the clash of sea on solid rock, but of the waves endlessly
rolling back millions of these paper-light pebbles with a sound some-
thing between a grind and a roar and a rustle as they absorb the energy
of the mighty sea, *oppositis debilitat pumicibus mare Tyrrhenum*. This par-
ticular is important as particulars usually are in Horace. The Tyrrhenian
waves are not 'derived from some Greek commonplace'. Horace is evok-
ing a scene familiar to many Romans, perhaps visible and audible from
the house where he sits or imagines himself sitting with Leuconoe.
'Look at us alongside the vastness of the world.'

    In the translation *sapias* is rendered 'Be wise' which is too solemn, but
less likely to be infuriating to Leuconoe than the more common version
'Be sensible'. Even so, after this daring advice, he immediately gives her
a job to do and takes her mind off the future. Again, unless Horace is
laying false clues, this tells us that Leuconoe is a slave, like Thaliarchus

51

in 1. 9 and Lyde in similar circumstances in 3. 28. In each case the beloved pours the wine. This done—Romans sometimes filtered their wine with muslin or snow—he tells her to prune long hope to a short stem (in horticultural terms hard winter pruning encourages growth) and the famous phrase *carpe diem*, 'harvest the day' is a metaphor from the vineyard. His proposal is that they should drink together and make love, but he speaks with such lightness and tact that it ought to have become a model for all subsequent writers on the subject.

By now we have some notion of Leuconoe and what she has been saying. We know something about her status, her relationship with Horace, the location, the weather, and the persona which Horace himself is presenting. We can also guess what time has to be envious about. Not bad for a dramatic monologue in eight lines.

Horace starts this ode with two prohibitions, one involving man's relationship with the gods and the other counselling against oriental superstitions. He follows these by a positive recommendation in general terms which takes us to the shore of the Tyrrhenian Sea and general reflections on life. He ends with three particular injunctions lightly laced with wine. The pacing and variation of tone in a poem are difficult to write about, but the metre is part of this dynamic and can be analysed.

XII

QVEM virum aut heroa lyra vel acri
    tibia sumis celebrare, Clio?
quem deum? cuius recinet iocosa
      nomen imago

aut in umbrosis Heliconis oris   5
aut super Pindo gelidove in Haemo,
unde vocalem temere insecutae
      Orphea silvae

arte materna rapidos morantem
fluminum lapsus celerisque ventos,   10
blandum et auritas fidibus canoris
      ducere quercus?

52

The long lines in 1. 11 (see the Appendix on Metres) start with a foot of two syllables and end with a foot of two syllables. The middle of each line is filled with three long feet, each long–short–short–long, known as choriambs. The importance of this is visible and audible in lines 5–6:

quae nunc   oppositis   debilitat   pumicibus   mare
Tyrrhenum.

The storms of winter are wearing out the Tyrrhenian Sea and the wearing-out, *debilitat*, fills a choriamb. So do the pumices, *pumicibus*. So does their opposition, *oppositis*, and this endless battle spills over into the next stanza in line 5 which is the only line in this poem with a break in sense at this point, after the third syllable. The choriamb is the key to the sound of this poem and the key unlocks another door. As the poem is read it has interjections at several points which give it a slightly jerky, dislocated rhythm. Many of these points are choriambs like those in line 5 where the feet begin and end where the words begin and end. *Scire nefas*, 'it is wrong to know' is a choriamb containing a moralization in a parenthesis, like *ut melius* and *quidquid erit* in line 3. Similar are *vina liques*, *dum loquimur*, and the famous *carpe diem*. These are facts. Their effects are inexpressible, but there they are in the poem.

XII

What man or hero do you choose, Clio,
to celebrate with lyre or shrill pipe?
What god? Whose name will the playful echo
      sing back

on the shady slopes of Helicon   5
or on Pindus or chilly Haemus
from where the wilful woods followed
      sweet-voiced Orpheus,

as by his mother's art he held back
swift winds and the rushing flow of rivers   10
and led the long-eared oaks with the charm
      of his singing lyre.

Iupiter

quid prius dicam solitis parentis
laudibus, qui res hominum ac deorum,
qui mare et terras variisque mundum   15
    temperat horis?

unde nil maius generatur ipso,
nec viget quicquam simile aut secundum:
proximos illi tamen occupavit
    Pallas honores.   20

Pallas

proeliis audax, neque te silebo,
Liber, et saevis inimica Virgo

Liber & Athena

beluis, nec te, metuende certa
    Phoebe sagitta.

Apollo.

dicam et Alciden puerosque Ledae,   25

Hercules & Dioscuri

hunc equis, illum superare pugnis
nobilem; quorum simul alba nautis
    stella refulsit,

defluit saxis agitatus umor,
concidunt venti fugiuntque nubes,   30
et minax, quom sic voluere, ponto
    unda recumbit.

Romulum post hos prius an quietum
Pompili regnum memorem an superbos
Tarquini fascis, dubito, an Catonis   35
    nobile letum.

Regulum et Scauros animaeque magnae
prodigum Paulum superante Poeno
gratus insigni referam Camena
    Fabriciumque.   40

hunc et incomptis Curium capillis
utilem bello tulit et Camillum
saeva paupertas et avitus apto
    cum lare fundus.

crescit occulto velut arbor aevo   45
fama Marcelli; micat inter omnis
Iulium sidus velut inter ignis
    luna minores.

What can I do but follow custom and praise first
the Father who governs the affairs of men
and gods, the land and sea and sky   15
    from hour to hour?

None of his children is greater than himself.
There is no other living thing like him
or second to him but at his side Pallas has taken
    the place of honour.   20

Nor shall I be silent about you, Bacchus,
bold in battle, nor the virgin goddess,
enemy of wild beasts, nor you, dread Phoebus
    with your unerring arrow.

I shall speak too of Hercules and of the sons   25
of Leda, famous for their victories, one with horses
the other with fists. As soon as sailors see
    their bright star shining,

the heaving sea streams down from the rocks,
the winds fall and clouds disperse   30
and when they will it, the towering wave
    subsides upon the ocean.

After these I wonder whether to speak of Romulus
or the peaceful reign of Numa Pompilius
or the proud rods of Tarquin   35
    or Cato's noble death.

With the glorious Muse of Italy I shall gratefully sing
of Regulus and the Scauri, of Paulus prodigal
of his mighty spirit in the Carthaginian victory
    and of Fabricius.   40

Like rough-bearded Curius sound in battle,
and like Camillus, he was born
of cruel poverty on his father's farm
    with household gods to match.

The fame of Marcellus grows like a tree   45
over time unseen; the Julian Star shines
among them all like the moon
    among the lesser fires.

gentis humanae pater atque custos,
orte Saturno, tibi cura[magni   50
Caesaris] fatis data: tu secundo
    Caesare regnes.

ille seu Parthos Latio imminentis
egerit [iusto domitos triumpho,]
sive subiectos Orientis orae   55
    Seras et Indos,

te minor] laetum reget aequus orbem;
tu gravi curru quaties Olympum,
tu [parum castis] inimica mittes
    fulmina lucis.   60

'What man or hero or god will you choose to sing?' Horace asks his Muse, and reverses the order as he answers, starting with the gods and moving to heroes and then men. A hero in this context is a demigod, like Hercules, son of Jupiter and the mortal woman Alcmena, and like Castor and Pollux, sons of Jupiter and Leda. At line 33 he turns to Rome and deals with the hero Romulus, son of Mars and the priestess Ilia, and then mortal men. The list ceases at 46 with the Julian family and the ode ends as it began with Jupiter, as Horace prays for the continued safety of the Julian Augustus, ruling the earth under the ruler of the gods. Whom is Horace to praise? The obvious answer is Augustus, but that answer does not come in any obvious form. The ruler of Rome is praised obliquely and with Pindaric elaboration in an ode which is meant to stand beside the greatest lyric poetry hitherto written. This purpose is declared in the first stanza, which is an adaptation of the opening of Pindar's second *Olympian*:

> Hymns that rule the lyre,
> what god, what hero, what man shall we proclaim?
> Zeus is lord of Pisa, Hercules established
> the Olympic festival as the first-fruits of war,
> but Theron must be celebrated for his victory . . .

No poet begins a poem like Pindar and Horace has seized upon this opening and subtilized it to begin his ode in praise of Augustus. Ezra Pound in *Hugh Selwyn Moberley* made fun of it, quoting the Greek (*Tina theon, tin'heroa, tin'andra . . .*) and punning:

O father and guardian of the human race,
offspring of Saturn, to you the Fates have given   50
care over great Caesar; may you reign
    with Caesar second to you.

Whether he routs the Parthians who threaten Latium,
or the Chinese and Indians lying close
to the East, subduing them   55
    in a just triumph,

as your subordinate let him rule a joyful world in equity:
you will shake Olympus with the weight of your chariot,
you will send down your angry lightning
    on the groves of the impure.   60

> What god, man, or hero
> Shall I place a tin wreath upon!

Horace had some fun with it too, but with wit and also with the respect which one great poet would show towards another. Pindar is a difficult and startling writer, principally because of the daring of his images and the subtlety of his transitions and Horace often speaks in tones which recall the boldness of his master. So, in this third stanza when the woods follow *temere*, 'rashly, pell-mell', is this an invitation to see them lumbering along and falling over their own roots? This seems to be confirmed, though we translators tend to avert our gaze in embarrassment, when Orpheus is said to have the charm to lead *eared* mountain oaks, *blandum ... auritas ... ducere ... quercus*. The Pindaric tone is maintained in the fourth stanza, 'What shall I say sooner than the accustomed praise of the Father ...?', which is an allusion to an established formula used in the opening of *Olympian* 2, quoted just above, and also, for example, in Theocritus' praise of Ptolemy Philadelphus (17. 1):

> Let us begin with Zeus, Muses, and with Zeus let us end.

Horace has followed this prescription in this ode at lines 13–18 and 58–60. This is precarious writing. Horace is drawing upon the Greek poetic tradition and aspiring to the sublime, Pindaric style, but not with total solemnity. 'Whom will you choose to celebrate' he asks his Muse and in line 13 it is Horace who is singing. The voice that echoes round the groves and cliffs of the great Greek poetic mountains where Orpheus worked his weird miracles is the voice of Horace.

He answers the question with which he begins by listing some warlike Greek gods including Apollo who won the victory at Actium for Octavian, then moving to formidable heroes. Why do Castor and Pollux, the junior members of this cast, receive the longest billing, being praised for their individual expertise and also for their manifestation as St Elmo's fire, the blue lights at the mast-heads which we have already met at 1. 3. 2? The centre of Horace's odes is often important (see Moritz). Here this eighth stanza of fifteen is a peaceful interlude between the Greek of the first half and the Roman of the second, and the transition is marked by a transition from the Greek Muse Clio in line 2 in her three Greek mountains to the Italian Muse *Camena* in line 39 of the Latin. We shall see the same transition at 3. 4. 21.

To the superficial eye the Roman part is a list of Roman worthies starting with Romulus, the founder of the city, and ending with Marcellus at the end of the third century BC. This eye is then bewildered by the breach of chronological order in the early placing of the Younger Cato who committed suicide in 46, the latest of all these great Romans. Scholars have agonized over this problem, questioning the structure of the argument or seeing Cato as a tactful stand-in for Brutus who drove out the Tarquins in 510 BC and whose descendant assassinated Julius Caesar in 44 BC. Some of the best Horatians solve the problem by condemning or emending the manuscript reading.

The problem was solved by Brown in 1991. Horace began the ode with a question: 'Whom shall I praise first, A, B, or C?' First he deals with the Greeks and then, after the lull in the middle of the poem, he turns to Rome and asks what amounts to the same question: *prius . . . memorem . . . dubito*, 'I am at a loss whether to sing first of A, B, C or D.' These four, including Cato, provide a chronological sweep of the history of Rome. The first of them, like the last of the Greeks, is a demigod, son of the god Mars and the priestess Ilia, founder of Rome in 753 BC. Numa was Romulus' successor, the pious, peaceful counterpoise to the warlike founder. The proud rods of Tarquin, *superbos Tarquini fasces*, must allude in some measure to the end of the monarchy with Tarquin the Proud, *Tarquinius Superbus*. The death of Cato could be seen as the end of the Republic. In this stanza therefore Horace is asking whom he shall praise and is surveying the range of possibilities. The stanzas that follow contain his answer. If, with Nisbet and Hubbard, we take the Scauri to refer to two brothers, his list of eight Greeks is followed in lines 37–46 by eight Romans of the Republican era, making a shapely structure.

Its finesse lies in the fact that Horace does not include in the list of Romans the man whom he wishes to praise, but chooses rather to arrive at Augustus by a cunning transition. The list of Roman warriors is not a list of unbroken successes. Regulus was famous for being tortured to death by the Carthaginians, Lucius Aemilius Paulus for his defeat at Cannae, Marcus Aemilius Scaurus and Fabricius for their frugality. It is as though Horace is providing an austere setting for the brilliance of Augustus. Fabricius, Curius, and Camillus are the first victors and they lead to Marcus Claudius Marcellus, consul five times between 222 and 208 BC, conqueror of the Insubrian Gauls and captor of Syracuse. Marcellus has led us to Augustus.

In 25 BC a descendant of this great Marcellus, who bore the same three names, married Augustus' daughter Julia. When Romans heard in lines 45–6 that the fame of Marcellus grows like a tree in hidden time, they knew that the Marcelli lapsed into obscurity in the second century BC, recovered to produce three consuls in the last years of the Republic, and now in 25 BC were being united in marriage with the ruling family of Rome. The Augustan theme is developed by the reference to the Julian Star. According to Pliny, *Natural History* 2. 94, on each of the seven nights of the games held by Octavian four months after the assassination of Julius in 44 BC, a comet was seen to blaze in the sky and the people believed that the soul of Caesar had been received among the immortal gods. Octavian rejoiced at this portent and exploited it. There are at least half a dozen sightings of this star in the *Aeneid* (see West, 1993). To spell out the implications—the fame of old Marcellus grows (with the marriage of young Marcellus to Julia, daughter of Augustus) and the Julian Star outshines other stars (as the Julians outshine the other families of Rome). Virgil's *Aeneid* is the story of Aeneas, son of Venus and ancestor of Julius Caesar and of his grand-nephew and adoptive son, now Augustus. Horace has here travelled the same genealogical route as Virgil at *Aeneid* 6. 855–64 in order to praise the Julians and in particular Augustus.

We remember the opening: 'What man or hero . . . what god?' The Greek list does not trouble with Greek men but ends with heroes who became gods, Hercules entering Olympus as the husband of Hebe, the goddess of youth, Castor and Pollux each spending six months of the year on Olympus and six in the Underworld. The Roman list ends, by implication, with Julius Caesar who was deified in 42 BC two years after his death. His adoptive son, Octavian, was soon known as the Son of the God, *Divi Filius*, and was himself clearly destined to be deified.

At the end of *Odes* 1. 2 Horace played with the idea that Augustus was already a god. By the time of the writing of this ode, presumably nearer the time of Marcellus' marriage into the Julian family in 25 BC, Augustan policy had become clearer. Horace now makes no such statement, but on the contrary stresses the supremacy of Jupiter. Augustus is subordinate, second not in power—line 18 tells us there is none such—but second in the sense that he rules the earth with the approval of the ruler of the universe. The last words of the stanza also suggest that Augustus rules with more benignity than Jupiter.

Here in the ending of this poem there are other rumbles of official Augustan policy. The stress on world conquest is central, although the claims about India and China are exaggerations. The reference to the fairness of Augustus in line 56 accords eloquently with the praise of Cato in line 36—praise of this Republican saint is evidence of the magnanimity of Augustus, the *clementia* and *iustitia* celebrated on the *Clupeus*

XIII

CVM tu, Lydia, Telephi
cervicem roseam, cerea Telephi
laudas bracchia, vae meum
fervens difficili bile tumet iecur.

tum nec mens mihi nec color   5
certa sede manet, umor et in genas
furtim labitur, arguens
quam lentis penitus macerer ignibus.

uror, seu tibi candidos
turparunt umeros immodicae mero   10
rixae, sive puer furens
impressit memorem dente labris notam.

60

virtutis, the shield presented to Augustus to commemorate his courage, clemency, justice, and piety (*Res Gestae* 34. 2). It also shows that the magnanimity of Augustus extends to allowing his poet to praise one who would surely have been a bitter enemy of the regime. Then in line 57 his rule over the world is advertised as being in accord with the will of Jupiter and we are told that the world accepts it joyfully. The emphasis throughout on the supremacy of the Olympian gods conforms exactly with Augustan policy, as does the aspersion on other cults at the very end of the ode. As Suetonius records in chapter 93 of the *Life of Augustus*, 'He treated with extreme reverence such foreign cults as were ancient and traditional, but all others he despised.' Finally the mention of impurity is a hint of Augustus' desire to raise the standards of sexual behaviour, a theme which was repeatedly stressed in the Roman Odes (3. 1–6), and which was to become official policy in 18–17 BC. Augustus is not specifically included in the list of Romans to be praised, but his moment comes at the end of the ode where his policies are commended and he rules the world under Jupiter.

XIII

When you praise Telephus's
rosy neck, Lydia, and Telephus's
   waxen arms, oh how my
liver boils in indigestible bile.

At such a time neither mind nor colour   5
stays in its fixed seat and moisture trickles furtively
   on to my cheeks making clear
how slow are the fires which torment me to the heart.

I burn if drunken
brawls sully your white shoulders   10
   or if that wild boy's tooth
prints the tell-tale mark upon your lips.

Odes 1. 13

non, si me satis audias,
speres perpetuum dulcia barbare
        laedentem oscula quae Venus   15
quinta parte sui nectaris imbuit.

felices ter et amplius
quos irrupta tenet copula nec malis
        divulsus querimoniis
suprema citius solvet amor die.   20

There are problems. In the fourth line the relation of bile to liver is
not clear in the Latin, which could mean either by, with, from or in
bile. In the second stanza how odd to say that neither mind nor colour
stays in its fixed seat, and how strange that a *furtive* tear should make
anything *clear*, least of all how slow are tormenting fires.

Light dawns when we pierce the veil of translation. In line 8 the word
'torment' loses the literal flavour of *macerare*, a technical term from cook-
ing in Latin as in English: 'to macerate, to soften by steeping in a liquid,
with or without heat' (*Oxford English Dictionary*). Varro (*Res Rustica* 1.
59. 3) macerates pears in the sun and Pliny (*Natural History* 28. 212)
macerates the bladders of wild boars in smoke. Sometimes the word is
used in its strict technical sense. Sometimes it is used as an active
metaphor. Sometimes it is a dead metaphor meaning simply 'to torment'
or 'to weaken'.

This raises a point of method. If a poet summons up remembrance of
the past, it would be foolish to insist that the reader should think of a
legal summons. But if he *summons up* remembrance to the *sessions* of
thought, it would not be foolish to be put in mind of a court case. If the
poet goes on as Shakespeare does in *Sonnet* 30 to use such words as date-
less, long since cancelled, expense, grievances, tell (in the sense of count),
account, fore-bemoanèd, pay, paid, restored, it would be foolish not to
be alert to legal implications. The poet is exploring resemblances
between the process of memory and the process of the law. The literal
sense of sessions is activated by cognate words in the context. So in *Odes*
1. 11 'Harvest the day', *carpe diem*, does not by itself demand exploration
of literal harvesting, but after 'cut back to a short length' and before
'trusting as little as possible to tomorrow' we are dozing if we do not
think of fruit, and in that context of the king of fruits.

Macerare is a surprising word. Its literal sense was well-known. Are
there any cognates in the context to help us to know whether that literal

62

If you would only listen to me
you would not imagine that he would be for ever
  barbarously wounding those sweet lips   15
dipped by Venus in the quintessence of her nectar.

Three times blessed and more than three
are those held in an unbroken bond, whose love
  untorn by ill-natured scolding
will not release them till their last day comes.   20

sense should be invoked? The symptomatology starts in the first stanza:
'my boiling liver swells in indigestible bile'. If liver were stewing in a pot,
on this interpretation bile would be the stock and the liver would cer-
tainly swell. Then in the next stanza, 'my mind does not stay in its fixed
place'. Nor would a boiling liver. 'My colour', similarly, 'does not stay in
its place'. Here the fit is not perfect, but the proposition that Horace
himself changes colour is not too far away and it suggests colour changes
in the cooking. Moisture trickles down furtively on to Horace's cheeks,
as moisture may trickle down the side of a simmering pot. Now we know
why tears are here referred to, very unusually, as moisture, *umor*. This
overflow demonstrates that the liver is being cooked through and
through, *penitus*, by a slow heat, *lentis . . . ignibus*, which is to say that
Horace's tears reveal the depth and the duration of his suffering. There
are half-a-dozen cognates and they all fit.

The heat of the process is mentioned in several other passages where
macerare is used. In Plautus, *Trinummus* 225 the slave is cooking himself
and macerating himself, *egomet me coquo et macero*. In Horace himself, in
Epode 14. 11–16, Anacreon's very frequent (*persaepe*) serenading is com-
pared to the *fire* of Maecenas' passion and Horace's own (gentler) mac-
eration. At *Ciris* 244 in the *Appendix Vergiliana* love macerates its victim
with its well-known fire, *macerat igni*. Even where the literal force is
touched upon very lightly, the slowness of the process seems to be hinted
at with the occurrence of words suggesting frequency, *satis iam, satis iam
hos multos dies, magis magisque, ab eodem saepe* (Plautus, *Captivi* 928,
Poenulus 1248, *Pseudolus* 4 and 9, Afranius 351–2, and Lucretius, 3. 75
and 826–7). The slowness of the suffering, which is crucial to line 8 of
our ode, seems to linger on in these passages where the metaphor may
well be otherwise inactive.

A quarter of a century has passed since I put forward this obvious
interpretation and argued for it at great length (West, 1967: 65–71). The

world was not then ready for it. Indeed it may never be. Most scholars have politely ignored it or cited it with an exclamation mark. But *macerare* is the indicator. Since the technical flavour of the word is so strong and the cognates in the context are so numerous, and since the startling and the surreal are part of the armoury of this poet, we should surely ask what effect the metaphor would have on the poem if it were active.

The symptoms of love had been a familiar theme of poets since Sappho saw her beloved girl sitting with a man and wondered at his imperturbability, to the extent of suffering ten different physiological disturbances including sweating, fluttering of the heart in the breast, and fire running under the skin. In Catullus 51 in similar circumstances the poet experiences six similar symptoms including flame flowing down into the body, but stopping short of the most severe. Horace had admitted the influence of Sappho at 1. 1. 34, and on other occasions, without admitting it, he imitates and tries to improve on Catullus. Here, like them, he essays the stock theme of the lover's symptoms. But Horace is Horace. He is not going to have trembling in his breast or go as green as grass or be near unto death as Sappho was and he is not going to end by being ashamed of himself like Catullus. He has his feelings and ruefully admits to them, but smiles at Sappho and Catullus and at himself as he does so, by expressing his suffering in this whimsically detailed metaphor from cooking. We shall see more of this attitude to love in 1. 16 and 1. 17.

The characterization is vivid. Lydia goes on about Telephus at the end of each of the first three lines (*Telephus . . . Telephus . . . meum*). Telephus

---

Σἀς φσ∂

XIV

O NAVIS, referent in mare te novi
fluctus! o quid agis? fortiter occupa
    portum! nonne vides ut
        nudum remigio latus,

et malus celeri saucius Africo,   5
antennaeque gemant, ac sine funibus
    vix durare carinae
        possint imperiosius

is very pretty. Besides, he is a boy (11)—a sensitive point for the ageing Horace. A tear comes to his cheek and he tries to conceal it but it gives him away (the furtive tear making clear). Telephus is violent, witness the weals on Lydia's shoulders (whether caused by assault or by erotic wrestling as scholars dispute) and the bruising on her lips. This reminds Horace of how sweet they were. He warns her that the affair with young Telephus will not last, without being confident that she will listen (line 13). He ends by offering a totally different kind of love.

A last problem for the palate. The translation claims that Lydia's kiss is the quintessence of Venus' nectar. This would refer to the concept of a fifth element, purer than earth, air, water, and fire, by which Aristotle explained the mysterious workings of the heavens and of the soul. Horace is mischievously suggesting that the mysterious workings of Venus are to be explained by some such fifth ingredient in her nectar and that Lydia's lips have been dipped in it. Some scholars reject this interpretation on the grounds that the Latin for 'essence' would be some such word as *corpus* or *elementum*. Horace's word is *pars* so they suggest that Lydia's kisses were dipped in a fifth part of the nectar of Venus. In effect they would then be one fifth as sweet as the nectar of Venus. But they were surely far sweeter than that. *Pars* is a perfectly acceptable and comprehensible word for *elementum* on the lips of a non-philosophical poetic lover. Neither Horace nor Lydia would have been content with a fifth. What they would demand is not immersion in a fraction of Venus' nectar but maceration in its most rarefied and potent element or part, its quintessence.

nicaean-ship q svave

XIV

> O ship! Will new waves carry you out to sea
> again? O what are you doing? Make boldly
>   for the harbour. Don't you see how
>   your side is stripped of its oars,
>
> your mast is crippled by the swift sou'wester,   5
> the yards are groaning and without roping
>   the hull has little chance of holding out
>   against the mounting tyranny

aequor? non tibi sunt integra lintea,
non di quos iterum pressa voces malo.　　　　　10
　　quamvis Pontica pinus,
　　　silvae filia nobilis,

iactes et genus et nomen inutile,
nil pictis timidus navita puppibus
　　fidit. tu, nisi ventis　　　　　15
　　　debes ludibrium, cave.

nuper sollicitum quae mihi taedium,
nunc desiderium curaque non levis,
　　interfusa nitentis
　　　vites aequora Cycladas.　　　　　20

As a boy at Harrow Winston Churchill was unable to believe in the
sanity of the Romans because on his first day of Latin he was called
upon to address a table, *o mensa*. 'O ship' is not English, but it is needed
because it personifies the ship from the first word and that personifica-
tion is the basis of the intense feeling that runs through the poem and
culminates in the last stanza. Ships were feminine in antiquity as they are
now. The first line shows her helplessness and the rest of the stanza
expostulates with her, telling her to act with speed and courage and make
a realistic assessment of her difficulties. We then learn what they are.
One part of her is naked (*nudum*); another is crippled (*saucius* (5) is lit-
erally 'wounded'); another is wailing; she seems scarcely able to hold out
as the sea becomes more and more bullying; she is calling on the gods as
Italian women still do in storms at sea and boasting about her ancestry
although at a time like this her ancestry will be as much use to her as her
cosmetics. This detailed personification leads to the climax in the final
stanza (literally): 'recently you were an anxious (*sollicitum*) distress to me,
now a longing and a care (*cura*)'. The translation took a risk in translat-
ing *cura* as 'love' but the word often means that and something has to be
done to step up from the recent anxiety (*sollicitum*) to the present *cura*.
In this context of female personification, love seems to be implied.

　　The personification is vital but the force of the poem comes also from
the vividness and drama of the description. Horace is on shore. The ship
has been coming in to harbour and has been swept out to sea again by a
heavy swell. A sailor who wants to cross the harbour bar in such condi-
tions has to have courage and he has to seize the right moment. Any old

of the sea. Your sails are unsound and so are the gods
you call upon in dire distress once again.   10
    Though you are a Pontic pine,
       daughter of a noble forest,

and boast your useless ancestry and name,
the frightened sailor puts no trust
    in painted sterns. Keep a look out,   15
       unless you owe the winds some sport.

Not long ago you were a worry and a weariness for me,
and now a longing and a deep love.
    So steer clear of the waters that swirl
       between the shining Cyclades.   20

Scottish fisherman will tell tales of men who drowned on the rocks just
below their own homes because they came down the wrong side of the
pier. *Fortiter occupa portum* is real. So were the ropes. Line 6 refers to the
ancient practice of frapping, of strengthening the hull with ropes as
when the sailors taking St Paul to Rome 'used helps, undergirding the
ship' (Acts 27: 17). The damaged gods of line 10 were images kept in
niches in the high stern of the ship. Persius, 6. 29–30 describes a ship-
wrecked sailor washed ashore at the foot of a cliff with the huge gods
from his ship's stern lying beside him (*iacet ipse in litore et una ingentes de
puppe dei*). The gods were there to protect the ship but the ancients well
knew that they did not always do so.

    The first impression is that this is a vivid account of a ship caught in
a storm. But this obvious interpretation does not work. The anxiety and
passionate longing of the last stanza are out of all proportion unless this
is a very special ship. We know what ship it is. This poem is, like 1. 7,
1. 9, and 1. 10, related to poems of Alcaeus now preserved in fragments:

This wave in turn comes (*like?*) *the previous one*, and it will give us much trouble *to
bale out* when it enters the ship's . . . *Let us strengthen* (*the ship's sides*) as *quickly* as
possible, and *let us race* into a secure *harbour*, and *let soft fear not seize* any of us;
for a great (ordeal) stands clear before us. Remember *the previous* (*hardship*): now
let every man show himself *steadfast*. And let us not disgrace (by cowardice) our
noble fathers lying beneath the earth, who . . . the city . . . being . . . from fathers
. . . our spirit . . . is like . . . swift . . . heart (?) . . . tyranny . . . and let us not accept

. . . (fragment 6; translated by D. A. Campbell with his supplements in paren-
theses.)

Odes 1. 14

I do not understand the set of the winds.
One wave rolls from one side,
the next from another, and in the middle of them
we are swept along with our black ship,
struggling desperately with the storm.
The bilge is up round the mast-block.
The sail is already wide open to the light
and there are great rents through it.
The anchors are working loose . . .

(Fragment 208)

In the first of these fragments the words italicized show how close the Horace is to the Alcaeus. The references to the city, to ancestors, and to tyranny (*monarchia* is the Greek word) suggest that Alcaeus' ship is the Ship of State and this is the unanimous view of ancient commentators on Alcaeus. This is also the unanimous interpretation of Horace's *Ode* 1. 14 in the ancient commentators. Quite apart from these poems the notion of the Ship of State was a familiar metaphor in Greek thought before Horace. It 'must have been fairly trite in Hellenistic disquisitions on politics' (Nisbet and Hubbard: 181).

Not all the details in Horace's scene make a precise fit with the political allegory, but the storm is war. The new waves are a renewed outbreak. Courage is needed. The vessel is in a sorry plight and there is wailing in lines 6 and 10. The growing tyranny of the sea is expressed by the word *imperiosius* in line 8. The painted prows in lines 12–15 hint at the impotence of the aristocracy (the entrance hall of the Roman aristocrat would be lined with the painted effigies of the ancestors of the house).

A recent study by Woodman has rejected the political interpretation and argued that the allegory of the ship applies not to the state but to a mistress of Horace's. 'You're being carried away again. Stay where you are. You're in no condition to start off on another affair. The gods won't help you out this time, your background won't save you, and your makeup will only put your new lover on his guard. It's true I was annoyed with you, but that's over now and I need you badly. Oh well, take care as you go.' According to the orthodox view the nautical details refer allegorically to the state. According to Woodman they refer to a woman.

In 1. 11 and in 1. 13 I held that a metaphor was confirmed by cognate allusions in the immediate context. Here it might be argued that there are enough allusions to love to confirm the erotic metaphor. On the other hand in 1. 11 the metaphor of pruning was vividly signalled at the begin-

68

ning by the notion of 'cutting back', and in 1. 13 the cooking notion was vividly signalled by boiling and confirmed by discoloration, overflow, slow heat, and maceration through and through. Here there is no indica-tor. On the contrary, Horace is starting from an Alcaean poem about the Ship of State and there is nothing to suggest to the reader that his own poem is going to take a different tack. Further, in the other two passages all the details conformed with the ruling metaphor whereas here there are several points which are grossly improper to the erotic interpretation. 'Boldly make for the harbour' makes sense but 'Be brave and come back to me' is such a strange invitation that Woodman's paraphrase changes it to 'Stay where you are'. The naked side of the lover makes no sense in this context whether or not we remember that *latus*, side, is often used as an obscene term for sexual intercourse. And what would Horace's mistress's mast be? What is her undergirding? What are these torn sails with day-light showing through? No lover would have any hope of effecting a rec-onciliation if he talked like this. It will be argued that this is to press the metaphor too hard. After all, these details do not have close correspon-dences to the Ship of State. On the other hand, if the poem is about the Ship of State, these details show vividly that the whole fabric of the state is in a sorry plight. They offer an appropriate general sense and there is little temptation to explore the detailed correspondences. But if these details refer to a mistress of Horace's, the correspondences cry out to be explored and lead us into absurdities. The metaphor makes nonsense. This is vividly illustrated by Jocelyn, who quotes among other passages a squib by Meleager in order to argue that whenever a ship metaphor is applied to a woman the tone is always scurrilous:

> Timarion, once a pinnace with a trim frame,
>   can no longer bear Aphrodite's rowing.
> Her back is bent like the yard-arm on the mast
>   and her forestays are grey and slack.
> Her flapping sails hang down as sagging breasts
>   and the brine has etched wrinkles in her belly.
> Below everything is full of bilge-water, the sea swills about
>   in her stomach and the brine shivers in her knees.
> The poor thing is still alive, but she'll soon be putting in
>   at Acheron's swamp, the twenty-oared hag.

(Meleager in *Palatine Anthology* 11. 60)

Scholars have asked what crisis of state could have provoked Horace's poem and made many guesses. The clues in the poem are so slight that certainty is not possible, perhaps not even probability. Nevertheless we should try. The emotion at the end of the poem may well apply not only to the state but also to its guardian, Augustus. In that case line 17 would imply that Horace had suffered anxiety and distress because of the continuance of civil war, and line 18 would suggest that when it broke out again he was concerned for his patron's safety. We are looking for a moment, perhaps between 30 and 23 BC, when war had broken out again or seemed to be breaking out again after an apparent lull and in such a way as to endanger Augustus. There are several such moments of which perhaps the likeliest (proposed by Kukula) is after the battle of Actium when Octavian travelled to Athens and then made his way to the island of Samos, a hazardous voyage already hinted at if our comment on 1. 3. 20 is correct. 'He had not been long in Samos when grave news reached him from Italy. The veterans (whom he had disbanded in Italy after Actium) were mutinous and even Agrippa could not handle them. Midwinter though it was, Octavian hurried back to Brundisium.' Official deputations flocked to greet him. 'So did the veterans but not so amicably. Concessions had to be made. Octavian agreed to distribute land, fully realising the storm of unpopularity that might break out round him ... This was the very action that had led to the war of Perusia.' (J. M. Carter, 228–9, using Dio Cassius, 51. 1–4 and Suetonius, *Life of Augustus* 17. 3–4.) With the benefit of hindsight we know that this storm blew over. But at the time it was menacing enough

2ª Asclp (nb y previous epc-ra)
VI

XV

PASTOR cum traheret per freta navibus
Idaeis Helenen perfidus hospitam,   interp
ingrato celeris obruit otio
    ventos, ut caneret fera

Nereus fata: 'mala ducis avi domum,   5
quam multo repetet Graecia milite,
coniurata tuas rumpere nuptias
    et regnum Priami vetus.   zeugma

to take Octavian on a winter's voyage 600 miles across the Mediterranean in which ships of his flotilla foundered in two storms off Greece and his own ship lost its rigging and broke its tiller. At such a time (it might even have been during the twenty-seven days Octavian spent at Brundisium) a poet who was a client of Maecenas might well have felt as Horace says he felt in this last stanza of 1. 14. Perhaps the Cyclades are a vital clue. What have these islands in the Aegean Sea some 100 miles to the south-west of Samos to do with the welfare of Rome? There is no trace of the Cyclades in the surviving fragments of Alcaeus. Perhaps Horace brought them into his Alcaean poem because a ship sailing from Samos to Brundisium would normally steer through the middle of them.

This is only a guess. There were other times in that decade when similar fears could reasonably have been felt for Augustus. It will be argued that by the time these odes were collected and issued in 23 BC the memory of this episode would have faded. On the other hand, the ode would have been powerfully relevant if written and read soon after the event, and even six years later it would still have worked as a general reminder of the dangers from which Octavian saved the state and as a statement of the importance of Octavian for the future of Rome. A totally different approach is adopted by Nisbet and Hubbard: 'The poet's immediate impulse was not a worsening political situation (which is why the date is so uncertain), but a perverse determination to write allegory.'

Bacchylides — allied
adversaries result ? of lost

XV

When the shepherd was dragging Helen off across the sea
on Idaean ships, a traitor carrying off the wife of his host,
Nereus subdued the swift winds to idleness
   against their will so that he could sing

the cruel fates: 'With an ill omen you take home a woman   5
whom Greece will come to claim with a great army,
swearing an alliance to break your marriage
   and the ancient kingdom of Priam.

heu heu, quantus equis, quantus adest viris
sudor! quanta moves funera Dardanae   10
genti! iam galeam Pallas et aegida
    currusque et rabiem parat.

nequiquam Veneris praesidio ferox
pectes caesariem grataque feminis
imbelli cithara carmina divides,   15
    nequiquam thalamo gravis

hastas et calami spicula Gnosii
vitabis strepitumque et celerem sequi
Aiacem; tamen heu serus adulteros
    crinis pulvere collines.   20

non Laertiaden, exitium tuae
genti, non Pylium Nestora respicis?
urgent impavidi te Salaminius
    Teucer, te Sthenelus sciens

pugnae, sive opus est imperitare equis,   25
non auriga piger. Merionen quoque
nosces. ecce furit te reperire atrox
    Tydides melior patre,

quem tu, cervus uti vallis in altera
visum parte lupum graminis immemor,   30
sublimi fugies mollis anhelitu,
    non hoc pollicitus tuae.

iracunda diem proferet Ilio
matronisque Phrygum classis Achillei;
post certas hiemes uret Achaicus   35
    ignis Iliacas domos.

The Trojan prince Paris visited Sparta and carried off Helen, the wife of Menelaus, the Spartan king. This ode purports to give the prophecy delivered to Paris on the voyage by the sea-god Nereus. The language of prophecies is often obscure and portentous and that is why Horace begins this poem with such an awkward first stanza. One of the difficulties is that the name of Paris is not given. He is simply 'the shepherd'. A quotation from Milton is illuminating:

Alas! Alas! for the sweat of horses and of men
and for all the deaths you bring to the people of Dardanus.   10
Pallas is already preparing helmet and aegis,
    her chariot and her madness.

Proud in the protection of Venus, in vain
will you comb your locks and set the songs
the ladies love to your unwarlike lyre.   15
    In vain will you hide in your bedchamber

to avoid the heavy spears and the barbs
of Cretan arrows, the din of battle and the speed
of Ajax's pursuit. But too late, alas! will you smear
    your adulterous hair in the dust.   20

Have you no thought for the son of Laertes, the doom
of your people? For Nestor of Pylos?
Pressing you hard are fearless Teucer of Salamis,
    and Sthenelus, expert in battle

and no sluggard if there is a call to govern   25
horses. Meriones too you will come to know. See there,
raging to find you is the fierce son of Tydeus,
    a better man than his father.

When you see him, like a cowardly stag seeing a wolf
on the other side of the hill, you will forget the grass   30
and run panting away with your head in the air—
    this is not what you promised your mate.

The anger of Achilles' fleet will postpone
the day of doom for Troy and the women of Phrygia.
After a fixed number of years Achaean fire   35
    will burn the homes of Ilium.'

        Sing, Heavenly Muse, that on the secret top
        Of Oreb or of Sinai didst inspire
        That shepherd who first taught the chosen seed
        In the beginning how the heav'ns and earth
        Rose out of chaos:

           (Milton, *Paradise Lost*, 1. 6–10)

That shepherd was Moses, who brought down the words of the Lord from Mount Sinai to the children of Israel in Exodus 24. By not providing the name of Moses in the text Milton gives his readers the thrill of recognition and the warm glow that comes from the exercise of knowledge. We have just met this device, 'antonomasia' in *pastor*, the first word of *Odes* 1. 15. The 'shepherd' is Paris, Idaean ships are Trojan ships made from timber cut on Mount Ida near Troy, the Dardan race (10) is the Trojans, the son of Laertes (21) is Odysseus, and the son of Tydeus (28) is Diomede. Homerists, enjoying the epic patronymics, will be delighted to remember that Horace is here correcting Agamemnon who said in anger that Tydeus was a better man than his son (*Iliad* 4. 399–40). Antonomasia poses a problem for translators. If they keep it readers may be baffled. If the normal names are tacitly substituted, they lose the pleasure of mental activity. I tend to take the latter course, not wishing to leave readers cold in the middle of a poem, thumbing through an index of persons.

But there are occasions when the antonomasia is a vital part of the poetry. The above passage from *Paradise Lost* is certainly one of these. Hesiod, the Greek poet who lived about 700 BC, was also a shepherd and one day when he was looking after his lambs on the holy Mount of Helicon, the Muses of Olympus came and taught him glorious song (*Theogony* 22–5). Milton knew this well and his strategy at this point in *Paradise Lost* is to assert that the Christian vision is in every respect superior to the pagan. The *Heavenly* Muse (singular) is superior to the nine Muses of Greece. Their home Mount Helicon may have been holy but it cannot compete with Oreb and Sinai. Moses taught the chosen seed, not pagan Greeks, and taught them not about the birth of the plural pagan gods as Hesiod did in the *Theogony*, but about the creation of the heavens and earth by the one God Jehovah. Here and throughout the preface to *Paradise Lost* Milton is trumping the pagan with the Christian. The antonomasia of 'shepherd' in line 3 is a calculated demotion of Hesiod.

Taking the opening of Horace's poem in the order in which it comes, after our first puzzle at the unnamed shepherd, we find another at *traheret* which means 'drag'. Shepherds do not drag, they drive. The mystery deepens when we learn that the dragging is done across the sea (what kind of shepherding is this?) and is solved when we learn that instead of a flock we have the most beautiful woman in the world, and realize at last that the shepherd is Paris, his shepherding is the abduction of Helen, and he is sailing on ships whose timber was cut on Mount Ida where he tended his flocks and judged the beauty of the three goddesses. All these false trails and paradoxes pave the way for the entry of the prophetic sea-god Nereus. Prophets speak in riddles. The beginning of his speech maintains the elevation and the paradox. The evil omen is literally an evil bird, *mala avi*, Greece is personified and her armies are expressed by a poetic singular 'many a soldier', *multo milite*. A striking linkage involving a verb governing in two different senses two different objects (Fowler discusses it under 'syllepsis') ends the stanza by breaking a marriage and a kingdom and the presence of sweat adds to the oracular mystification, literally 'What sweat is present for horses! What for men!' Another syllepsis ends the next stanza as Pallas prepares chariot and madness. The voice of the prophet is heard again in the last stanza, again with characteristic obscurity. How could Paris have begun to understand that the fleet of Achilles would *postpone* the doom of Troy? He could not at this moment have had any notion that Achilles would weaken the Greek armies by retiring in high dudgeon to his tent and thus postpone the fall of Troy. Besides, he would certainly take *classis*, as the translation does, in its normal sense of 'fleet' and have been mystified since Achilles was not known for his maritime exploits. He could not possibly have gone back, as we now do, to its rare and ancient sense of 'a body of citizens summoned for military service'. *Classis* is an oracular obfuscation. The prophet means 'contingent' but everyone would take him to mean 'fleet'.

The middle of the poem moves more into the epic mode with conventional epic epithets and the patronymics such as Laertiades which we have already looked at. It finishes with an epic flourish. In the last line *ignis* ends with a short syllable and that is contrary to the metre. If the next word *Iliacas* began with a consonant, that consonant would lengthen the final syllable of *ignis*. The flourish is that in Homer, Ilium and words derived from it *would* be treated as though they began with a consonant, the obsolete digamma (pronounced like our -w-). Horace has then scanned *ignis* before *Iliacas* as though he were writing Greek (J. P. Postgate). The ode ends with the very intonation of the voice of Homer.

Why did Horace write this poem? Most scholars explain it purely as an attempt to imitate earlier Greek poetry (notably the fifth-century Bacchylides of Ceos) and muster lists of poems which contain prophecies. 'He seems to have recaptured perfectly the tepid elegance of the Bacchylidean style', say Nisbet and Hubbard. This is like the approach instanced at the end of the comment on 1. 14 and it is an approach often adopted by the best scholars. Of course poets are often inspired by their predecessors and often try to imitate them, emulate them, criticize and correct them, converse with them or simply ring their own changes. But the best and deepest poets go beyond such dealings with their predecessors. Great poets—and this includes Horace and Milton—write because they have something of their own to say.

The central bulk of our poem is a meditation on one aspect of the *Iliad*—the abduction of Helen by Paris, its baneful effects upon his own people and also the Greeks, the fearful armoury of the goddess of war, the impotence of the goddess of love, the uselessness of Paris's carefully groomed hair and prettily scored music (in lines 14–15 he combs the one and divides the other), and his vain attempts to avoid the horrors of battle. Then, after a muster of the formidable enemies who are hunting him down, the prophecy ends with an image of his cowardice. Why did Horace write about this? He was obviously moved by Homer and relished the challenge to present this aspect of the *Iliad* in such vivid pic-

---

Alcaics

XVI

O MATRE pulchra filia pulchrior,
quem criminosis cumque voles modum
    pones iambis, sive flamma
      sive mari libet Hadriano.

non Dindymene, non adytis quatit   5
mentem sacerdotum incola Pythius,
    non Liber aeque, non acuta
      sic geminant Corybantes aera,

tristes ut irae, quas neque Noricus
deterret ensis nec mare naufragum   10
    nec saevus ignis nec tremendo
      Iuppiter ipse ruens tumultu.

fertur Prometheus addere principi
limo coactus particulam undique
    desectam et insani leonis   15
      vim stomacho apposuisse nostro.

41.6,
117

tures, but why choose this topic? The poem is a meditation on the dis-
astrous results of adulterous lust as pursued by Paris in the *Iliad*. Perhaps
we should read the poem alongside the treatment of love which Horace
has already provided in 1. 5, 11, and 13, and which he is about to offer
in 1. 16 and 17. There are also two relevant political considerations: first,
a corner-stone of Augustan propaganda against Antony and Cleopatra
was the extravagance of their love, adulterous as it was because Antony
was married to Augustus' sister Octavia; second, an important part of
Augustus' social policy was his concern with sexual behaviour. The mar-
riage legislation of the *Leges Iuliae* was still in the future (18 BC accord-
ing to Badian) but adumbrations of it are already beginning to appear in
these odes, as we have already seen at 1. 12. 59 and 1. 13. 17–20. We
may even remember that we found reason to suggest on 1. 6. 15–16 that
Meriones and Diomede seemed to be the Iliadic analogues of Agrippa
and Augustus.

XVI

Daughter lovelier than your lovely mother,
put an end to those scurrilous iambics
  however you wish, whether in the fire
    or in the Adriatic sea.

Neither the goddess of Mount Dindymus, nor the dweller in Delphi   5
so shakes the minds of his priests in their shrine,
  neither Liber nor the Corybantes so violently
    twin their shrill bronzes

as does intemperate anger. Neither does sword
of Noric steel deter it, nor ship-shattering sea,   10
  nor raging fire, nor Jupiter himself
    rushing down in fearful tumult.

They say Prometheus had to add to the primeval slime
a particle cut from every animal
  and grafted the violence of a rabid lion   15
    on to our stomach.

irae Thyesten exitio gravi
stravere et altis urbibus ultimae
   stetere causae cur perirent
      funditus imprimeretque muris   20

hostile aratrum exercitus insolens.
compesce mentem: me quoque pectoris
   temptavit in dulci iuventa
      fervor et in celeris iambos

misit furentem: nunc ego mitibus   25
mutare quaero tristia, dum mihi
   fias recantatis amica
      opprobriis animumque reddas.

W hat is the story? Who wrote the scurrilous iambic poems of the first stanza? The culprit must be Horace, particularly if we remember, as Horace so often did, the poetry of Catullus. In *Poem* 36 Lesbia had threatened to throw Catullus' vicious iambics into the fire. This seems to be the same situation. Horace proceeds to deliver a mock-serious sermon on the evils of anger, softens it by admitting that he too had once succumbed when he wrote the offending verses, and pleads for a reconciliation. On this interpretation the scurrilous iambics of lines 2–3 are the swift iambics of line 24.

There are difficulties about this reconstruction. It does not involve the mother mentioned in the first line, but we shall soon try to suggest an explanation of her presence. It also posits a very leisurely time-scale for this love affair. He sent these poems in his youth, and now he asks for a reconciliation apparently many years later. Such things do happen. But other reconstructions have to be considered. Jenkyns (1982) for example, has suggested that Horace had sent the poems to the mother and is now asking the daughter to destroy them and become his mistress.

The sermon which makes up the bulk of the poem is clearly a burlesque. In lines 5–6 Cybele is not named, but referred to by the name of her holy mountain in Phrygia, and another antonomasia denotes Apollo by an allusion to the frenzy of his priestesses who prophesy in convulsions in his shrine at Delphi. There is some more mock elevation in the forced linkages which seem to credit Cybele with causing the prophetic convulsions experienced in Apollo's cave at Delphi so graphically described in Virgil, *Aeneid* 6. 77–101. Similarly Bacchus is credited with the clashing

Odes 1. 16

Anger laid Thyestes low in a heavy doom
and has stood as the final cause by which
  lofty cities were razed to the ground
    and insolent armies drove   20

the enemy's plough down upon their walls.
Subdue your mind. I too was assailed by the fire
  of passion in my breast in the sweet days
    of youth and driven raging

to swift iambics. I now wish to change   25
from harshness to gentleness, if only,
  my insults recanted, you become my friend
    and give me back your heart.

of cymbals which is characteristic of the Corybantes, the priests of
Cybele. In the next stanza the rhetoric swells to Jupiter himself, but the
translation has had to blur the outlines of the Latin rhetoric, which works
by producing a string of four negatives with *non* in lines 5–7 and follows
that by a string of four negatives with *neque* and *nec* in lines 9–11.

Religion is mocked. Philosophy is the next target, with the sudden
intrusion of the creation myth to explain the presence of anger in the
human breast. 'Plato had twisted the crude legends of archaic Greece to
recommend a more popular morality, and the technique must have
proved congenial to the popular teachers of the Hellenistic age' (Nisbet
and Hubbard).

In the next stanza it is the turn of tragedy and epic. The *Thyestes*
which Horace has in mind is presumably none of the dozen other ver-
sions we know of (see Tarrant) but the *Thyestes* of Varius which has
already been alluded to at 1. 6. 8. Thyestes seduced the wife of his
brother Atreus. Atreus banished Thyestes. Thyestes sent Atreus' son to
murder him but instead Atreus killed his own son without recognizing
him. In revenge Atreus served Thyestes a meal of his own children. The
fun lies partly in Horace's cheerful vagueness. The Latin suggests that
the anger of Thyestes is at issue but the final decisive anger was that of
Atreus. When we come to the fall of cities, we must think of the para-
digm of fallen cities, the lofty city of Troy and the *Iliad* which com-
memorated it. Horace recalls the story in an elaborate sustained
metaphor. Thyestes is *laid low* in a *heavy* doom. There are *standing*
causes for the perishing *to the depths* (*funditus*) of *lofty* cities, and the

enemy plough *presses down* upon their ruined walls. The Romans famously ploughed the site of Carthage with salt in 146 BC. (The causes are final causes in what is perhaps a parting dig at the final causes of the philosophers.) These are all absurdly lofty matters to compare with Horace's little local difficulty.

From religion, philosophy, tragedy, epic, and a high point in Roman history, Horace turns to Catullus. In *Poem* 36, mentioned above, Lesbia has made a vow that if she and Catullus were reconciled, she would burn the choicest poems of the worst poet, meaning of course Catullus. Catullus prays that the goddess Venus should accept as payment of the vow the burning of the poems—not his own, of course, but those of the unfortunate Volusius. This is a witty poem in which Catullus mocks a rival poet and teases his own mistress. It expresses no tenderness.

Horace never lays out a schematic account of his view of love and it would be foolish to produce one for him. Nevertheless, in the love poems we have so far met in this book a picture is building up. Essential features which are conspicuous in this ode are his abhorrence of extremes and his good humour. Throughout the sermon in this poem the gross disparity between the portentous analogies Horace suggests and the situation to which he applies them, is surely meant as fun. After the gods, Prometheus, Thyestes, Troy, and Carthage, when he comes to the *Ich-Schluss* in line 22, *me quoque*, 'me too', surely he says it with a smile.

The mother raises a fascinating possibility. The most famous palinode or recantation in classical poetry was written by Stesichorus, who lived at

---

q invitam in Ellis — crowd + live in country (4H).

Meaие

XVII

Italia
VELOX amoenum saepe Lucretilem
Ne ——— mutat Lycaeo Faunus et igneam
defendit aestatem capellis
usque meis pluviosque ventos.

impune tutum per nemus arbutos   5
quaerunt latentis et thyma deviae
olentis uxores mariti,
nec viridis metuunt colubras

the beginning of the sixth century BC. He first wrote a poem attacking Helen and according to legend as a punishment was blinded by her brothers Castor and Pollux. He then wrote a palinode (fragment 192) in which he recanted his criticisms:

> It's not true that story.
> You didn't sail on the well-benched ships
> and you didn't go to the citadel of Troy.

Readers will note that Helen, daughter of Tyndareus, is conspicuous in 1. 15, and Tyndaris, which means daughter of Tyndareus, is Horace's beloved in 1. 17. The oddity is that the first line of our poem 1. 16, 'Daughter lovelier than your lovely mother', would make an apt and beautiful tribute to Horace's mistress called Tyndaris, in that Helen, the loveliest of women, was the daughter of Leda, herself known as a beauty. A wild guess would bring all this together. The tribute to Horace's Tyndaris would be all the more apt if the first line of Horace's poem was a translation of a line from the palinode of Stesichorus.

That is speculation. What is clear is that Horace's word *recantatis* in the second-last line, a word not used before in surviving Latin, is a Latin translation of the Greek *palinode*. We do not know how close this ode is to the fragmentary palinodes of Stesichorus, but it is a palinode. Horace is begging to be forgiven the errors of his youth. He understands the lady's anger. He was angry then himself, but he now wishes her to forget all that and love him once again.

XVII

Swift Faunus often exchanges Lycaeus
for my lovely Lucretilis and never fails
   to keep the fiery heat and rainy winds
     from my kidlings.

The wives of stinking billy straggle   5
safely everywhere in the security of my wood
   looking for thyme and arbutus
     and the kids are not afraid of green snakes

nec Martialis haediliae lupos,
utcumque dulci, Tyndari, fistula   10
  valles et Vsticae cubantis
  levia personuere saxa.

di me tuentur, dis pietas mea
et Musa cordi est. hic tibi copia
  manabit ad plenum benigno   15
  ruris honorum opulenta cornu:

hic in reducta valle Caniculae
vitabis aestus et fide Teia
  dices laborantis in uno
  Penelopen vitreamque Circen: 20

hic innocentis pocula Lesbii
duces sub umbra, nec Semeleius
  cum Marte confundet Thyoneus
  proelia, nec metues protervum

suspecta Cyrum, ne male dispari   25
incontinentis iniciat manus
  et scindat haerentem coronam
  crinibus immeritamque vestem.

The first three stanzas describe how the Greek god Pan comes in a moment from Arcadia to Italy, from Lycaeus to Lucretilis, as the Italian god Faunus, to protect Horace's Sabine farm. After the central pivot of the poem in lines 13–14 we read Horace's invitation to Tyndaris to visit him there in his country paradise. The subtlety lies, according to many readers, in the skilful interweaving of two poetic forms, the pastoral and convivial. They are certainly bound together by correspondences. Many details in the first three stanzas reappear later to imply, with tongue slightly in cheek, that the divine protection granted to Horace's goats is available also to Tyndaris—security, protection from heat, fodder, mating (polygyny for the billy, polyandry and polygyny on the Sabine farm), absence of fear (*metuunt* and *metues* in 8 and 24), Mars, music, and green Circe after the green snakes. Most important of all is Tyndaris, who ends the third stanza and dominates the last three.

But this explanation of the poem as a blend of two genres is the usual scholastic heresy. Poets often respond to technical challenges and they

nor the wolves of Mars
whenever the valleys and smooth rocks   10
   on the slopes of Ustica ring, O Tyndaris,
     with the sweet pipe of Faunus.

The gods are guarding me. My piety and my Muse
are near to their hearts. Here for you a rich abundance
   of the glories of the countryside will pour   15
     from the full horn of plenty.

Here in my sequestered valley you will escape
the heat of the Dogstar and sing to the Teian lyre   *Anacreon*
   of Penelope and sea-green Circe,
     both suffering over one man.   20

Here in the shade you will drink cups
of harmless Lesbian wine. Semele's son, Thyonian Bacchus,
   will not join with Mars to stir up battles
     and you will not be afraid

of the suspicions of that hot-head Cyrus. He will not   25
lay a hand on you in passion—a hand you can't resist—
   or tear the garland plaited in your hair
     or the dress that has not deserved such treatment.

are often aware of the work of their predecessors, but writing poetry is
not simply a matter of shuffling and redealing the old cards. Good poets
blend their experience of literature and their experience of life in a hugely
complex operation which they themselves do not fully understand. As
Horace might have put it, the poet was under the guidance of the Muse
who led him where he did not know that he wanted to go. The inter-
weaving of poetic elements, forms, or genres is only that tiny part of the
business which is most accessible to scholarly analysis. Shakespeare
knew that the poet is of imagination and emotion all compact
(*Midsummer Night's Dream*, 5. 1). We have not gone very far when we
have traced his work to previous work which it resembles.

   To sense the thrust in this poem we have to remember the person to
whom Horace addressed this collection, his patron Maecenas. We also
have to remember the gratitude Horace felt to Maecenas for the gift of his
beloved Sabine farm. Horace is the master of tact. Not for him to write: 'I
am terribly grateful to you for this farm. I am enjoying it very much and

writing well. I enclose a specimen.' These are sophisticated people and they speak in a sophisticated code. When Horace writes that the gods love him and his Muse and that Faunus protects his flocks, Maecenas knows perfectly well what was meant. Faunus protects. Maecenas gave.

Horace had received the Sabine farm (either directly or indirectly, see Bradshaw, and Cairns, (1992) 107–9) as a reward for his poetry and as an incentive to write more. This ode informs his patron that he is doing so. It expresses his gratitude, his contentment, and his continued dedication to the Muse. In *Satire* 2. 6 published seven years before in 30 BC, he had spoken in the same way and had made it clear that he wanted no more (the passage is cited on *Odes* 1. 31). His only prayer to Apollo was that he would make his flocks fat and his Muse slim. So here his goats are feeding well, Horace is enjoying the plenty of the country *and* he is writing. 'My piety and my Muse are dear to the gods.'

He ends the poem by announcing one kind of poetry he is writing and Maecenas and Augustus must have been pleased to hear it. It is poetry of love, not adolescent or 'elegiac' love, riven with suspicion and violence, but gentle and serene, enjoying the light poetry and music of Anacreon of Teos and the benign, sweet wine from the island of Sappho and Alcaeus. At the end the passionate youngster is once again put in his place. Horace did not go in for tearing dresses.

The last three stanzas of this poem are not a definition of love. Horace does not define. But they are an example of the sort of love he approved. This collection of poems is like nothing which had ever appeared before. It starts with a parade of nine poems in different metres, six of the first seven addressed to some of the most important men in Rome. By the time Roman readers reached this seventeenth poem, they would have some notion of the range of Horace's work and the persona he was presenting. Ten of these poems have to do with love and they give a consistent picture. In 1. 5 he says goodbye to stormy passion where the innocent boy is at the mercy of a temperamental mistress and in 1. 6 he describes love as he will treat it. In 1. 8 he is amused by the power of a woman over a youngster. In 4 and 9 there are indications that homosexuality is part of this world. In 11 there is kindness between lovers and Horace sees life *sub specie aeternitatis*, urging Leuconoe to enjoy his love while they are both able to do so. In 13 he has fun at his own expense as he describes his jealous symptoms and once again he rejects the violence of young love, promising rather a love which is harmonious and constant unto death. In 15 we read how adultery brought down the city of Troy in Homer's epic. In 16 the bitter anger of his mistress is humorously compared with religious frenzy and explained in terms of solemn popular philosophy. It is then set beside the wildest horrors of Greek tragedy and the sack of cities before Horace enters an appeal for reconciliation and a return to love. Now in 17 the passionate youth is again shown the door as Horace gives a positive notion of some of the pleasures of mature love.

Scholars have not thought highly of Horace's love poetry. Kenney is a distinguished example: 'Horace was undoubtedly a poet and erotic themes are to be found in his poems; but that he ever wrote anything which in the ordinary acceptance of the term could be called a love poem, I do most earnestly deny.' Perhaps such scholars have been looking for a kind of love that Horace did not want.

We noted on 1. 5 that Horace's view of love as there presented had some affinity with recent and contemporary Graeco-Roman thought, notably in Epicurean philosophy. The fullest surviving statement of Epicurean recommendations for male sexual behaviour occurs at the end of the fourth book of Lucretius' *De Rerum Natura*. This starts (4. 1058–72) with an austere physiological analysis to support the proposition that a man should not have a single lover but should dispose of his semen by casual sex. There follows a devastating indictment of the folly of such infatuation as we find in the elegiac lover, and also in the adolescent rival in Horace. But Horace swore no oath of allegiance to any philosophical master. He is always his own man. Close as he was to his admired Lucretius in his attitude to 'elegiac' love, the quality of the relationships he posits in these poems is worlds away from the joyless functionalism we find in the Epicurean texts (see Brown's commentary).

The question is still asked how Horace can movingly plight his undying troth to Lydia at the end of 1. 13, and at 1. 11 and 1. 17 be loving Leuconoe and Tyndaris. This question in turn tends to lead to the conclusion that these are not love poems but literary exercises. This is to raise yet again the spectre long-since-laid of the autobiographical fallacy. We know nothing of Leuconoe, Lydia, Tyndaris, Thaliarchus, or Ligurinus, not even what we are told in the poems. We do not know whether they existed or whether there ever existed any persons to whom Horace attached these names. We do not know whether Horace ever made love to woman or boy or ever wanted to. Horace is not writing a history of his love affairs. In 1. 11 and 1. 17 he visualizes situations with Y and Z. In 1. 13 he visualizes a phase in a relationship with Z. This last poem is inconsistent with the two others. That does not matter. What does matter is whether the poems demand our attention, move well, interest us, draw us into the life they represent, stir us, linger with us—whether they work as poems.

XVIII

NVLLAM, Vare, sacra vite prius severis arborem
circa mite solum Tiburis et moenia Catili.
siccis omnia nam dura deus proposuit, neque
mordaces aliter diffugiunt sollicitudines.

quis post vina gravem militiam aut pauperiem crepat?   5
quis non te potius, Bacche pater, teque, decens Venus?
ac ne quis modici transiliat munera Liberi,
Centaurea monet cum Lapithis rixa super mero

debellata, monet Sithoniis non levis Euhius,
cum fas atque nefas exiguo fine libidinum   10
discernunt avidi. non ego te, candide Bassareu,
invitum quatiam, nec variis obsita frondibus

sub divum rapiam. saeva tene cum Berecyntio
cornu tympana, quae subsequitur caecus Amor sui
et tollens vacuum plus nimio Gloria verticem   15
arcanique Fides prodiga, perlucidior vitro.

W ine is a consolation and a delight given by the gods (1–6) and
there are ample warnings not to misuse it (7–11). I shall never
commit impiety against you, Bassareus (11–13). Keep your drunken rout
in check (13–16).

The wine-god has four different names in this short poem. In lines 6
and 9 he is called approvingly by names common in Rome, Bacchus and
Liber. As the focus turns to the misuse of wine in lines 9–11, Euhius and
Bassareus are Greek titles used in the orgiastic cult of Dionysus.

The first line is a literal translation of fragment 342 of Alcaeus, adding
only the address to a Varus (perhaps the Quintilius whose death is
mourned in 1. 24) and the word *sacra*, 'holy', which gives the opening
prohibition a not entirely serious touch of sternness. The second line
takes us from Greece to the Romans' favourite hill-town founded by
Catilus (see 1. 7) where Varus presumably had an estate. The smiling
gravity resumes with the third line, literally: 'the gods have put all things

misuse? *re wine - held in religious circumstance*
— misuse
— unflattering kinds 'cellar' drinkers
— holiness (sacre)

XVIII

Plant no tree, Varus, before the holy vine
in the kindly soil around Tibur and the walls of Catilus.
For god has put nothing but obstacles in the way of sober men
and only wine puts biting cares to flight.

After wine who harps on about the harshness of soldiering or poverty? 5
Who does not rather speak of father Bacchus, and lovely Venus?
And the fatal brawl Lapiths fought with Centaurs over unmixed wine
gives warning that no man should go beyond the rituals of

moderate Liber. Euhius, too, gives warning, scourge of Thracians
when in their greed for lustful pleasures they draw a narrow line 10
between right and wrong. I will not shake you, fair Bassareus,
against your will, nor will I drag out into the light of day

what is screened by your varied leaves. Keep in check
your wild drums and Berecyntian horn with their retinue
of blind Self-love, Vainglory raising her empty head absurdly high 15
and Trust betrayed, squandering secrets, more transparent than glass.

hard before the sober'. This is a cheerful perversion of Hesiod's advice to
his idle waster of a brother in *Works and Days* 289–90: 'The gods have
put sweat in front of virtue. The path to it is long and steep and rough
in the beginning'. The praise of wine then comes to a climax in line 6
with the names of two of Horace's favourite gods, of whom we are about
to hear more in the next two poems.

The first example of the misuse of wine is the story of the battle
between Lapiths and Centaurs at the wedding of Pirithous and
Hippodamia. The Centaurs came to the wedding, drank wine, and
attempted to ravish the bride. Fighting broke out. *Rixa* means a brawl,
and the prefix in *de-bellata* indicates that they fought to the finish, the
killing of the Centaurs. The scene is gloriously portrayed in sculptures
which Horace must have seen *in situ* on the metopes of the Parthenon
during his stay in Athens in his early twenties and which we can now see
in the British Museum. The second example refers to the Sithonians, a

Thracian tribe. 'Thracians like other northern barbarians were famous for heavy drinking', write Nisbet and Hubbard, and produce evidence to prove it. In this particular instance, where Euhius was harsh to the Sithonians when their lust led them to confuse right and wrong, Horace seems to be alluding both to Sithon who loved his own daughter and was killed by Dionysus (Nonnus, 48. 93) and to Lycurgus who alleged that the god of wine was no god, drank wine, and then ravished his own mother (Hyginus, 132. 1). These first hazards of excessive drinking appear therefore to be fighting and incest, not hazards which pose an immediate threat to Horace.

At line 11 he turns to his own case with a long *Ich-Schluss*. At one level he is saying that he will not irreverently drag jar upon jar out of the cellar for coarse drinking. At another level he will not shake the god or blurt out the secrets of the Dionysiac Mysteries. In these rites the worshipper waved the thyrsus, a branch tipped with ivy leaves, which was believed to be in some sense the god. Sacred objects (the ancient sources mention pomegranates, poppies, a phallus, and a snake) were moved from the shrine and carried in procession in a basket. To move the sacred objects was therefore a technical term which indicated the beginning of the sacred procession. So when Horace says he will not shake the god against his will, it is not clear whether he is referring to the thyrsus, or to the god thought of as the thyrsus, or to the sacred objects in the basket (perhaps these too, thought of as having become the god). Similarly when Horace tells us that he will not drag out (perhaps from the basket) what is screened in varied leaves, we are not told what these things are, nor what are the varied leaves demanded by the ritual. This may be obscure, but it is not the obscurity so common in modern poetry; it is caused by our ignorance rather than any incompetence or discourtesy of the poet. By his veiled language Horace is demonstrating his resolve not to reveal the Mysteries. The obscurity supports the sense.

Horace now prays to the god to keep in check the wild music of the Bacchic rout, provided by the *tympanum*, the hoop covered by a single hide, and the two pipes of the Berecyntian horn, of which one was curved at the end like the saxophone, and like the saxophone produced a weird, disturbing timbre. The poem ends with an unflattering account of the participants. They are led by the blind, by Self-love. Vainglory raises her head absurdly high, a sign of pride no doubt and unsuitability for leadership, but also the typical stereotype of the Maenad baring her white throat to the moon in her Dionysiac orgies. In Latin tables are feminine and beds are neuter, *mensae* and *cubilia*,—gender then had no necessary connotation of sex. But here Horace exploits the feminine nouns *Gloria* and *Fides*. *Gloria* we saw as a Maenad, and now *Fides*, more transparent than glass, is another. In Latin loose women famously wear transparent clothes, often of silk from the Greek island of Cos.

'It may be asked what this poem is about', write Nisbet and Hubbard with characteristic boldness, and they give short shrift to some of the interpretations that scholars have tried. Their view is that Horace is ringing the changes on 'the old commonplace which praised the moderate, but not excessive use of wine' in a poem which 'depends for its effect on an intricate network of allusions'. 'Horace is playing a complicated literary game.' 'Where the commonplaces are less esoteric it is easier to persuade oneself that he is speaking from the heart.' 'Horace's tapestry tells no story, points no moral, and is not particularly beautiful; but one may admire all the same the *poikilia* of the needlework.'

Surely we can do better than this. The obvious first step is to relate the poem to Horace's own time, his interests, and the conditions of his life. Horace lived with the great, ate with them and drank with them, and was deeply conscious that living with the great was an art. He deploys that art in the second book of the *Satires*:

> quicumque obvius est me consulit: 'o bone, nam te
> scire, deos quoniam propius contingis, oportet,
> numquid de Dacis audisti?' nil equidem. 'ut tu
> semper eris derisor!' at omnes di exagitent me
> si quicquam. 'quid, militibus promissa Triquetra
> praedia Caesar an est Itala tellure daturus?'
> iurantem me scire nihil mirantur ut unum
> scilicet egregii mortalem altique silenti.

(Satires 2. 6. 51–8)

Everybody who meets me asks me questions. 'My dear fellow, you must know, being in such close contact with the gods, have you heard any news from Dacia?' 'Not I.' 'You will always have your joke.' 'May all the gods hound me if anything at all . . .' 'What about the land Caesar has promised to his veterans? Is it going to be in Sicily or in Italy?' When I swear I know nothing they look at me in amazement as though I were the one and only mortal capable of such profound and extraordinary silence.

Horace gives express recommendations in his advice to the client in the first book of his *Epistles*:

> arcanum neque tu scrutaberis illius umquam,
> commissumque teges et vino tortus et ira;
>
> . . . .

> percontatorem fugito, nam garrulus idem est,
> nec retinent patulae commissa fideliter aures.
>
> (*Epistles* 1. 18. 37–8, 69–70)

You will never ask him questions about private matters and anything he entrusts to you, you will keep secret whether tortured on the rack of wine or anger . . . Beware of people who ask a lot of questions. For they are gossips and flapping ears do not faithfully retain what is entrusted to them.

The most important statement of this principle is also in an *Ich–Schluss* in the second of the Roman Odes:

> est et fideli tuta silentio
> merces: vetabo, qui Cereris sacrum
>   vulgarit arcanae, sub isdem
>   sit trabibus . . .
>
> (*Odes* 3. 2. 25–8)

> There is for faithful silence, too, a secure reward.
> I shall not allow the man who has made public
>   the sacrament of Ceres to be under the same roof
>   with me . . .

It therefore looks as though this condemnation of self-love, vainglory, and blabbing disloyalty has a direct bearing on Horace's own life.

We may be able to come closer. The above quotation from the Roman Ode starts with a line which is a literal translation of Simonides, fragment 582, and this fragment was quoted in Greek by Augustus in a conversation recorded by Plutarch in his *Apophthegms of Kings and Emperors* 207 C. What is more, Augustus himself was an initiate of the Eleusinian Mysteries of the goddess Ceres in Attica, and took the cult seriously

(Suetonius, *Life of Augustus* 93). Further, in, or soon after 23 BC, the year of the publication of these odes, Aulus Terentius Varro Murena, an acquaintance of Horace's (see *Odes* 3. 19) and brother-in-law of Maecenas, conspired with Fannius Caepio against Augustus. The conspiracy was detected and both men were executed.

Augustus was a man of few words. On matters of importance he even wrote the text of what he was going to say to his own wife and read it out to her in case he should say too little or too much if he spoke extempore (Suetonius, *Life* 84). In such a political climate, where Augustus was surrounded by flatterers and gossips and schemers, the client of Maecenas and protégé of Augustus has made it clear, in his own Horatian way, that he wanted nothing to do with self-love and pride and could be trusted to keep silence. He would drink with the great but he would not retail their conversation. Such qualities were much appreciated by the Romans (see Skutsch on Ennius, *Annales* 266–85) and much appreciated by Augustus. The proof is the surviving letter in which Augustus asked him to become his private secretary. This poem is not just a literary game, nor is it simply a piece of flattery from client to patron. We saw when Horace borrowed his first line from Alcaeus, that he added to it the concept of holiness. Religious terms abound in the poem. It is god that makes life hard for teetotallers in line 3. The blessings of wine and of love are spoken of as gods in line 6. Bacchus is a father, Liber is moderate. Venus is *decens*, a term which implies a degree of decorum. Euhius points a moral explaining what is acceptable and unacceptable to the gods, *fas* and *nefas*. Bassareus is *candidus*, 'fair-skinned and beautiful'. The villains of the piece are not the gods, but their drunken followers. This is not just literary furniture. In his cups and in his lovemaking, Horace sensed the presence of something more than human.

XIX

MATER saeva Cupidinum
Thebanaeque iubet me Semelae puer
    et lasciva Licentia
finitis animum reddere amoribus.

    urit me Glycerae nitor   5
splendentis Pario marmore purius:
    urit grata protervitas
et vultus nimium lubricus aspici.

    in me tota ruens Venus
Cyprum deseruit, nec patitur Scythas   10
    et versis animosum equis
Parthum dicere nec quae nihil attinent.

    hic vivum mihi caespitem, hic
verbenas, pueri, ponite turaque
    bimi cum patera meri: 15
mactata veniet lenior hostia.

Horace is under orders. The gods who surround him are a formidable combination. Venus is the cruel mother of Desires, *Cupidinum*, and these come in visible form as the rascally Cupids so common in Roman art. We know these boys and the mischievous delight they take in human anguish, from Cupid's naughtiness in Virgil, *Aeneid* 1. 690 where he struts around copying Iulus' walk and laughing as he rehearses the treachery which will destroy the queen of Carthage. Love and wine are dangerous allies, all the more so if wine, too, is seen as a boy (*puer*, 2), the young Bacchus, born of one of the great love stories of antiquity. The pregnant Semele was tricked by Juno into demanding to see her divine lover. Jupiter duly appeared as a flash of lightning and as his beloved perished in the fire, he rescued the embryo of the god of wine from her womb and stitched it into his thigh, till its time would come. The third god giving orders to Horace is the untranslatable *lasciva Licentia*, whose sacraments, familiar as they were, enjoyed no state cult, and if they did, Licence would scarcely be in a position to give orders. Horace had given up love, but how could an old man defy such a trinity?

    The second stanza is also a triad, the shining white of Glycera's skin,

XIX

The cruel mother of Desires,
Theban Semele's boy and amorous Licence
  order me to give my heart
to love, long since ended.

Glycera sets me on fire, the sheen   5
of her fair skin, flawless as Parian marble,
  her delicious naughtiness,
her face so hazardous to look at.

Venus has deserted Cyprus and rushes
upon me with all her force. She will have no talk   10
  of Scythians or of Parthian horsemen
aggressive in retreat, or anything else bar love.

Put here for me, lads, a piece of living turf,
some greenery here for a sacrifice,
  and incense with a bowl of two-year-old wine.   15
I'll kill a victim and she will come more gently.

her eager naughtiness (*protervitas* in 7 is another untranslatable), and her
face, an interesting and credible list. The translation fails yet again, first
in losing the rhetoric at the beginning of lines 5 and 7: 'Scorches me her
sheen . . . Scorches me her naughtiness' and then in line 8 where *lubri-
cus* means 'slippery'. To look at that face is to step on a slippery slope, or,
in view of line 6, perhaps a slippery floor of Parian marble.

  Greek gods moved freely from shrine to shrine and in the third stanza
Venus has left her beloved Cyprus and rushed upon Horace with full
force. Some scholars think of Venus as swooping like a bird of prey, but
the word *ruens* (12) was used in 1. 16. 12 of Jupiter's lightning flash, and
that is surely the picture we should have in mind here after Semele's
incineration in line 2 and the scorching of Horace himself in lines 5 and
7 of the Latin. When Horace says that Venus does not allow him to
speak of Scythians and Parthians, we remember that Augustus recorded
in his *Res Gestae* 31. 2 the embassy he received from the Scythians and
other northern peoples in 25 BC. We have already seen elsewhere in this
book in 2. 22 and 51, and in 12. 53 that the Parthians were a burning
issue in the mid-20s. But not here for Horace. Love is forbidding him to

93

write poems about them or about anything which is not relevant to his love, or as he says in a crushingly colloquial phrase, *nec quae nihil attinent*, 'and things which having nothing to do with it'. This third stanza, like the first two, contains a triad: Scythians, Parthians, or anything else. It ends with the Parthian, literally, 'spirited when his horses have turned', *versis animosum equis Parthum*. This is of course an oxymoron, a 'sharp-blunt'. Most warriors are frightened when they run away. When the Parthian has turned his horse, he is about to show his courage. Look out for the Parthian shot. Oxymoron is a favourite Horatian figure. This poem begins with a savage mother, continues with Licence giving orders and in the second stanza has pleasing naughtiness. All this demonstrates Horace's taste for the paradoxical and surreal. He likes surprises.

The fourth stanza also contains a triad: turf, greenery, and incense with wine. But the tone is vitally different. The poem starts with a sophisticated and perhaps gently self-mocking reference to gods. The

XX

VILE potabis modicis Sabinum
cantharis, Graeca quod ego ipse testa
conditum levi, datus in theatro
    cum tibi plausus,

clare Maecenas eques, ut paterni   5
fluminis ripae simul et iocosa
redderet laudes tibi Vaticani
    montis imago.

Caecubum et prelo domitam Caleno
tu bibes uvam: mea nec Falernae   10
temperant vites neque Formiani
    pocula colles.

In these twelve lines, as Cairns well sees, the client makes at least a dozen points in praise of his patron. The first is the first word. Horace pays Maecenas the compliment of inviting him to come and drink an inferior (*vile*) wine with him, so demonstrating his confidence that second stanza is a sensuous and beautifully organized description of the attractions of the beloved. The third conveys the irresistible force of love's onset and Horace's total submission to it at the cost of all other interests. But now in the fourth stanza we see him praying to be saved from the violent effects of love as presented in lines 1, 5, 7, 8, and 9. We leave the theology of Hellenistic Greece, the ravishment of the senses, and the world of politics to be with the poet on his Sabine farm telling his young slaves to set up a simple turf altar, bring the statutory greenery for a sacrifice with a libation dish of wine of a modest age, no doubt of his own bottling as we may guess from the opening of the next poem. The last of the four triads in the poem is complete and for the first time a sentence ends in mid-stanza, leaving the last line in telling isolation. He hopes that if he sacrifices an animal, the love goddess will come upon him not like a flash of lightning, but in a gentler mood.

XX

You will drink from plain cups an inferior Sabine wine
I put into a Greek jar and sealed
with my own hands the day you, Maecenas,
    knight of great distinction,

were given such applause in the theatre   5
that the banks of the river of your fathers
and the playful echo from the Vatican Mount
    joined in your praises.

You can drink your Caecuban and the grape
tamed in the Calenian press;   10
no Falernian vines or Formian hills
    soften my wine.

Maecenas can rise above pomp and luxury and enjoy simple friendship. The third word strengthens the message. They will drink not from engraved silver, but from plain (*modestis*) cups.
    The second word in the ode, *potabis*, is not simply 'you will drink' but

'you will drink heavily'. The hint is confirmed by *cantharis*, the large drinking-cups, so large that they needed two handles. This is serious drinking, a great bond between those who practise it, whether it be wine or other intoxicants:

> And at his elbow Souter Johnny,
> His ancient, trusted drouthy crony;
> Tam lo'ed him like a vera brither—
> They had been fou for weeks thegither.

> (R. Burns, 'Tam O'Shanter')

The easy assumption of intimacy from the humble poet—such is Horace's *persona*—to the great patron is another oblique compliment.

The fourth word, *Sabinum*, is also a form of praise. It seems to imply that Maecenas is being asked to come and visit Horace on his Sabine farm, but whether or not that is so, the wine they will be drinking is Sabine wine transferred to jars on the estate which Maecenas gave to Horace and which he so loved. In 1. 17 he has expressed in his own way his gratitude for the gift. Now he comes back to the theme. The warmest word in these two lines is *ipse*. Horace put the wine into an amphora and sealed it *himself*, with his own hands corking the jar and smearing the cork with pitch (cf. 3. 8. 10). Gratitude can be expressed without being stated.

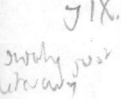

Why did Horace put his wine into Greek jars? Greek wine was often salted to preserve it, and it has been suggested that Horace's Sabine, being an inferior wine with little staying power, would be preserved by the salt lingering in the Greek jars. This is not likely. If you want to add salt to wine, you do not cart Greek jars up into the mountains of central Italy, but add salt or sea-water, as Cato, for instance, recommends in his *De Re Rustica* 24. It is more likely that Horace is using Greek jars to improve the flavour of his ordinary local wine. This zest for seeing to the wine on his Sabine farm demonstrates to Maecenas that his client is not only grateful, but is satisfied. He is not asking for more and better. He enjoys what he has as he demonstrates three years later in *Epistles* 1. 14. 39 when his country neighbours gather round to laugh at him shifting clods and boulders.

Sandwiched between the vinous beginning of this poem and its vinous end, there is praise of Maecenas, but tact is preserved. Even that is not from the lips of Horace, but from the throats of the Roman people, and from the River Tiber and the Vatican Mount. Horace discovered that on the day he had drawn off his wine into jars on his Sabine farm, Maecenas had gone to the theatre after recovering from an illness and had been loudly and joyously acclaimed by the audience. A more subtle point of praise lies in the address at the beginning of the second stanza. *Clare*, 'distinguished' is an adjective normally reserved for senators but Maecenas never accepted a seat in the Senate. If this event took place in 29 BC when Maecenas was left in charge of Rome during the absence of Octavian (as seems to be indicated by *Odes* 3. 8), we have to visualize the scene when the most important man in the city enters the theatre after a serious illness and goes to his seat, not in the orchestra with the senators but only in the fourteen front rows of knights, the *Equites*. This praise of his modesty is sharpened by *paterni*, the last word of the same line. Maecenas was of Etruscan descent and the first line of this book and the first line of 3. 29, inform us that the ancestors of this *eques* were kings. The reference to the Tiber, sometimes called the Etruscan river, as the river of his fathers, is a delicately pointed allusion to his royal ancestry. The truly royal is unmoved by rank.

In this apparently simple, but densely allusive poem, we should remember the delight Horace takes in activating the etymology of words. The Vatican Mount refers not to the present Vatican which is too far north to give an echo from Pompey's theatre in the Campus Martius, but to the Vatican Field, the present Gianicolo. According to Varro (in Gellius, 16. 17. 1), the most learned man in Rome in Horace's day, the Vatican Field was so called because of the vaticinations, the prophecies which were made there by the power and the inspiration of the god Vaticanus. Horace may be humorously insinuating the infallibility of the crowd's favourable judgement of Maecenas.

The last stanza begins with an acknowledgement of Maecenas' wealth and good taste. When you are at home, 'you can drink the great wines from the south of Rome, Caecuban and Calenian from Latium, Falernian and Formian from Campania, but up here in the Sabine mountains you will drink my Sabine.' The poem ends as it began with the suggestion that for Maecenas connoisseurship is less important than friendship. The great man has the humility to come and soak up his friend's *vino locale*.

A vital aspect of Horace's clientship is that he refuses to give up his independence. He insists upon this point in two great poems, at the end of the Maecenas ode, 3. 29, and in *Epistle* 1. 7. Here the point is made in a code of wines. Maecenas' grape is pressed and tamed, *prelo domitam* (9) but nothing *temperat* the vines of Horace. I translate this as 'softens'. Fraenkel (344) takes the verb to mean 'renders less violent, intense, rigorous, or burdensome'. What underlines this message by a touch of the surreal is that Maecenas' great wines would be much stronger than Horace's Sabine, according to Galen the thinnest of the Italian wines (in Athenaeus, 27B). Falernian, for instance, is called *severus, ardens, fortis* at 1. 27. 9, 2. 11. 19, and *Satires* 2. 4. 24. If there was any softening it would be the other way round, but Horace is defiant and persists in keeping his inferior product as it is. Horace is grateful, admiring, affectionate, but he is his own man. This, of course, reflects well on Maecenas, that he should be happy with a client who adopted this attitude. We should also remember that the word 'Sabine' spoke of probity, simple living, and independence. The wine code is hinting that Horace possesses the same qualities, and so showing appreciation of the liberality of Maecenas in being happy with a client who adopted this attitude.

There are two other points of praise. First, this reminder of the patron comes at the beginning of the second half of the book; and second, it is a tiny poem, the shortest so far: it looks like a slight poem and yet it is addressed to his great patron. The flattery comes in the unspoken confidence that Maecenas will understand and be amused.

It would be wise to suspect the above discussion. Is it overinterpretation? Some scholars have marked the poem down as a tissue of commonplaces, which it is. Like the music of Mozart. Happily there is a control at hand, 'one of the prototypes', as it has been called. The Epicurean philosopher Philodemus had addressed a very similar poem to Lucius Calpurnius Piso, consul 58 BC, using many of the same themes, to invite him to celebrate the birthday of Epicurus at a vegetarian dinner on the 20th of the month:

> Tomorrow your Muse-loving friend is carrying you off,
> after the ninth hour, dearest Piso, to his simple hut,
> for the annual dinner on the Twentieth. If you leave
> your dish of udders and your toasts in the Chian wine of Bromios,

you will at least see companions wholly true, you will at least   5
hear talk honey-sweeter than the land the Phaeacians knew.
But if you ever turn your eyes, Piso, even upon us,
we shall hold a rich Twentieth instead of a simple.

(*Palatine Anthology* 11. 44)

This is a pleasant piece, beginning with the humorous notion that the
Greek philosopher is going to be dragging the great Roman to dinner,
the skittish reference to Piso's carnivorous diet as opposed to the vege-
tarianism of Philodemus and his friends, the mythological pomp of his
Greek vintages (*Bromios* being a title of Dionysus, the Greek Bacchus),
and the literary fun with the *Odyssey* in line 6. Macleod is a little hard in
saying that Philodemus succeeds only in abasing himself. The last line is
surely asking for the wealth of Piso's presence not for a subsidy, but com-
pared with the Horace this is thin fare. Philodemus offers no grounds for
honouring Piso, very little evidence of Piso's regard for himself, and only
the wine and the udders in the fourth line to set against the subtleties of
Horace's wine code. Horace's poem is a completely different object. The
density of the nuances is far beyond Philodemus. But the crucial differ-
ence is that Horace is talking about a real friendship. His humour is not
simply literary or philosophical or playful flattery by a dependant.

Some readers, for the best of reasons, will find words addressed by a
client to a patron to be distasteful. Judgement in such matters tells us
more about the judges than the accused. For what it is worth, I like
Horace's poem because it shows in eloquent human details how he and
Maecenas crossed social barriers and barriers of wealth to enjoy each
other's friendship. I suppose it is the warmth of the poem that raises it
and this warmth lasted. Maecenas died in 8 BC, fifteen years after this
poem was published, and according to the Suetonian *Life of Horace*, his
will, as quoted in the Introduction to this book, included the request to
Augustus, 'Be mindful of Horace, as though he were myself', *Horati
Flacci ut mei memor esto.*

XXI

DIANAM tenerae dicite virgines,
intonsum, pueri, dicite Cynthium
    Latonamque supremo
      dilectam penitus Iovi.

vos laetam fluviis et nemorum coma,   5
quaecumque aut gelido prominet Algido
    nigris aut Erymanthi
      silvis aut viridis Gragi.

vos Tempe totidem tollite laudibus
natalemque, mares, Delon Apollinis,   10
    insignemque pharetra
      fraternaque umerum lyra.

hic bellum lacrimosum, hic miseram famem
pestemque a populo et principe Caesare in
    Persas atque Britannos   15
      vestra motus aget prece.

Variety is one of the principles by which Horace orders his books of poems. After three love poems and two different kinds of drinking-poems Horace now in this next ode offers a sacred poem in which he asks the unstained maidens and boys of Rome to pray to Diana and her brother Apollo of Mount Cynthus in Delos. The solemn sacral tone is conveyed by the balanced Latin in which one half-choir is asked to make its response to the other. The first line is echoed by the second. The opening of the second stanza is echoed by the opening of the third and the first line of the last stanza has its own balance as the supplications focus on the god Apollo.

As often, Horace is inspired by Catullus. His *Poem* 34 demonstrates this formal hymnic style as it prays to Diana, who was born (9–12):

to be mistress of hills	montium domina ut fores
and green forests	silvarumque virentium
and secret groves	saltuumque reconditorum
and sounding rivers.	amniumque sonantum.

Horace adopts this sculptured style but, as usual, his model is there to

XXI

a political express of
faith that makes use
of an ancient poetic
form   —Williams

Sing, tender virgins, of Diana.
Sing, boys, of unshorn Cynthius
    and of Latona, dear to the heart
        of supreme Jupiter.

You girls, sing of the goddess who delights in rivers   5
and whatever foliage of trees stands out
    on chilly Algidus, or in the dark woods of Erymanthus
        or of green Mount Gragus.

You boys, raise Tempe no less often with your praises,
and Delos, birthplace of Apollo,   10
    his shoulder shining with the quiver
        and his brother's lyre.

He will drive war with its tears and famine and pestilence
with their misery, far from the people and from Caesar
    the princeps, to the Persians and Britons,   15
        moved by your prayer.

be departed from. The complexities of his second and third stanzas have
driven commentators to wonder whether Erymanthus is green and the
woods of Gragus are black and to differ about *insignemque umerum*—'and
the notable shoulder of Apollo' as I have taken it, or 'and Apollo notable
as to his shoulder'. Horace seems happy to set up these post-Catullan
ambiguities. There can be no doubt that sophistication is part of his strat-
egy. *Gelido . . . Algido* (7) offers an etymology for the word *Algidus*. The
mountain is called the Cold (*Algidus*) because it is chilly, *gelidus*. This
alerts us so that when we come to the rattling phrase *Témpe tótidem tóllite
laúdibus* we are bound to remember that Tempe in north Greece, where
Apollo slew the Python, is the archetypal beautiful *valley*. 'Lift up the val-
ley of Tempe' is a play upon words, and it sets up his next. *Delos* is the
Greek for clear, conspicuous, and the Latin word *insignis* means conspic-
uous, distinguished. So in lines 10–11 the boys are asked to praise Delos,
the conspicuous island, and the conspicuous shoulder of Apollo. Another
Horatian play is the juxtaposition *natalemque mares* in line 10. Here *mares*,
'males' is a surprising way to address the boys, and coming as it does
between the two words denoting the birthplace of the male god, it is

bound to activate the connection and fix our minds firmly on the male half-choir, *natalemque, mares, Delon*. Horace now leaves the boys with the ghost of a smile, reminding them of an episode in the story he touched upon in 1. 10. There the naughty baby Mercury stole Apollo's cattle and quiver and Apollo laughed. The story goes on that to appease his big brother Mercury presented him with the lyre. We have come a long way from Catullus.

In the ravishing stanza quoted above from Catullus we have an echoing list of four of the areas governed by Diana. In the second stanza of the Horace we have not only music, but also stimuli for the eye. To say that Mount Algidus is cold is not far from hinting that it will at times be snow-covered. At such times the conifers which clad long ridges of that range will stand out black against the snow. Erymanthus is 'the wildest and most impassable mountain in Arcadia' (Nisbet and Hubbard), so we may imagine that its conifers, too, would often look vividly black. Gragus, on the other hand, is on the south coast of Asia Minor and the Romans would naturally think of it as being green, and untouched by snow.

Algidus is not far from Italy's most famous temple of Diana, at Aricia by the Alban lake south-east of Rome, where there lived:

Sapphics.

XXII

INTEGER vitae scelerisque purus
non eget Mauris iaculis neque arcu
nec venenatis gravida sagittis,
    Fusce, pharetra,

sive per Syrtis iter aestuosas   5
sive facturus per inhospitalem
Caucasum vel quae loca fabulosus
    lambit Hydaspes.

namque me silva lupus in Sabina,
dum meam canto Lalagen et ultra   10
terminum curis vagor expeditis,
    fugit inermem,

Odes 1. 22

> The priest who slew the slayer
> And shall himself be slain.

Apart from this mountain all the place-names are Greek until the last stanza, but Algidus has sounded the Italian note which now takes over the poem. Apollo was credited with giving Octavian the victory at Actium, as we noted at 1. 2. 32. So 'tearful war', *bellum lacrimosum* in line 13 is no ornamental epithet. Romans had been weeping for generations because of civil war. The allusion to pestilence has no known contemporary Roman relevance, but recalls Apollo's role as healer and bringer of plague. The prophecy that Apollo will protect Augustus is no empty pietism. Romans had only to look up to the Palatine Hill where Augustus lived and where he had dedicated the magnificent temple of Apollo to commemorate the victory which had made him the most powerful man in the world and left no enemies except the remotest peoples of the West and East, the Britons and the Persians. On the day of its dedication, 9 October 28 BC, there was much singing in praise of Augustus and in gratitude to Apollo (see *Odes* 1. 31 and Propertius, 4. 6). This poem is an echo from that great day.

XXII

The man who is pure of heart and innocent of evil
needs no Mauretanian spears, Fuscus,
nor bow nor quiver heavy
    with poisoned arrows

whether he is setting out across   5
the sultry Syrtes or inhospitable
Caucasus or lands licked
    by the fabled Hydaspes,

for as I wandered far from my farm
in Sabine forest singing of my Lalage   10
without a care to burden me, a wolf ran from me
    unarmed as I was—

103

quale portentum neque militaris
⸿ Daunias latis alit aesculetis
nec Iubae tellus generat, leonum   15
    arida nutrix.

pone me pigris ubi nulla campis
arbor aestiva recreatur aura,
quod latus mundi nebulae malusque   two nons
    Iuppiter urget;   20

pone sub curru nimium propinqui
solis in terra domibus negata:
dulce ridentem Lalagen amabo,
    dulce loquentem.   22

The second song in my well-thumbed sixth edition of the *Scottish Students' Songbook* (1897) is a setting of this ode in Church Hymnary style, and Nisbet and Hubbard tell us that it used to be sung at German and Scandinavian funerals. Such solemn views must lean on the lofty opening with its version of a notion dear to Stoic philosophers that the virtuous man (whom we shall meet again at the beginning of 3. 3) will be happy on the rack. This philosophical undertone might be strengthened in line 6 by the recollection of the famous march of Cato the younger, the archetypal Stoic, along the shore of the Great Syrtes (modern Gulf of Sirte in North Africa) in 47 BC from Berenice (Benghazi) to Lepcis Maior, some 700 miles in thirty days at the head of 10,000 troops. The hardships of this march became an inspiration to the Republican cause in the 40s and were an important feature in the idealization of Cato as a Republican hero. This observation is typical of the fundamental contribution of the Nisbet and Hubbard commentary to the understanding of these poems.

But Nisbet and Hubbard do not take even the first line wholly seriously. It could be rendered literally as 'Whole of life, of evil pure'. The genitive case 'of life', instead of the ablative 'in life' is 'mannered'. The chiasmus (ABBA arrangement) is 'grandiloquent'. From the beginning Horace is having a dig at the pretensions not only of Stoic philosophers but, at the same time, at extravagant lovers like Catullus and the elegiac poets. The man who wrote the first twenty-one poems in this book would not have walked in a dangerous forest singing about his Lalage, and if he had he would not have expected his singing to frighten away a

such a monster as warrior Daunia
does not feed in her broad oak-woods
nor does the land of Juba, dry nurse of lions,   15
    give it birth.

Set me on barren plains where no tree
is revived by a summer breeze,
in a zone of the earth oppressed by clouds
    and a hostile Jupiter;   20

set me right under the chariot-wheels of a sun   *i.e. uninhabitable places.*
in a land where no man can build a home—
I shall love my Lalage sweetly laughing,
    sweetly speaking.

wolf. Such experiences are reserved for more solemn lovers such as
Propertius (3. 16. 11–18) and Tibullus (1. 2. 27–8). Ovid, like Horace,
has some fun with the idea: 'You, too, will be brave,' whispered Cupid to
the trembling poet, then:

> nec mora, venit amor: non umbras nocte volantis,
>   non timeo strictas in mea fata manus.
>
>   (*Amores* 1. 6. 13–14)

In an instant came love. I do not fear shades that fly by night.
  I do not fear swords drawn to kill me.

The ode is full of genial exaggerations, many of them associated with
a pair of sustained metaphors. The doting lover is seen as a soldier.
Hence the spears, bows, and arrows of the first stanza. Poison arrows,
being attested for Libya by Silius Italicus (15. 681), are perfectly at home
with Mauretanian spears. Hence, too the famous march of Cato, still in
North Africa, then the transfer to the River Hydaspes in the Punjab,
scene of the famous victory of Alexander the Great over Porus and his
elephants in 326 BC. In the next stanza, cares are *expeditis*, 'rendered
light'. *Expediti* in Latin are light-armed troops. *Inermem* (12), 'unarmed'
continues the fun. Daunia, the wild mountainous area of south Italy near
Horace's birthplace, Venusia, is called 'military' and Juba takes us back
to Africa. This was Juba II of Numidia, who fought for Octavian at
Actium and in due course became king of Mauretania. The other
metaphor seems to me to begin with *Daunias alit* (14). Once again, as at
the end of 1. 18, grammatical gender is in play with sex. *Daunias* is used

as a feminine noun and when a female *alit*, she gives suck. This is supported by *generat* (15) and the oxymoron, 'dry [because desert] nurse'. At this point this tremendous arc of the sentence comes to an end and is sharply followed by the rhetorical commands with *pone*, 'set', at the beginning of each of the last two stanzas.

The decisive proof of the cheerful interpretation of this poem is its addressee. Aristius Fuscus had a sense of humour. In *Epistles* 1. 10. 5 he and Horace sit together nodding like a pair of old pigeons who know each other very well. In *Satire* 1. 9 Horace is stuck with a terrible bore who has been following him around the streets of Rome:

> ecce
> Fuscus Aristius occurrit, mihi carus et illum
> qui pulchre nosset. consistimus. 'unde venis?' et
> 'quo tendis?' rogat et respondet. vellere coepi,
> et prensare manu lentissima bracchia, nutans,
> distorquens oculos, ut me eriperet. male salsus
> ridens dissimulare.

> (*Satires* 1. 9. 61–6)

Along comes Fuscus Aristius, a friend of mine, who knew the fellow perfectly well. We stopped. 'Where have you been?' and 'Where are you going?' he asked and answered. I tugged at his toga. I clutched his arms. They stayed

3ʳᵒ (Asclepiad) *[handwritten marginal note, illegible]*

XXIII

VITAS inuleo me similis, Chloe,
quaerenti pavidam montibus aviis
    matrem non sine vano
        aurarum et siluae metu.

nam seu mobilibus vepris inhorruit   5
ad ventum foliis seu virides rubum
    dimovere lacertae,
        et corde et genibus tremit.

limp. I nodded and screwed up my eyes to get him to rescue me. The swine laughed and pretended not to notice.

In the end Fuscus refuses to go with Horace and talk business because it is a Friday, the sacred day of the Jews. Horace of course protests that he is not superstitious:

> 'nulla mihi' inquam
> 'religio est.' 'at mi: sum paulo infirmior, unus
> multorum: ignosces: alias loquor.'
>
> (*Satires* 1. 9. 70–2)

'But I am,' says Fuscus; 'I'm one of the weaker brethren, an ordinary chap. Do forgive me. I'll talk with you some other time.'

Surely this Aristius would have been smiling before the end of the first line of our ode.

When we reach the last two lines, we must yet again, as in 1. 13, 1. 16, and 1. 21, remember Catullus. Lalage's sweet laughter is an echo of Catullus 51 where Catullus' rival looks at Lesbia and listens to her as she laughs so sweetly, *dulce ridentem*. Here Catullus is translating from Sappho's account of her ten acute symptoms when she sees and hears the woman she loves sitting laughing and chatting with a man. Horace shows no respect.

XXIII

You avoid me, Chloe, like a fawn looking for her mother
who has run off in fright into the trackless mountains,
    and the fawn panics needlessly
      at breezes and at the wood.

Whether the fluttering leaves of the thorn tree   5
shudder in the wind or green lizards
    part the brambles, she trembles,
      heart and knees.

atqui non ego te tigris ut aspera
Gaetulusve leo frangere persequor: 10
tandem desine matrem
tempestiva sequi viro.

A deeply problematical poem. First of all, where is the mother? Most translators and editors talk as though fawn and doe are both on the trackless mountains but a careful reading of the Latin gives a much better picture. Since the fawn is looking for its mother, the ready inference is that the mother is absent, and the sandwich word-order of the Latin, 'the frightened in the trackless mountains mother', *pavidam montibus aviis matrem* suggests that the doe has been frightened and made off for the mountains leaving her fawn standing abandoned and terrified below the wood-line among thorn trees and brambles. 'Trackless' is then the fawn's focalization (as in 1. 2. 11–12), giving her view of the vast mountain wastes where she dares not go because she knows she would soon be lost. This *mise-en-scène* exactly fits the fragment of a poem from which Horace appears to have started:

> Gently, like a new-born sucking fawn,
> terrified, having been abandoned
> in a wood by its horned mother . . .
>
> (Anacreon, fragment 408)

The second grave problem is the thorn tree in line 5. The manuscripts have no thorn tree in the wind, *vepris . . . ad ventum*, but the arrival of spring, *veris . . . adventus*. Many Latin scholars have been reluctant to accept the arrival of spring. There are good parallels for the metaphor and the personification, but the difficulty is that the arrival of spring is said to shudder or shiver in the leaves. Latin is a very literal-minded language. Can an arrival shiver or shudder in leaves? And if it could what would the fawn be hearing? A fawn might well be upset by the lizards (a nice plural) which keep flickering through the bramble leaves, particularly if they are green lizards (*virides* is no ornamental epithet), but how would the arrival of spring in the leaves upset a nervous animal? Here I join the ranks of those who believe that the manuscripts do not make satisfactory sense and add an argument in favour of the reading *vepris*, conjectured independently by several scholars including Richard Bentley in his famous edition of 1711. In defence of this reading we might invoke the precise workmanship of these two stanzas. There is an obvious symmetry between lines 4 and 8. The fear of breezes and wood,

Yet I am no man-eating tiger or Gaetulian lion
hunting you down to crunch your bones.   10
   It is time to stop going with your mother.
   You are ready for a man.

aurarum et silvae metu, is answered by the fluttering of the heart and the trembling of the knees in line 8, *et corde et genibus tremit*, with a nice chiasmus of plural and singular answered by singular and plural. More to our point is the other symmetry, whereby the fear of (even slight) breezes is picked up by the rustling of the thorn tree and the fear of the wood is picked up by these little green animals darting through the green leaves of the bramble—one invisible flash and then nothing. The logic is now tight and the sensory data precise, as we have come to expect in this poet. Bentley's own defence of the conjecture is worth translating from his robust Latin:

As for the old reading, there are many reasons for the sensible man to reject it. Neither can the arrival of the spring bristle on the leaves since at that time there are no leaves; nor do fawns look for their mothers because hinds do not give birth until spring is well advanced; nor do lizards part the brambles since they do not emerge as soon as that from the lairs in which they hibernate; nor indeed, if you remove all these objections can you say in Latin 'The arrival of spring bristles on the leaves' when the correct Latin would rather be 'The leaves bristle at the arrival of spring' . . . Absolutely nothing can be more certain than this conjecture and it proves itself by its own light as surely as though it were produced from a hundred manuscripts.

Another intriguing question about this poem is the manipulation of the simile. The details of the descriptions are as vivid and telling as the detail in the great epic similes of Homer and Virgil, but in the limited compass of a dozen short lines it may surprise us to read that Horace has not made up his mind between thorn trees and brambles or between tigers and lions. To compare himself to a tiger or Gaetulian lion startling a fawn is one of the many epic touches in this passage and the alternatives contribute to the mock-heroic flavour. Compare the simile when young Ascanius appears in the thick of battle:

> qualis gemma micat fulvum quae dividit aurum,
> aut collo decus aut capiti, vel quale per artem
> inclusum buxo aut Oricia terebintho
> lucet ebur;

(Virgil, *Aeneid* 10. 134–7)

like a jewel parting tawny gold,
an ornament for neck or head, or like
glowing ivory concealed with great art in boxwood
or in Orician terebinth;

Such is the manifold beauty of Ascanius that Virgil has not adjudicated between gold and ivory, between head and neck, between boxwood and terebinth. Such alternatives are common in Virgilian similes, particularly in the later, military books of the *Aeneid*. In this tenth book of the *Aeneid*, for instance, there are in all fourteen similes and eight alternatives are offered (the above three and those at 273, 603, 723, 766, and 806).

The last delight in this poem is the movement into and out of the simile. No 'Just as a fawn . . .' picked up by 'just so do you . . .'. No recap of detailed resemblances. Four Latin words take us into the simile: 'You

XXIV

Qvis desiderio sit pudor aut modus
tam cari capitis? praecipe lugubris
cantus, Melpomene, cui liquidam pater
    vocem cum cithara dedit.

ergo Quintilium perpetuus sopor   5
urget! cui Pudor et Iustitiae soror,
incorrupta Fides, nudaque Veritas
    quando ullum inveniet parem?

multis ille bonis flebilis occidit,
nulli flebilior quam tibi, Vergili.   10
tu frustra pius heu non ita creditum
    poscis Quintilium deos.

quid si Threicio blandius Orpheo
auditam moderere arboribus fidem,
num vanae redeat sanguis imagini,   15
    quam virga semel horrida,

110

avoid me, Chloe, like a fawn' and we emerge for a moment at line 9: 'I do not pursue . . . you'. But where do we re-emerge to the literal after the tigers and lions? The orthodox view is that lines 11–12 are devoted to Horace and Chloe, but it may be better to allow the fawn to have a share in line 11. Chloe is clearly nervous, but it is the fawn rather than Chloe whose habit it is to trot along behind her mother. The clear emergence from the simile comes with a thump at the last word *viro*. Chloe is old enough for a man.

It would add to our understanding of contemporary social life if we could determine whether Chloe was a free Roman or a freedwoman or a slave, but such enquiries make the bold supposition that Chloe once existed.

(Readers should be warned that the translation cheats by making the fawn explicitly feminine.)

XXIV

Why should our grief for a man so loved
know any shame or limit? Teach us sad songs,
Melpomene. Your father gave you a clear voice
    and with it the lyre.

So a sleep that will not end bears down   5
upon Quintilius. Honour, Incorruptibility,
sister of Justice, and naked Truth—
    when will they ever see his equal?

Many good men will weep at his death,
but none weep more than you, Virgil. Your piety   10
counts for nothing as you ask the gods for Quintilius.
    They did not give him on such terms.

What if you were to tune a sweeter lyre than Thracian Orpheus
and trees came to listen? Would blood come back
into the empty shade which Mercury has once herded   15
    into his black flock

111

non lenis precibus fata recludere,
nigro compulerit Mercurius gregi?
durum: sed levius fit patientia
quidquid corrigere est nefas.   20

This poem begins by speaking of a grief that can know no limit and
ends by explaining how such grief becomes lighter. This does not
mean that Horace is a hack contradicting himself as he rings the changes
on the commonplaces of consolation. Only by sharing Virgil's grief can
he claim the right to suggest how grief can be contained. This is the
rhetoric of friendship and the ancients knew it (Theon, 2. 117. 16, cited
by Nisbet and Hubbard).

The second stanza was criticized in words attributed to Boccaccio by
Walter Savage Landor in *Pentameron* 4, 'What man on such an occasion is
at leisure to amuse himself with the little plaster images of Pudor and
Fides, of Justitia and Veritas . . .?' But it is wrong to think of plaster images
or frigid abstractions. The Romans were accustomed to visualize such enti-
ties as gods. Incorruptibility, justice, and truth are the qualities for which
Horace and Virgil admired their friend and which Horace was to com-
memorate about half a dozen years after the publication of these odes:

> Quintilio si quid recitares, 'corrige, sodes
> hoc' aiebat 'et hoc': melius te posse negares,
> bis terque expertum frustra, delere iubebat
> et male tornatos incudi reddere versus.
> si defendere delictum quam vertere malles,
> nullum ultra verbum aut operam insumebat inanem,
> quin sine rivali teque et tua solus amares.

> (*Ars Poetica* 438–44)

If you recited something to Quintilius, 'Correct that please,' he would say,
'and that.' You might reply that you had tried two or three times and could not
do any better. He would tell you to delete it and take your badly turned verses
back to the anvil. If you defended what you had done wrong rather than
change it, he would not say another word or waste his time on you but would
leave you alone to love yourself and your own creations without a rival.

This ode, like for example 1.4, is *ad hominem* poetry and there is
another man to consider. In the centre of the poem, where Moritz has
taught us to look for the important name, we find Virgil. The allusion to
the story of Orpheus which follows would take the mind of the contem-
porary Roman to Virgil's version of the story of Orpheus and Eurydice

with fearful crook? Prayers do not easily
persuade him to open the gates of death.
It is hard. But by enduring, we can make lighter
    what the gods forbid us to change.   20

at the end of the fourth book of the *Georgics*. These poems appeared in
29 BC and became an instant classic, being studied in the schools under
Caecilius Epirota (Suetonius, *On Grammarians* 16). The argument of
this ode runs, 'Do not hope, Virgil, to achieve anything by piety [11] or
poetry [13]. You cannot bring back Quintilius. Even the great Orpheus,
as you know better than anyone, failed to bring Eurydice back to life.'
But this is Horace and the argument is not spelled out. Nevertheless, line
17 of the ode, *non lenis precibus fata recludere*, must take us back to Virgil's
description of the scene in *Georgics* 4. 470 when Orpheus approaches the
gods below:

> nesciaque humanis precibus mansuescere corda.
> and the hearts which are not softened by the prayers of men.

Once the link is made, we see at line 11 that Virgil asking for
Quintilius is like Orpheus asking for Eurydice. Horace is reasoning with
Virgil from Virgil's own text. Music is powerless. Not even Orpheus
could make the blood return to the empty phantom of Eurydice. In this
context the mention of piety reminds us of its importance in the *Georgics*
and we can be sure that Horace was aware that the standard epithet for
Aeneas, the hero of the epic which everyone knew Virgil was writing,
would be *pius*. The repeated weeping, *flebilis, flebilior*, in lines 9 and 10
reminds us that the fourth *Georgic* is awash with tears. For instance
between lines 505 and 514 Virgil asks what weeping, *fletu*, could move
the Shades, then Orpheus is said to have wept, *flesse*, for seven long
months, as the nightingale weeps, *flet*, all night long for the nestlings she
has lost. We may then think back also to the first stanza, to Melpomene,
later to become the Muse of Tragedy. Again Landor's Boccaccio is on
the warpath, 'What man immersed in grief cares a quattrino about
Melpomene?' The answer is that Horace did and Virgil did. Poet is
speaking to poet and asking how they are to be taught to mourn in verse
the man they loved. The end of the poem utters a truth which is not new
or rare but it would have been near to the heart of the author of the
Aeneid. He was to express it himself in the words of old Nautes as he
comforted Aeneas in *Aeneid* 5. 709–10:

nate dea, quo fata trahunt retrahuntque sequamur;
quidquid erit, superanda omnis fortuna ferendo est.

Son of the goddess, let us follow the Fates, whether they lead us on or lead us back. We must overcome everything that Fortune brings, whatever it may be, by enduring it.

This ode, then, is a consolation *ad hominem* to Horace's friend Virgil, which works by asking him to reflect upon his own great poem. Contemporary readers would have understood some of this. Even the little we can detect is vital.

It is not rare for men to grieve at the death of friends, or for a comforter to show great delicacy. What makes this poem rare is, as ever, the texture of Horace's thought and the vitality in his language. It opens with a rhetorical question, a prayer, and an exclamation in lines 5–6. Here the weight of the language comes partly from the metre and 1. 11. 5 is our guide. Two choriambic feet (–◡◡–) fill the centre of each of the first three lines of each stanza, but only in lines 5 and 18 is each choriamb occupied by one word. The inevitability of these statements is reinforced by the sound of the verse, *Quintilium perpetuus, compulerit Mercurius*. In the obituary which follows, Horace not only pays tribute to Quintilius but also presents a vivid tableau of the Roman mourners round a corpse. Here again, as at the end of *Odes* 1. 18 and 22, grammatical gender merges into sex. *Pudor* is masculine but the merger comes at *Fides*, the *sister* of *Iustitia*, and is exploited at naked *Veritas*. Truth has rent her clothes in grief. The end of the poem too is enriched by the intensity of Horace's senses. After the music in 13–14, we are asked to imagine blood coming back into an empty phantom and we shudder at *horrida*. The last stanza gives us mildness in line 17, where Mercury is 'not mild to open . . .' and then blackness, hardness, lightness, and the will of the gods in the last word *nefas*.

It is never possible to define how poetry works, but contrast and comparison can on occasion help it to work. Shelley clearly knew this ode:

I weep for Adonais—he is dead!
O weep for Adonais! though our tears
Thaw not the frost which binds so dear a head!
And thou, sad Hour, selected from all years
To mourn our loss, rouse thy obscure compeers,
And teach them thine own sorrow, say: 'With me
Died Adonais; till the Future dares
Forget the Past, his fate and fame shall be
An echo and a light unto eternity!'

In this first stanza of his 'Adonais', Shelley has heard the variation of *flebilis* and *flebilior* and followed the indicative 'I weep' with the imperative 'weep'. At 'so dear a head' he has literally translated *tam cari capitis* of Horace's second line. Where Horace has asked the Muse to teach sad songs, Shelley has asked the Hour to teach its compeers its sorrow. His last three lines personify with all the boldness of Horace's second stanza, but his metaphors are richer and seem more profound than Horace's as they survey the Hour, the years, the Future, the Past, and all eternity. But the hope at the end of the poem, the fate and fame, an echo and a light, throw into starker relief the end of the ode, where Horace speaks the plain, bleak, truth.

Something of the power of Horace's poetry can be measured by the frequency with which those who know it call it to mind. Kipling is a prime witness. The depth of his response can be gauged by a marginal jotting against this ode in one of his many copies of Horace:

They pass, O God, and all
    Our grief, our tears,
Achieve not their recall,
    Or reach their ears.
Our lamentations leave
    But one thing sure.
They perish and we grieve
    But we endure.

XXV

Parcivs iunctas quatiunt fenestras
iactibus crebris iuvenes protervi,
nec tibi somnos adimunt, amatque
    ianua limen,

quae prius multum facilis movebat   5
cardines; audis minus et minus iam
'me tuo longas pereunte noctes,
    Lydia, dormis?'

invicem moechos anus arrogantis
flebis in solo levis angiportu,   10
Thracio bacchante magis sub inter-
    lunia vento,

cum tibi flagrans amor et libido,
quae solet matres furiare equorum,
saeviet circa iecur ulcerosum,   15
    non sine questu

laeta quod pubes hedera virenti
gaudeat pulla magis atque myrto,
aridas frondis hiemis sodali
    dedicet Euro.   20

This poem 'has no merit and may be omitted with advantage' wrote
Page in 1883, and Wickham in 1892 omitted it. In 1962
Commager valued it rather as a philosophical metaphor, a plea for the
acceptance of human nature, a critique of 'rigidity in a world of change'.
But such philosophical interpretations are too general to be of any inter-
est and are remote from the text. Nisbet and Hubbard see the poem as
an elaboration of traditional motifs, a weaving together of diverse poet-
ical strands which, not surprisingly, fails to achieve complete consis-
tency. 'Horace does not persuade us that his conventional formulas
reflect real feelings.' But there is surely a better way of looking at the
poem. Horace is no part of this amorous imbroglio. We are not told that
he had ever loved Lydia or been refused by her or envied her lovers. He

very Love — human comedy
— much old & —94
— " younger — elegiac poets
— ar door ...

XXV

The wild young men are not so eager now
to rattle your closed shutters with volleys of pebbles
and disturb your sleep. The door that once
    moved so very easily

on its hinges, now hugs the threshold.   5
Less and less often do you hear the cry
'I'm dying for your love, Lydia, night after long night
    and you lie there sleeping.'

Your turn will come, when you are an old rag
in some lonely alley-way, weeping at the insolence of lovers   10
as the wind from Thrace holds wilder and wilder orgies
    between the old moon and the new

and your burning love, the lust
that drives the mothers of horses to madness,
rages round your ulcerous liver,   15
    and you will not fail to complain

about the cheerful youngsters who take pleasure
in green ivy and dark myrtle
and dedicate dry leaves to the east wind,
    winter's crony.   20

is rather adopting his accustomed role as Professor of Love, *Praeceptor Amoris*, and dispassionately observing the human comedy.

The poem begins with three nouns passing in close order, each with its own epithet. The shutters are closed (*iunctas* means joined), the volleys of pebbles are frequent, and the young men are wild. This pat arrangement may be a clue. The poem is not mocking Lydia only. The behaviour of young men in love is also ridiculed, particularly as depicted in Roman comedy and elegy. The first books of Tibullus and Propertius have come out while Horace is writing these odes and their notion of love is not his, as we have seen, notably in 1. 16 and 17.

The satirical note becomes clearer where Lydia's door now loves, *amat*, 'hugs' its threshold. How different from the old days when these two were often parted to admit her lovers. The amorous metaphor continues with 'easy', *facilis*, an adjective commonly applied in Latin to compliant women, women of *easy* virtue. Strictly, the Roman door did not have hinges as we normally understand them, but projections which rotated in sockets in threshold and lintel. These often became stiff and would grind and squeal, but not Lydia's in the old days. Now, however, things have changed and less and less often does she hear the moaning of a lover on the doorstep at his night-long winter vigil—the plural *noctes* is sardonic; this lover says he has been on the doorstep for several nights. The song at the closed door, the *paraclausithyron*, is a staple theme of Roman elegy (Horace writes his own at *Odes* 3. 10) and here he gives a short snatch of one, beginning with a mock-poignant juxtaposition, *me tuo*, '*me*, being *yours*, dying throughout long nights', and again the punch comes in the short line, 'you, Lydia, are asleep'. The Professor of Love is smiling at the beginners.

Now the pivot. One emphatic word, *invicem*, 'you in your turn', governs the whole of the huge sentence which takes up the rest of the poem. The time will come when Lydia will want love, but lovers will be insolent. No longer will they besiege her house. She will have to take to the streets, weeping as she stands in a north wind growing wilder towards the dark nights between the old moon and the new, and she will be *levis*, 'worthless, despised'. The literal sense of the word 'light' hints that she will be blown by the wind from Thrace as though she were a scrap of rubbish in her lonely alley-way, *in solo levis angiportu*. Thrace was the home of the Bacchic rites which drove women into the mountains in mystic frenzy. This is a Thracian wind and is not surprisingly engaged in a Bacchic orgy. Lydia is caught up in it.

When Horace was writing these odes, the most famous poem in Latin, as we have just noted on 1. 24, was the *Georgics* written by his friend Virgil. There we read that all animals are subject to love:

Surely the wildest of all is the frenzy of mares

. . . . . .

Love leads them across Mount Gargara and the roaring river
Ascanius. They climb mountains and swim rivers
and when the flame is applied to the lusting marrow of their bones
(but mostly in spring because heat returns to their bones in spring),
they instantly stand on high rocks, their faces turned towards the west
and catch the gentle breezes, and often without mating,

by some strange miracle, they conceive by the wind
and scatter over rocks and cliffs and deep valleys
not towards your rising, wind of the east, nor the rising sun,
but towards Caurus and Boreas in the north and where the south wind,
blackest of all, is born and darkens the sky with chill rain.

(Virgil, *Georgics* 3. 266, 269–79)

This passage is surely in Horace's mind. He has two winds to Virgil's four. He has mares, referred to in mock-heroic terms, 'the mothers of horses', the burning of love, and its raging. There are two main differences. First, in Virgil mares are impregnated by spring Zephyrs from the west whereas Lydia will not be impregnated and will know nothing of the gentle western breezes but be exposed to blasts of the north wind and consigned at the end to the east. Second, in Virgil mares feel the heat of love in their bones, whereas it rages round Lydia's ulcerated liver. Horace has shifted the seat of love no doubt to accommodate the brutal adjective. It is easier to think of an ulcerated liver than ulcerated bone marrow. Horace, the detached observer, sees the three phases of Lydia's life, her past when lovers beat a path to her door, the present when their visits are less frequent, and the future when she will long for love and not receive it.

This is not a pretty matter and there is no way of dressing it up as though it were. But three considerations apply. First, satire at the expense of old women is a stock type of poem in some of the Greek poets whom Horace is attempting to rival in Latin. His ambition was to complete his portfolio. This he does with greater subtlety and fairness in this poem than we find in the surviving examples in the *Palatine Anthology* (11. 66–74). Second, Horace is even-handed in that he ends the poem with a sardonic look at the men in the case. They are cheerful, *laeta*, and they find their pleasure, *gaudeant*, not in dry leaves but in evergreen foliage, the ivy of Bacchus and the myrtle of Venus. The sardonic observation gains edge from the other sense of *laeta*, fertile, fruitful. It is as though they forget that they are subject to the same natural laws of growth and decay as govern Lydia. Horace is not condemning or abusing anyone, but smiling at the silliness of the love poets and giving a realistic picture of the behaviour of young men and the career expectations of women like Lydia. Third, our very revulsion at his cruelty is testimony to the power of what he writes.

Alcaic

XXVI

Mvsis amicus tristitiam et metus
tradam protervis in mare Creticum
    portare ventis, quis sub Arcto
        rex gelidae metuatur orae,

quid Tiridaten terreat, unice   5
securus. o quae fontibus integris
    gaudes, apricos necte flores,
        necte meo Lamiae coronam,

Pimplei dulcis! nil sine te mei
prosunt honores: hunc fidibus novis,   10
    hunc Lesbio sacrare plectro
        teque tuasque decet sorores.

For Horace the Muses are an antidote to misery, so here, as their friend, he consigns fear and gloom to boisterous winds to carry far away to the stormy seas off Crete. He is supremely unconcerned about local difficulties at the limits of the Roman world, but commentators need to give them a short paragraph. The Parthians were the great power in Asia and between 31 and 26 BC. Tiridates had twice rebelled and taken the throne and twice been expelled and fled to the Romans. During that period he must have had many things to be afraid of but the chattering alliteration in line 5, *quid Tiridaten terreat*, tells us that what terrified Tiridates did not worry Horace. In the north some king is causing alarm but Horace is so blasé that he does not even tell us his name. It was probably the Dacian Cotiso, who according to *Satires* 2. 6. 53 was the talk of Rome when that book was published in 30 BC and whose eventual defeat was a great relief in the capital according to *Odes* 3. 8. 18. Nor does he tell us what ice-bound shore or river bank is referred to in line 4 but again the reference may be to the Dacians who lived north of the Danube or to the Bastarnae who crossed the Danube and the Haemus and had to be quelled by a Roman expedition in 29–28 BC (Dio Cassius, 51. 23).

Horace's insouciance about these matters is advertised in the reference to the far north in line 5 of the English and line 3 of the Latin, *sub Arcto*, literally under the Bear, presumably the Great Bear in the celestial North

120

XXVI

I am a friend of the Muses. Gloom and fear I shall throw
to the wild winds to carry off to the Cretan sea,
 supremely uninterested
  in what king is alarming

some ice-bound northern shore and what is terrifying   5
Tiridates. You who delight in pure fountains,
 weave flowers grown in the sun,
  weave a garland for my Lamia,

sweet Pimpleis! Without you the honours
I confer are worthless. To sanctify this Lamia   10
 by a new lyre and by a Lesbian plectrum
  becomes you and becomes your sisters.

Pole, apparently so far away as to be off Horace's map. He is perhaps extracting a little surreal fun from this by teasing us to imagine the constellation as an animal—a standard conceit in astrological poetry in Greek and Latin. Ovid, for example, employs it at *Metamorphoses* 2. 173–5 when the chariot of the Sun hurtles out of control towards the celestial north and warms up Draco, the eternally hibernating Serpent, and makes him angry; or at 2. 199 when the sight of Scorpio makes Phaethon drop the reins. Horace plays the same game at 3. 29. 18 when Canicula, the Little Dog, becomes rabid. Here in 1. 26, we can scarcely become agitated about strange people who live under a bear. Thanks to the Muse all these quaint, remote, and unimportant anxieties leave Horace supremely unperturbed, *securus*, and his unconcern is emphasized by the placing of the word at the end of a long sentence in line 6 of the Latin and before heavy punctuation after the first word in the line. In Horace such clashes between line-ending and punctuation sometimes seem to suggest excitement or exaltation, as for example in the Bacchic frenzy of 3. 25. 8–14 or the drunken shouts of 3. 19. 10–22, perhaps even in similar circumstances in our next ode, 1. 27. 1–14. Here, in 1. 26, the exaltation comes as Horace turns to address the Muse.

This address is full of the language of the kletic hymn, as we shall describe it on 1. 32. It opens with an impassioned *O* introducing the addressee, followed by the adjective clause introduced by *quae*, then the

121

fountains which are the home of the divinity; the request, here insistently redoubled in the repetitious action, *necte* ... *necte*, weave ... weave; the laudatory adjective *dulcis*, sweet, and at the end of a long sentence an oblique indication of the divinity, again by means of her home, here Pimpla near the Pierian fountain of the Muses on Mount Olympus. Remembering how often Horace plays with the etymology of Greek proper names, I have kept the spelling of manuscript B, *Pimplei*, our lady of Pimpla, to hint at the verb *pimplemi*, I fill. In this context this would be plausible as a learned suggestion that the fountain of the Muse was ever full and ever flowing. More repetitions in the last two lines maintain the elevated tone, particularly the hymnal repetition of the second-person pronoun in *teque tuasque* and this is confirmed in line 11 by *sacrare*, hallow, consecrate.

So much for the sublimity of tone, but this invocation of the goddess of poetic inspiration is also a programmatic statement. For those with ears to hear Horace is explaining his poetic intentions. The fresh fountains and the new strings stress his originality. The double weaving suggests artistic elaboration. The sweetness of the Muse hints at the sweet music of the verse. The coronet or chaplet of flowers which the Muse is asked to weave for Horace is not, of course a chaplet, but a poem. This ode is the fulfilment of the prayer it contains. The new strings (not the Greek lyre or the cithara but the Latin *fides*) beside the Greek plectrum demonstrate that Horace has accommodated Greek music to Latin measures. At the end the hallowing of Lamia, perhaps for his victories as legate in Spain in 25–24 BC (hence the triumphal garland of line 8, see Nisbet and Hubbard, 301) hints at the immortality which poetry can confer, and the term, *Pimpleis*, unparalleled in extant Latin as a personal name, is a piece of mythological erudition. All of this demonstrates Horace's affiliation with the poetry produced in Alexandria at the end of the fourth century BC, particularly by Callimachus. All of these images and motifs can be exemplified from his work. This whole passage displays also Horace's regard for another master, namely Lucretius, the great Roman philosophical poet of the previous generation:

Odes 1. 26

iuvat integros accedere fontis
atque haurire, iuvatque novos decerpere flores
insignemque meo capiti petere inde coronam
unde prius nulli velarint tempora Musae.

(Lucretius, 1. 927–30)

I delight in approaching pure fountains
and drinking deeply. I delight in plucking fresh flowers
and finding a glorious chaplet for my head with such blooms
as the Muses have never before given to veil the temples of any other man.

On the other hand Horace has written a number of poems in which a distinguished Roman is urged to enjoy convivial pleasures. The formula is that he is told to forget his political concerns for a time, and these are usually connected with incidents far from Rome. Garlands of flowers or greenery are provided for his head. There is lyre music and ladies to play it and sing. This may be another reason for the unheard-of name Pimpleis, which sounds as though it could be one of those exotic names affected by Greek ladies of pleasure (for which see Lyne). Clio or Calliope or any of their seven sisters would have led the mind too strictly to the Muse. Pimpleis is the lyre-player. This poem therefore has much of the equipment and all the zest for a *convivium*.

It is an act of joyous worship, a celebration of the creative experience of writing poetry, a tribute to a friend, a proud programmatic statement, a declaration of poetic affiliation, and a subtle evocation of the pleasures of a Roman *convivium*. Nisbet and Hubbard formulate their view of it with lapidary eloquence: 'the ode lacks content, in spite of all its elegance. Poetry is not the best subject for poetry, and Horace's greatest odes are not written simply about poetry.' Kiessling–Heinze's commentary is perhaps nearer the mark in calling it a Horatian masterpiece in miniature, *ein Meisterstück horazischer Kleinkunst.*

XXVII

NATIS in usum laetitiae scyphis
pugnare Thracum est: tollite barbarum
   morem, verecundumque Bacchum
     sanguineis prohibete rixis.

vino et lucernis Medus acinaces   5
immane quantum discrepat: impium
   lenite clamorem, sodales,
     et cubito remanete presso.

vultis severi me quoque sumere
partem Falerni? dicat Opuntiae   10
   frater Megillae, quo beatus
     vulnere, qua pereat sagitta.

cessat voluntas? non alia bibam
mercede. quae te cumque domat Venus,
   non erubescendis adurit   15
     ignibus, ingenuoque semper

amore peccas. quidquid habes, age
depone tutis auribus. a! miser,
   quanta laborabas Charybdi,
     digne puer meliore flamma.   20

quae saga, quis te solvere Thessalis
magus venenis, quis poterit deus?
   vix illigatum te triformi
     Pegasus expediet Chimaera.

In dramatic monologues the poet addresses a third party, and our plea-
sure as readers comes largely from piecing together scraps of evidence
in the words we overhear to build up our understanding of the scene, the
action, and the characters involved. In Robert Browning's 'My Last
Duchess', for instance, we know without being told that a duke is show-
ing a picture of his dead wife to a visitor because the first lines read:

> That's my last duchess on the wall,
> looking as if she were alive.

Pny of Love.
— Owed solemnity of older man
amongst youthful symposiast company
— of Syme wit jutting out of hand
of cork

XXVII

—Cups are made for joy. Only Thracians use them
for fighting. Put a stop to that barbarous practice.
   Keep Bacchus respectable. Don't let him near
      brawling and bloodshed.

Wine and lamplight don't belong in the same world   5
as a Persian dagger. Moderate
   your unholy noise, friends,
      and keep the weight on the elbow.

—You want me to join you in that grim Falernian?
—Let's hear from Megilla's brother from Opys.   10
   What's this wound he's lucky enough to have?
      What's this arrow he's dying from?

—You're hanging back? No more drink
for me. These are my terms. Whatever Venus
   is taming you, you don't need to blush   15
      about your burning passion, since any lover you fall for

is always well-born. Whatever it is, come, tell me
your secret. It's safe with me. —O you poor devil!
   What a Charybdis you've been caught in! You poor boy!
      You deserve a better flame than that.   20

What witch can free you? What Thessalian magician
with his potions? What god? Not even Pegasus
   will find it easy to disentangle you from the coils
      of that triple Chimaera.

We know what the visitor says because of lines 12–13:

             so, not the first
      Are you to turn and ask thus.

We gather what sort of man the duke was and what happened as a result
from his words to his visitor:

           Oh sir, she smiled, no doubt,
      whenever I passed her; but who passed without
      Much the same smile? This grew; I gave commands;

Then all smiles stopped together. There she stands
As if alive.

The last lines of the poem complete the dossier on the character of the duke:

Notice Neptune, though,
Taming a sea-horse, thought a rarity,
Which Claus of Innsbruck cast in bronze for me.

Scene, actions, and character are all conveyed to the reader, as though overhearing, and the same technique is used in Horace, *Odes* 1. 27. Here, too, we have the added pleasure at the five points marked with dashes in the translation of filling in for ourselves unstated words of the listeners in the scene.

Our first challenge is to supply the noise of an incipient drunken brawl before Horace even begins to speak. Our second is to appreciate the persona Horace is presenting in this little drama. We are helped in this by what we have already seen earlier in this book of his distaste for the extremes of youthful behaviour, his tact and his sense of humour. So here when sententious moralizing opens each of the first two stanzas and is followed in each of these stanzas by two imperatives, addressed to his *sodales*, his drinking companions, we are surely to understand this as mock solemnity. Horace is the elder statesman of the symposium bringing the youngsters to order with a smile. Civilized people do not brawl at symposia. That's the behaviour one expects from drunken northerners like Thracians, and Horace impresses his young friends by conjuring up for them a scene he no doubt remembers from his own student days in Athens, namely the moment in the battle in Thessaly at the wedding of Pirithous and Hippodamia when a Centaur is about to crash a great jar down on the head of a Lapith on his knees before him. Horace could have seen this on the ninth metope on the south side of the Parthenon.

On that same day he could have gone into the Parthenon and seen the *acinaces*, the straight, short, Persian sword which was displayed there in commemoration of the Persian War, as recorded in Greek inscriptions cited in Liddell and Scott's *Greek Dictionary*. This is the first use of the word in surviving Latin and it is hardly ever heard of again. Horace is appealing to intellectual pretensions of these young men—they understand about such things—and asking them to remember the standards of Graeco-Roman civilization. They are not expected to behave like barbarians, northern or eastern. He is also telling us what is happening. The *acinaces* is a clue for the reader and the obvious interpretation is that somebody has brought an *acinaces* along to the party, perhaps as a curio or a memento of his travels. There has been a difference of opinion and the sword is being waved around. People start shouting and getting up from their couches. The old boy calls upon them to remember that they are Romans, not barbarians. They know that Bacchus can be a dangerous god and they must keep him respectable, and not allow him near any brawling. Shouting at a symposium is not only barbarous, it is also impious. Horace's final vivid instruction is to put their left elbows back where they belong, on the couches, to leave their right arms free for their proper duties.

Romans who took part in drinking-bouts were even more subject to social pressures than we are. The king or arbiter of the drinking (*rex* or *arbiter bibendi*) decided the speed of the drinking and the strength of the wine. This party is just moving on to the Falernian. Pliny tells us in his *Natural History* 14. 62 that in his day no wine was more esteemed than Falernian from the Faustus estate. He also adds mysteriously that it was the only wine which ignited when a flame was applied to it. The joke is that the Latin word *severum*, which here means 'dry and powerful' is more often used in a moral sense meaning 'strict' and is regularly applied to teetotallers. What Horace is saying, but saying with a non-serious frown, is that if the hubbub doesn't stop, he is not going to stay for the Falernian.

But here at the middle of the poem he deftly turns the minds of his young friends from Bacchus to Venus. He is not going to stay unless Megilla's brother tells them whom he is in love with. 'Megilla's brother' is an extraordinary expression. Patronymics are common, but sororonymics unheard of. This little touch is as much as to say 'Of course, we all know Megilla . . .'.

At the beginning of line 13, the boy very wisely refuses to be drawn. Horace then wheedles him with the oiliest and most transparent flattery, spread over the longest sentence in the poem and the only sentence which spans two stanzas. This is totally unscrupulous manipulation, as emerges in line 18. He has asked his victim to deposit his secret in Horace's safe ears, *depone tutis auribus*. The moment he hears it he starts a long tease which makes it abundantly clear that he has no intention of honouring the confidence.

Charybdis and Chimaera are names given elsewhere to Greek ladies of pleasure. Charybdis, being the whirlpool which Odysseus avoided in *Odyssey* 12. 234–59, would drive a man giddy before she sucked him down, and the Chimaera, 'in front a lion, at the rear a snake, in the middle a goat' as described by Homer in *Iliad* 6. 181, would entangle him in her coils before consuming him. Line 19 contains a delicious use of the imperfect tense, *laborabas*, 'you were toiling', which conveys with Latin economy the notion, 'So that's what was troubling you!' The effect is heightened by the metre. The Alcaic stanza often exploits the difference in weight between its third and fourth lines. Here, in *quanta laborabas Charybdi*, only the third and third-last syllables are short. In *digne puer meliore flamma*, the line trips off with two dactyls. Similarly the third line of the last stanza gives due weight to the triform entanglement, while the last line speaks of release by a flying horse. Such effects scarcely bear talking about because sounds do not convey sense. They only add an inexpressible tone and vitality to the utterance. They cannot be expounded, but they must be heard.

In the last stanza Pindar joins the fun. His second *Olympian Ode* opens by asking: 'What god, what hero, what man shall we proclaim?' and Horace uses the formula to begin *Odes* 1. 12, 'What man, what hero . . . what god?' Now, he applies it mischievously to this frivolous occasion and laces it with a typical absurdity. Bellerophon rode the winged horse Pegasus to destroy the Chimaera. Horace now suggests that not even *Pegasus* would be able to release this unfortunate boy from the coils of the Chimaera. That never was the function of the horse.

It may be that we should here ask a question. Why does Horace cast himself in this role? Why does one of the two great poets of the age present himself as going to drinking-parties with young men and competing with young men for the love of women? An answer might start from the last poem in his first book of *Epistles*. Here, as he sends his book out into the world he tells it what to say about himself, if asked:

> me libertino patre natum et in tenui re
> maiores pennas nido extendisse loqueris,
> ut quantum generi demas virtutibus addas;
> me primis Urbis belli placuisse domique;
> corporis exigui, praecanum, solibus aptum,
> irasci celerem, tamen ut placabilis essem.
>
> (*Epistles* 1. 20. 20–5)

that I was born in humble circumstances of a freedman father
and my wings became too big for the nest
(so underestimating my ancestry and exaggerating my virtues);
that I pleased the leading men of the city in war and peace;
was small in stature, prematurely grey, enjoyed the sun,
was quick to anger, but easily appeased.

He knows how important it had been for him to please the leading men
of the city and has the candour to declare it. On the other hand, his
greatest contribution was his creation of a lyric poetry in Rome which
could stand beside the dazzling lyric poetry of Greece, including the
poems of love and conviviality by Sappho, Alcaeus, Archilochus, and
Anacreon. But they wrote for their friends and lovers of the same age as
themselves, the young men and women who were characters in their
poetry. Horace had the more delicate task of bringing Augustus,
Maecenas, Agrippa, and a large number of the senior consulars of Rome
into his amatory and convivial verses. This he negotiated with his
famous tact, but in order to give himself more freedom to transplant this
poetry of love and friendship to Roman soil, he found it convenient to
represent himself as enjoying such relationships among the younger
generation. Hence the persona of the tolerant, worldly-wise, middle-
aged hedonist, the Professor of Love, *Praeceptor Amoris*. Even so, the
question just discussed and the answer offered may seem to be over-
simple. It may, however, receive some support from the large number of
young addressees in *Epistles* 1 (20 BC) and *Odes* 4 (13 BC). By now
Horace is the Poet Laureate, the Augustan *vates*. His material is often
not quite appropriate to the *dignitas* of the senior political figures of the
Augustan regime, but it may have been thought that it did not damage
their sons to be tactfully shown in some relationship to the activities
depicted in the previous Golden Age of lyric poetry.

Note, yet again, that this account is not falling into the autobiograph-
ical fallacy. It does not presuppose that Horace ever went to such a sym-
posium or ever loved or ever drank wine. He may have. He may not have.
Nothing of this is known. For Horace throughout, read the persona pro-
jected by Horace. We have before us the world he created for his poetry,
not a case history of his private life.

TE maris et terrae numeroque carentis harenae
    mensorem cohibent, Archyta,
pulveris exigui prope litus parva Matinum
    munera, nec quicquam tibi prodest

aerias temptasse domos animoque rotundum   5
    percurrisse polum morituro.
occidit et Pelopis genitor, conviva deorum,
    Tithonusque remotus in auras,

et Iovis arcanis Minos admissus, habentque
    Tartara Panthoiden iterum Orco   10
demissum, quamvis clipeo Troiana refixo
    tempora testatus nihil ultra

nervos atque cutem morti concesserat atrae,
    iudice te non sordidus auctor
naturae verique. sed omnis una manet nox   15
    et calcanda semel via leti.

dant alios Furiae torvo spectacula Marti;
    exitio est avidum mare nautis;
mixta senum ac iuvenum densentur funera; nullum
    saeva caput Proserpina fugit.   20

me quoque devexi rapidus comes Orionis
    Illyricis Notus obruit undis.
at tu, nauta, vagae ne parce malignus harenae
    ossibus et capiti inhumato

particulam dare: sic, quodcumque minabitur Eurus   25
    fluctibus Hesperiis, Venusinae
plectantur silvae te sospite, multaque merces
    unde potest tibi defluat aequo

ab Iove Neptunoque sacri custode Tarenti.
    neglegis immeritis nocituram   30
postmodo te natis fraudem committere? fors et
    debita iura vicesque superbae

XXVIII

Measurer of earth and ocean and numberless sand,
  Archytas, you are now confined
near the Matine shore, by a little handful of dust duly sprinkled,
  and it profits you nothing to have probed

the dwellings of air and traversed the round vault of heaven   5
  with a mind that was to die.
The father of Pelops also died, boon companion of the gods,
  and Tithonus, though carried off into the winds,

and Minos, though admitted to the secrets of the gods.
  Tartarus keeps the son of Panthous,   10
though he was twice sent down to Orcus and called the Trojan Age
  to witness by unfastening his shield to prove

that he had given nothing but flesh and sinew to dark death,
  and in your eyes he was no mean teacher
of truth and of nature. But one night waits for all of us   15
  and all must walk the path of death once.

The Furies give some men over to stern Mars for his games.
  The greedy sea is the death of sailors.
Young and old together, the funerals come thronging. Proserpina
  is merciless and runs away from no man.   20

I, too, was overwhelmed in the Illyrian waves by the south wind,
  wild comrade of Orion as he descends.
But you, sailor, must not be sparing, do not grudge me a little
  of this drifting sand for my head and bones.

So, for all the threats of the east wind on the western waves,   25
  may you be safe when the woods
of Venusia are lashed, and may great profit flow down
  upon you from whatever giver,

from favouring Jupiter and from Neptune, guardian of Tarentum.
  Do you not care that you are doing a wrong   30
that will hurt your innocent descendants? It may be
  that a debt of justice and a reward for your pride

131

te maneant ipsum: precibus non linquar inultis,
    teque piacula nulla resolvent.

quamquam festinas, non est mora longa; licebit   35
    inecto ter pulvere curras.

1–15   You died, Archytas, and so did Tantalus, Tithonus, Minos, and
        Pythagoras.
15–22 All men must die. I too died, of drowning.
23–36 Sprinkle my corpse with sand, sailor, as you pass.

This brutal skeleton of argument shows that the poem starts with twenty lines of philosophizing. It is not till line 22 that we realize that a dead man is speaking. The interpretation has been hotly disputed, but the simplest solution is to assume one speaker, a drowned man, musing to himself until about line 17 where he begins to speak to a passing sailor.

There is nothing unusual about the opening. To list the names of great men who have died is a common feature of the literature of consolation. Lucretius, for example, in persuading his reader to accept the inevitability of death, follows such a list with the question at 3. 1045:

> tu vero dubitabis et indignabere obire?
>
> Will you then hesitate and protest about dying?

Nor is there anything at all unusual about the appeal from the corpse to the passer-by. Book 7 of the *Palatine Anthology* is full of such poems. What is unusual is the combination of the two motifs and the seemingly awkward and unbalanced structure of the ode.

Why are these five presented as examples of great men who have died? Archytas of Tarentum won fame as a mathematician in the first half of the fourth century BC and is chosen partly because of the irony of the contrast between his cosmic achievements and his insignificant end. He calculated the numberless, and in his astronomical studies is said to have dared to traverse the skies and scrutinize the abodes of the gods, but the mind that achieved all this was doomed to die and his body to be confined by a little dust. Tantalus, father of Pelops, appears because he had to die, although he had communed with the gods and dined at their table. Tithonus was carried off by Eos, goddess of the dawn, in her chariot (Statius, *Silvae* 1. 2.45) and the familiar story tells how he received immortality but, having failed to ask for eternal youth, faded away to nothing. Despite being carried off into the air by a goddess, Tithonus still died. Minos was admitted to the secrets of Jupiter (the language is

are waiting even for you. If you abandon me, my curses will not go
    unheard, and no expiation will ever acquit you.
Although you are in haste, it would not delay you long. You can   35
    throw three handfuls of dust and go speeding on your way.

almost political, as at 3. 25. 6 where Augustus is to be included in the
council of Jupiter, *inserere et consilio Iovis*). Pythagoras (532/1–497/6 BC)
believed that the human soul was a portion of the divine enclosed within
the body as a tomb and condemned to a cycle of reincarnation. One day,
among the dedications in a temple in Argos he saw a shield which he
realized he himself had carried in the Trojan War centuries before, in a
previous existence as Euphorbus, son of Panthous. Sure enough, when
he took it down the name Euphorbus was inscribed on the inside of it.
But despite his two lives, argues the dead sailor, he still had to die. So
these five examples are chosen because the first four are men who had
close contacts with gods and the fifth is a man who seemed to have
proved that he had lived twice.

The dead man now concludes his list by pondering the universality of
death. It may seem surprising that he says in line 16 that all men have to
tread the path of death *once*, immediately after having discussed
Pythagoras who is claimed to have trodden it twice. The best explana-
tion is that this is a pointed response by the speaker. Archytas may
believe Pythagoras' story, but the drowned man is replying sceptically.
Either he rejects Pythagoras' demonstration with the shield or he implies
that his first death did not take Pythagoras all the way along the path of
death. No matter what the truth of the Euphorbus story, Pythagoras,
too, has now taken the road to death.

At line 23 the dead man is addressing a passing sailor and asking him
to throw on his corpse some of the sand blowing about on the shore.
Line 30 tells us that the sailor is preparing to hurry on his way without
complying with the request. The dead man now warns him that a simi-
lar fate may be in store for him, and curses him if he fails to perform the
rite. At line 35, he softens his approach and ends with an appeal. We
have seen already in the previous ode that in reading dramatic mono-
logues we have to be alert to the implied responses of the silent listener
or listeners. Here too, by this alertness, we can make sense of the poem,
and in this case can explain the slightly disjointed utterances of the last
dozen lines as being desperate manœuvres by the dead man in response
to the apathy of the one person who can help him. True to form, the
dramatic monologue lets us know what is said by the interlocutor though

it does not report it, and true to form it gives a notion of the character and mood of both the speaker and addressee.

On this view (call it the minimalist interpretation) the address to Archytas with which the poem starts is a misleading clue. He is simply one of the five examples of dead worthies. Perhaps the address is not a real address, but the common Latin trick of enlivening the utterance by pretending to speak to a person not present, as in 1. 12, 21–4, where in a list of third-person gods Horace suddenly addressed Liber, Diana, and Phoebus Apollo.

But is the clue so misleading? Does it not fit certain other clues in the poem? We note that the scene is firmly set in the south of Italy. Archytas was a Tarentine, the most famous son of his city, seven times elected as its leader, *strategos*. No doubt his tomb was at or near Tarentum, a famous seaport in the Bay of Taranto, the arch of the foot of Italy. Pythagoras spent most of his working life at Croton, across the bay, but in the second half of the fourth century BC, no doubt because of the earlier influence of Archytas, Tarentum became the centre of Pythagorean teaching. The list of five worthies begins and ends in line 14 with an address to Archytas. Perhaps this is not just a Latin convention. Indeed, Horace could be accused of deceiving his readers if it were so. The suggestion clearly is that the dead man has been washed up on the shore near Tarentum and for the first sixteen lines is musing about death and addressing his thoughts to the great Archytas in his tomb. If Nisbet and Hubbard are right in placing the Matine shore in the Bay of Taranto, then line 3 is another clue which supports this reconstruction.

At about line 17 a sailor comes in sight and the dead man begins to talk to him. 'There are different ways of dying. We sailors die on the sea . . . so please perform the necessary rites for my corpse.' We are given other topographical clues. The speaker was drowned in the Adriatic, the Illyrian Sea (22), which is near enough to consolidate the general picture. The passing sailor is a merchant sailing out of Tarentum (line 30), else why should the guardian god of the city be asked to ensure his prosperity, and he is on a trip to the north, up the Adriatic, where at the back of the heel of Italy the east winds can make the crossing to Greece extremely difficult, blowing onshore towards Apulia. Here Horace again particularizes, referring to the woods of Venusia, and he does not use the term in ignorance, since Venusia was his birthplace.

This dramatic monologue is more complex than the previous poem 1. 27, in that the addressee switches in the middle of the poem. It is almost as though Horace is teaching us to read such poems by gradually moving towards the more subtle example. Just so, we observed that 1. 25 was a complex amalgam of motifs from the *Palatine Anthology*, and here too, in 1. 28, Horace has taken different motifs from different sources, including the *Palatine Anthology*, and produced a complex, intriguing, and moving poem. This interpretation explains also the apparent imbalance and awkwardness in the general structure. Nisbet and Hubbard note: 'The two parts of the poem do not perfectly cohere.' The two parts are somewhat disjointed because the dead man's talk to Archytas is suddenly interrupted by a new arrival who gives him some hope of proper burial and consequently peace in death. He therefore stops his long musing to the dead Archytas and tackles this merchant sailor in a hurry.

XXIX

Icci, beatis nunc Arabum invides
gazis, et acrem militiam paras
   non ante devictis Sabaeae
      regibus, horribilique Medo

nectis catenas? quae tibi virginum   5
sponso necato barbara serviet?
   puer quis ex aula capillis
      ad cyathum statuetur unctis,

doctus sagittas tendere Sericas
arcu paterno? quis neget arduis   10
   pronos relabi posse rivos
      montibus et Tiberim reverti,

cum tu coemptos undique nobilis
libros Panaeti Socraticam et domum
   mutare loricis Hiberis,   15
      pollicitus meliora, tendis?

Iccius is a young man who had been an eager student of philosophy but is now agog to join an expedition to the East, presumably the Arabian expedition of 26–25 BC described by Strabo, 16. 779–80, by which Augustus seems to have attempted to take over the huge revenues exacted by the Shebans, *Sabaei*, from the spice trade. The attempt failed and Dio, 53. 29 gives a vivid account of the sufferings of the legions, but it was still presented as a victory. In *Res Gestae* 26 when Augustus has described the extension of Roman power in the west, north and east he claims in the south to have killed vast numbers and captured many towns of the Ethiopians as far as Nabata and of the Sabaei as far as Mariba.

Scholars have sometimes taken this poem seriously. Goar sees it as raising the problem of 'the intellectual who abandons his cultural ideals' and finds even more profoundly that 'it calls into question the moral validity of culture'. For McKay and Shepherd it is 'a complaint against aggressive imperialism' and Perret would agree, finding 'dépréciation de la vie militaire'. So Commager talks of 'a sense of disenchantment with Rome's national progress'. This commentary takes the more

XXIX

Iccius, are you now envying the rich treasures
of Arabia, preparing a ruthless campaign
   against the kings of Sheba never before subdued,
      and weaving chains

for the fearsome Mede? What barbarian virgin will be   5
your slave, mourning her bridegroom killed in battle?
   What boy of the court brought up to stretch
     Chinese arrows on the bow of his fathers

will take his place by your cup with rich oils
on his hair? Who would deny that down-rushing rivers   10
   can flow up steep mountains
     and Tiber reverse his course

when you are in such haste to exchange for Spanish breastplates
the Socratic school and the works of great Panaetius
   collected from all over the world—   15
     you promised better things.

orthodox view that Horace is bowing in the direction of this not very
impressive Augustan military venture and is gently making fun of a
young friend and gratifying him by including him in his volume of
poems.

The fun may begin as soon as the first line when Iccius is asked if he
envies wealth. No philosopher, certainly no follower of the Stoic
Panaetius, would admit to such a thing. And it is no ordinary wealth
which Iccius has in mind but the proverbial riches of the East. This part
of Arabia was known as Arabia Felix, *felix* like *beatis* in the first line of
this ode referring not only to happiness or bliss, but also to wealth, and
gaza is a Persian word suggesting exotic oriental treasures. The satire
continues with the notion that Iccius could be preparing a fierce cam-
paign. But if young Iccius gave up his philosophical studies and took to
war, he would be a junior and inexperienced officer, probably on the staff
and certainly not in the forefront of those likely to cause anxiety to kings
hitherto unconquered or to fearsome Medes. In lines 4–5 the mockery is
double-edged. The *weaving* of chains is an oddity. In Latin one weaves
cloth, garlands, flowers, or nooses, but the weaving of metal may sound

a little impractical. And why the fearsome Mede? The expedition of 26–25 BC was south into the Yemen in the kingdom of the Sabaei. Why is the target now the Parthians in the east and why are they dignified by an affecting poetic singular and expressed in terms which associate them with the glorious Greek victories over the Medes and Persians (as in 1. 2. 51)? All this mock-heroic elevation is of a piece with Iccius' young page in line 9 and his Chinese arrows (the Latin word is *Sericas*, referring to north-east China). Horace is having fun by inflating the sphere of operations beyond all possibility. Augustus in *Res Gestae* 31 records the visit of embassies from Indian kings, but not even Augustus claims to have had dealings with the Chinese.

'Which barbarian of the virgins' is how the Latin runs in lines 5–6 and Nisbet and Hubbard interpret: 'The genitive is grandiose; its conjunction with the nominative *barbara* makes the style still more mannered.' This grandiose tone is heightened by the mock-epic flavour of the question. Wright, 47, for instance cites Briseis' lament from Homer's *Iliad* 19. 291–2:

> I saw the man to whom my dear mother and father gave me
> cut to pieces with sharp bronze in front of the city.

In this elaborate teasing Horace would surely not expect his readers to shed a tear for the barbarian virgin and the court page from north-east China. Surely part of the fun is that Horace has already gone a long way towards convincing us that Iccius is in no danger of achieving these ends and that it is not even very likely that he ever entertained such high hopes. The role of the barbarians in the poem is rather to inform us that Iccius is forgetting the Stoic virtues and turning his mind towards luxury, exotic sexual pleasures, not without the pleasure of wine. The anointed hair makes it quite clear that the wine-bearer is a Ganymede. The love is not all heterosexual. Horace now professes to find Iccius' volte-face impossible to believe and launches into one of the standard examples of the figure of thought known as the *adynaton*, the impossible. This figure is common in erotic elegy, as for example when Propertius asserts that he will love till the rivers flow backwards (1. 15. 29–31) or that rivers will flow backwards as soon as the lusts of a woman can be checked (3. 19. 5–10). In Horace the picture is full of movement. *Down-flowing* rivers can *glide* backwards *up* steep mountains now that Iccius *is rushing* into war, *tendis* being the emphatic last word in the poem.

Horace, in his familiar role as *Praeceptor Amoris*, the middle-aged friend and amused adviser of youth, as in 1. 25 and 1. 27, proceeds to smile at Iccius' boyish enthusiasms and his tendency to pursue them by means of expensive acquisitions. In his recent philosophical phase Iccius has made a collection from all over, *undique* (13), of the works of Panaetius of Rhodes, the famous Stoic philosopher of the second century BC and now he is in a hurry to trade them in to buy not one breast-plate but several, and not in any ordinary, serviceable metal but in the most fashionable modern Spanish steel. The Socratic house, *Socraticam ... domum*, poses a problem. Alongside the books of Panaetius this seems to refer to Iccius' book collection, for example the Socratic dialogues of Plato, a philosopher highly respected by Panaetius (see Cairns, 1976: 73). Iccius has collected the works of Plato and others and he is now swapping that Socratic household for armour.

This comment began by referring to the views of scholars who took a serious ethical view of the poem. More circumstantial interpretations have been advanced by Wright and by Cairns. Wright suggests that the ode may be referring specifically to Stoic doctrine. The opening *beatis ... gazis*, might hint at the Stoic 'Blessed Life', *vita beata*, and Stoics disapproved of envy, of excessive desire for wealth, of luxury and sensual indulgence, of conquest and the enslavement of the conquered. Cairns collates such views in the ode with what is known of the thinking of Panaetius, particularly as it is conveyed by Cicero in *De Officiis*, citing for example the need for decorum, for consistency of behaviour, and for standing by one's decisions.

These interpretations seem to be too heavy a load for this little poem to bear. We know from line 15 that Iccius has had a craze for Panaetius and Horace is clearly inviting us to enjoy the clash between his new ambitions and the lofty aspirations of the Stoics. But the philosophical ideas in the poem are so general that they could be attached to almost any of the contemporary schools. The Epicureans, for instance, would take up exactly the same position with regard to envy, luxury, conquest, consistency of behaviour, and they would be equally cautious about sensual pleasures. In general, in the hubbub of ethical generalizations which were the stock-in-trade of philosophy at Rome in Horace's day, it is very difficult to separate out the influence of the different schools in any non-technical text like this. Horace is dealing airily with Stoic philosophy, not facing a student with a catechism of his failure to live up to the tenets of his sect. This may be confirmed by *Epistles*, 1. 12. In this letter written by 20 BC, three or four years later than these odes, we are shown an Iccius who needs to be reminded about the beauties of the simple life, who relishes luxury and would like to be wealthy, not the adherent of any particular school:

FRVCTIBVS Agrippae Siculis quos colligis, Icci,
si recte frueris, non est ut copia maior
ab Iove donari possit tibi. tolle querelas:
pauper enim non est cui rerum suppetit usus.
si ventri bene, si lateri est pedibusque tuis, nil   5
divitiae poterunt regales addere maius.
si forte in medio positorum abstemius herbis
vivis et urtica, sic vives protinus ut te
confestim liquidus Fortunae rivus inauret,
vel quia naturam mutare pecunia nescit,   10
vel quia cuncta putas una virtute minora.
miramur, si Democriti pecus edit agellos
cultaque, dum peregre est animus sine corpore velox,
cum tu inter scabiem tantam et contagia lucri
nil parvum sapias et adhuc sublimia cures;   15
quae mare compescant causae, quid temperet annum,
stellae sponte sua iussaene vagentur et errent,
quid premat obscurum lunae, quid proferat orbem,
quid velit et possit rerum concordia discors,
Empedocles an Stertinium deliret acumen.   20
verum seu piscis seu porrum et caepe trucidas,

(*Epistles* 1. 12. 1–21)

The income you are collecting from Agrippa's estates, Iccius,
if you used it properly, Jupiter could grant you
no greater plenty. No more complaining.
The man who has what he needs is not poor.
If your stomach, lungs and feet are sound, there is nothing
greater that the wealth of kings can provide.

If in the middle of plenty you live off herbs
and nettles, enough said, you will live in such a way
that the streaming flood of Fortune will plate you in gold,
either because money cannot change your nature
or because you think that everything comes second to virtue.   II
Are we surprised that Democritus' flocks ate all his crops
while his swift mind left his body and took off on its travels,
if in the midst of such contagion and pollution from lucre
you think of nothing mean and still attend to what is sublime?
What causes calm the stormy sea? What guides the year?
Do stars move about and wander of their own accord or under orders?
What conceals the dark side of the moon? What reveals its sphere?
What means this discordant harmony? What is its purpose?
Is Empedocles raving or is it the brilliant Stertinius?
But whether you're murdering fish or leeks and onions . . .

The reference to virtue in line 11 points to Stoicism, but Epicurus is
never far away; at the end of this extract Empedocles and the Stoic
Stertinius are both suspected of insanity, and the last line quoted takes
us firmly towards the reincarnation and Pythagoras. Following the hint
of this letter we should guess that Iccius of 20 BC was not a Panaetian, or
even an Eclectic, but a philosophical dilettante, and that Horace found
that quite amusing. So should we.

   Even the rhetorical organization of the poem supports the more light-
hearted interpretation. The first large question expounds the situation.
The next (*quae virginum?*) is followed by the longer and more elaborate
question (*puer quis?*), which swells to the fourth, most crushing and
longest of all (*quis?*) with the sad shaking of the head at the end. These
fireworks read effectively as mock indignation. It would be more diffi-
cult to hear them as a philosophical critique.

Gk.

XXX

O VENVS, regina Cnidi Paphique,
sperne dilectam Cypron et vocantis
ture te multo Glycerae decoram
    transfer in aedem.

fervidus tecum puer et solutis   5
Gratiae zonis properentque Nymphae
et parum comis sine te Iuventas
    Mercuriusque.

S hort poem, slight poem. A common notion, and false.
    Fraenkel held that Horace had forgotten the centuries of scepti-
cism and returned to an age in which the gods granted mortals the bless-
ing of their presence. It is true that the poem contains traditional
religious formulas, the names of the places the god is asked to leave and
the list of the followers of the god, but there is nothing here to take the
mind back to these early days of blissful innocence. The arrival of Cupid,
the Graces, and the Nymphs at the home of a *hetaera*, a woman of plea-
sure, belongs to a much more sophisticated age.

Other scholars have invoked a fragmentary poem or part of a poem by
Sappho (fragment 2):

> Come here from Crete to this holy
> sanctuary where you have your lovely grove
> of apple trees and altars
>   steaming with incense.
>
> In it the water murmurs through branches
> of apple trees, all the place
> is shaded by roses and sleep falls
>   from quivering leaves.
>
> In it a meadow where horses graze
> blooms with spring flowers
> and the winds breathe sweetly
>
>   .   .   .   .   .
>
> There, Cyprian Goddess . . .
> with good will gently pour nectar
> in golden winecups to mingle
>   for our festival.

142

XXX

Venus, queen of Cnidos and Paphos,
abandon your beloved Cyprus and move
to the lovely shrine of Glycera, who summons you
    with clouds of incense.

Your ardent boy must hurry along with you   5
and Nymphs and Graces with their girdles loose
and Youth, so uncongenial without you,
    and Mercury.

This is a gorgeously sensuous evocation of a place 'instinct with the spirit of Aphrodite' (Jenkyns, 1982: 32). The only resemblances in Horace's poem are the mention of the places the goddess is to abandon and the adjective 'lovely' describing the shrine of Glycera. Sappho's poem is a feast for the senses, of sight and smell and sound and taste, of light and movement and sleep. If it influenced Horace, it influenced him to produce something entirely different.

Editors tell us also that Horace is imitating an epigram by Posidippus:

> O goddess who visits Cyprus and Miletus and
>   Syria's lovely plain loud with the hooves of horses,
> come in kindness to Callistion who never
>   turned her lover away from her door.

(Palatine Anthology 12. 131)

The argument is simply that the goddess of love should come kindly to Callistion because she has always allowed her lovers to come to her. Nisbet and Hubbard incline to believe the ancient view that this ode of Horace has taken the argument a step further by summoning Mercury, the god of profit, in solitary emphasis in the last line of the poem. Quinn goes further still. He notes that Glycera calls upon the goddess 'with much incense' and takes this to refer to repeated invocations. Venus is invited so often that she would be well advised to come with her retinue and take up permanent residence, to 'transfer herself' (*te . . . transfer*) to Glycera's establishment. Mercury would then be 'the divine pimp to manage the business side' and Glycera 'a *demi-mondaine* whose business is booming'.

This last interpretation can be rejected. It turns the poem into a

143

superficial satire whose cynical purpose seems to be completely out of
harmony with the pictures in the poem and the tone in which they are
presented. Even Nisbet and Hubbard's view of the poem fails to con-
vince. If Mercury is to be thought of as the god of gain, why did Horace
write this poem? Why should a client write what Fraenkel justly calls 'a
little poem, a perfect creation' in order to pray for the profitability of a
professional lady?

There is another approach. Start with Glycera. We have met her
before in 1. 19 where Horace is ablaze with love for her and sacrifices to
Venus in order to persuade the goddess to visit him gently and kindly.
Now he is praying to Venus to suggest the manner of her visit to
Glycera.

The Romans freely personified abstract qualities. We have just seen
Honour, Justice, Loyalty, and Truth in 1. 24. Centuries of classicizing
have intervened and we tend to feel that such entities are frigid fancies,
'plaster images', but for the Romans they were presences, often divine.
So here when Horace, who was burning with love for Glycera in 1. 19.
5 and 7, prays for the presence of Venus' ardent boy, Cupid, *fervidus
tecum puer*, he is praying that Glycera should burn with love for him.
When he prays for the Nymphs and Graces to hurry along, and to have
their girdles loose, in bald terms we could say that he is praying that
Glycera will be impatient with desire, gracious and uninhibited in her
loving. Youth, *Iuventas*, was an ancient Roman god, for whom Augustus
established a festival to celebrate the day on which he donned the toga
of a man, the *toga virilis*. The presence of the Augustan god in the
entourage of Venus need not surprise. Horace is well aware that he is a
little old for such activities, but now that he has unexpectedly been called
to give his heart to love which he thought had ended long ago (1. 19. 5),
what more natural than that he should pray that the spirit of youth
should be present there to bless him in the house of his beloved?

Mercury clinches the case. Horace is Mercury's man, *Mercurialis vir*
in 2. 17 where Faunus, acting on Mercury's behalf, saved him from a

falling tree. It is Mercury, he says, who saved him from death in battle in 2. 7. The hymn to Mercury at 1. 10 celebrates the god's gifts to man, eloquence, civilization, the lyre, and cheerful rascality. Each of these may be helpful on this occasion. Eloquence, for instance, under the name *Suadela*, Persuasion, is coupled with Venus in *Epistles* 1. 6. 38 and Peitho, the Greek Persuasion, was, as Nisbet and Hubbard say, 'a traditional member of Aphrodite's train'. But Horace is Mercury's man and prays that Mercury will be there with all his gifts to look after him in his lovemaking. The punch is in the short last line of the Sapphic stanza.

Stripped of its theology, that is to say violated and diminished, 1. 30 means that Horace wishes to find Glycera passionate, uninhibited, gracious, and joyous, and that he himself longs for the return of his vitality, charm, and youthfulness. This interpretation of *Ode* 1. 30 seems to be nearer the poetic world which Horace has elsewhere created than the other interpretations sketched above. It also gives more relevance and savour to the details of the poetry.

How does the first stanza now look? The important word comes at the beginning of the second line. *Sperne* means 'to despise, to reject with disdain', yet in this passage, without good reason, commentators remove the element of disdain. Give the word its normal sense and we have before us one of Horace's stock themes, the antithesis between Greek and Roman. The goddess Aphrodite is invited under her Roman name to reject her beloved Greek sanctuaries in the eastern Mediterranean, in favour of the house of Glycera in Rome, 'transfer yourself to Glycera's lovely shrine'. In the phrase *sperne dilectam Cypron*, 'despise the beloved' is a pointed paradox, and the use of the Greek form of the accusative case, *Cypron* (for *Cyprum* as at 1. 19. 10 and 3. 26. 9) is perhaps part of the fun. Horace is implying that the Golden Age of Greek lyric poetry, when hymns were sung by Alcman and Sappho to Aphrodite, is now over, and that hymns far beyond the powers of Hellenistic epigrammatists such as Posidippus are now being sung by a Roman poet.

XXXI

QVID dedicatum poscit Apollinem
vates? quid orat de patera novum
    fundens liquorem? non opimae
      Sardiniae segetes feraces,

non aestuosae grata Calabriae   5
armenta, non aurum aut ebur Indicum,
    non rura quae Liris quieta
      mordet aqua taciturnus amnis.

premant Calenam falce quibus dedit
fortuna vitem, dives et aureis   10
    mercator exsiccet culillis
      vina Syra reparata merce,

dis carus ipsis, quippe ter et quater
anno revisens aequor Atlanticum
    impune. me pascunt olivae,   15
      me cichorea levesque malvae.

frui paratis et valido mihi,
Latoe, dones, et, precor, integra
    cum mente, nec turpem senectam
      degere nec cithara carentem.   20

On 9 October 28 BC Augustus dedicated on the Palatine a great temple to Apollo, god of music, medicine, and prophecy. This temple, set in a spacious piazza with the house of Augustus on one side and the new libraries of the Greek and the Latin classics on the other, gleamed with gold and ivory and Carrara marble, and was full of works of art not only of classical Greece but also of the Augustan Renaissance. This was the showpiece of the Augustan rebuilding of Rome as the most splendid city that had ever been, the shrine of the god Apollo who, it was claimed, had won the day for the forces of Western civilization against the hordes of the East led by Cleopatra at Actium.

    Augustan poets responded. On the Shield of Aeneas Virgil visualized Apollo's share in the battle:

Dec 4 Tq Neville 28 BC
- H asks for modest life
- in 19's
— political in sense of civil
arbit

XXXI

What does the bard ask from Apollo whose temple
is now dedicated? What does he pray for
    as he pours the new wine from the bowl? Not
      the fertile crops of wealthy Sardinia,

not the lovely herds of sultry   5
Calabria, not Indian gold or ivory,
    not land gnawed by the quiet waters
      of the silent river Liris.

Let those to whom Fortune grants it prune the vine
with the Calenian sickle, and let the rich merchant   10
    drain from golden goblets the wine
      he buys with Syrian merchandise—

darling of the very gods, visiting
the Atlantic three or four times a year
    and surviving. I eat easily digestible   15
      olives, chicory and mallows.

Grant, son of Latona, that I may enjoy what I have
with good health and, I pray, with sound mind,
    and that my old age may not be squalid
      and not without the lyre.   20

Actius haec cernens arcum tendebat Apollo
desuper; omnis eo terrore Aegyptus et Indi
omnis Arabs, omnes vertebant terga Sabaei.

          (*Aeneid* 8. 704–6)

Seeing this, Apollo of Actium drew his bow high above them.
In terror at the sight every Egyptian and Arab,
all the Indians and Shebans turned their backs.

The victory of 31 BC was followed by a triple triumph in 29 BC. This too
appears on the Shield, followed by a scene in which the conquered
peoples climb the Palatine in a long procession to present gifts to the
conqueror:

ipse sedens niveo candentis limine Phoebi
dona recognoscit populorum aptatque superbis
postibus.

(Aeneid 8. 720–2)

He himself sitting in the gleaming doorway of bright Phoebus
received the gifts of the peoples and nailed them
to the proud doorposts.

Propertius, too, celebrates the temple in poems of direct praise, 2. 31 and 4. 6, describing the golden chariot on the roof and the famous ivory doors.

Commentators are embarrassed by Virgil's account and many of them conclude that this presentation is a figment of poetic imagination because the dating is wrong. The triumph was celebrated on 13–15 August 29 BC, thirteen months before the dedication of the temple. But Virgil could not have put this scene on the prophetic Shield of Aeneas if it never took place. Prophecies after the event are never wrong. The mistake is to assume that the temple was finished on the occasion of the presentation. Virgil's description of the splendour of the doorway does not preclude the possibility that the scaffolding was still up round the back. This is superb theatre and Augustus was not the man to miss the chance of celebrating his temple when only its façade with its glorious doors and doorposts was finished.

What does our bard, our *vates*, ask Apollo for? The Augustan *vates* is poet, priest, and prophet. The expectation is that he will utter some profound and ennobling Augustan piety, worthy of Apollo, the god of prophecy. But in lines 2–3 our expectations are deceived. The question 'What does he pray for as he pours the new liquor from the bowl?' sounds no less lofty, with its sacramental libation dish, the *patera*, and *liquorem*, a solemn name for wine, but it teases us by turning from 9 October to 11 October, from Apollo of Actium to Apollo the god of healing. On this day, the Meditrinalia (from *medeor*, 'I heal'), the festival of the new wine, people recited the ancient formula preserved in Varro, *De Lingua Latina* 6. 21:

novum vetus vinum bibo
novo veteri morbo medeor.
I drink wine new and old.
I heal disease new and old.

The ode has turned sharply from the public to the personal, from the formal to the folk, from panegyric to meditation.

148

omani)

It proceeds with a list of things Horace is not going to pray for: not the fertile grain crops of Sardinia (and wealthy, *opimae* (3) is the first word in the list); not the lovely herds of battle bred in the sultry countryside of Calabria (and we know from 1. 17 how he delights in the cool valleys of his Sabine estate); not gold or ivory from India (and here he is gently making it clear that the splendours of the city of Rome and its glorious new temple are not for him); not the rich land between Latium and Campania which grew the grapes for the great Italian wines listed by Pliny in his *Natural History* 3. 59, Setine, Massic, Falernian, Calenian, and Caecuban (precious soil no doubt, but the vigneron had to watch it being silently eroded by the sluggish river Liris in lines 7–8). The hint throughout is that his heart is in his Sabine estate where the mountain streams go rushing down the valleys. He does not want to travel—the plethora of distant place-names shows that. He does not want wealth or risks or worries or a prestigious status in the Augustan hierarchy.

Horace now puts the matter positively, working backwards through the examples. 'Let others undertake the drudgery of keeping the great vines in check.' He prefers the particular to the general, so mentions only Calenian, and the verb *premant*, 'keep in check' hints at the drudgery of pruning rampant growth. 'Let the rich merchant risk his life to bring home merchandise which he can sell in order to be able to afford to drink from golden *culilli*.' These were ritual earthenware cups, as used by priests and Vestal Virgins, of which the *nouveaux riches* might have vulgar reproductions in gold. Horace's desires are much more modest. What he eats is olives, chicory, and mallows, and the adjective *leves*, 'light, easily digestible' makes it clear to us that he prefers sound sleep to rich dinners. But he is not simply telling us about his indigenous vegetarian diet. Horace's diet is often a code for his whole way of life, here the simple self-sufficient life he loves to lead in the Italian countryside. There may be a hint of something more. This praise of plain living near the end of a poem which moves to a climax on Horace's lyre, his poetry, is probably suggesting that he does not wish to write in the heavy style of mythological epic or of love elegy or the gross style of direct panegyric, but rather in the plain style which Callimachus taught the Romans (see Mette).

Confirmation of this last interpretation may be found in the final stanza, where the poem comes full circle. Horace's first prayer is for health and it answers, with a philosophical tinge, the second question in the poem—he wishes to be able to enjoy what he has, sound in body and in mind. His second prayer ends with the lyre and so picks up the allusion to Apollo the god of poetry in the first question, *Apollinem vates*.

In *Satires* 2. 6. 13–15, addressing Apollo, Horace has already stated his poetic ideal in philosophical and dietetic terms:

> si quod adest gratum iuvat, hac prece te oro:
> pingue pecus domino facias et cetera praeter
> ingenium, utque soles custos mihi maximus adsis.

> If I am happy with what I have, this is my prayer to you:
> to make my flock fat for their master, and everything else
> except my poetic talent, and to be my protector, as hitherto.

This is a statement of poetic intent and affiliation. In the programmatic opening of his *Aetia* Callimachus writes:

> When I first placed a tablet on my knees, Lycian Apollo
> said to me: '. . . feed up your sacrifice to be as fat as possible,
> but, my dear chap, do keep your Muse slender'

> · · · · · · ·

>   Let me be the light one, the dainty one . . .
> yes indeed, that I may sing and live
> off a free diet of dew from the divine air,
> and then cast off old age, which weighs upon me
> like the Triangular island on fierce Enceladus.
> No need to worry! For if the Muses have looked
> not unkindly on you when you were a child,
> they will not reject their friends when they are grey.

> (Callimachus, *Aetia* 1. 21–4 and 32–8)

XXXII

> Poscimvs si quid vacui sub umbra
> lusimus tecum, quod et hunc in annum
> vivat et pluris, age dic Latinum,
>   barbite, carmen,
>
> Lesbio primum modulate civi,   5
> qui ferox bello, tamen inter arma
> sive iactatam religarat udo
>   litore navim,

Horace knew this Callimachus and it conformed to his poetic pro-
gramme. He imitated it in his *Satire*. It lies behind the end of *Odes* 1. 31.

A poem which starts as though it is to be a patriotic celebration of the
achievements of the regime, its military success and its wealth, has pro-
posed a different ideal. It would be easy, but wrong, to find tension here
between the poet's true wishes and his duties as client and to read into
the *Odes* overtones of opposition to the regime. The proof is that such
writing was entirely acceptable to Augustus. If it had not been accept-
able he would never have invited Horace to become his private secretary.
It is also revealing that Horace was not afraid to decline the invitation.
Nor did he suffer for it. Again, in 17 BC for the third day of the supreme
Augustan festival, the *Ludi Saeculares*, he was invited to provide the
Carmen Saeculare, a national ode for a choir of boys and girls to sing in
the temple of Palatine Apollo. The explanation is simple. At the centre
of Augustan ideology was the need for an end to the ambition and strug-
gle for wealth and power which had helped to cause the Civil Wars and
imperil the future of Rome. A defence of the simple life accorded well
with this programme. Augustus proposed also a harmony within the
state to take the place of the competition and strife which had prevailed.
Augustus and Maecenas were the patrons of Horace. To maintain a poet
who was free to write in praise of chicory and mallows so near the dedi-
cation of a great Augustan showpiece, was a demonstration of the liber-
ality and tolerance of the new age. In short, a non-political poem dated
to October 28 BC was a political statement in support of the new regime.
The client had the courage to speak with his own voice and his patrons
had the intelligence to be happy with that.

XXXII

We pray, if ever we have relaxed with you in the shade
and played a melody that may live a year
or more, come and sound
    a Latin song, my Greek lyre,

first tuned by a citizen of Lesbos, fierce in war,   5
who, whether he was in the intervals
of war or had tied up his battered ship
    on the spray-soaked shore,

Odes 1. 32

Liberum et Musas Veneremque et illi
semper haerentem puerum canebat   10
et Lycum nigris oculis nigroque
    crine decorum.

o decus Phoebi et dapibus supremi
grata testudo Iovis, o laborum
dulce lenimen, mihi cumque salve   15
    rite vocanti.

This is a kletic hymn addressed by Horace to his lyre, his *barbitos* (and *lyra* and *barbitos* are both Greek words), asking it to play a Latin song. We have met this prayer form before, notably in 1. 2. 30–52, 1. 10, and 1. 30 and the time has come to compile a check-list of standard elements. This is best done by laying out a scheme based upon Catullus, 34:

We are in Diana's hands
girls and boys without a stain.
Boys and girls without a stain,
    let us sing of Diana.

O daughter of Latona, great
offspring of greatest Jupiter,
whom your mother laid upon the ground
    by the olive tree on Delos,

to be mistress of mountains
of green forests
of lonely valleys,
    of sounding rivers

You are called Juno Lucina
by women in childbirth.
You are called Mighty Trivia and Luna
    whose light is not her own.

Goddess, measuring in monthly course
the journey of the year,
you fill the farmer's barns
    with fine harvests.

Dianae sumus in fide
puellae et pueri integri:
<Dianam pueri integri>
    puellaeque canamus

O Latonia, maximi   5
magna progenies Iovis,
quam mater prope Deliam
    deposivit olivam,

montium domina ut fores
silvarumque virentium   10
saltuumque reconditorum
    amniumque sonantum:

tu Lucina dolentibus
Iuno dicta puerperis,
tu potens Trivia et notho es 15
    dicta lumine Luna.

tu cursu, dea, menstruo
metiens iter annuum,
rustica agricolae bonis
    tecta frugibus exples.   20

152

would still sing of Bacchus and the Muses,
of Venus and the boy who is always by her side,   10
of Lycus with his jet-black eyes
    and jet-black hair.

O glory of Phoebus, lyre welcome at the feasts
of Supreme Jupiter, O sweet easer of my labours,
grant me your blessing whenever   15
    I duly call upon you.

By whatever name you decree,	sis quocumque tibi placet
be hallowed and as in days of old	sancta nomine, Romulique,
protect the race of Romulus	antique ut solita es, bona
by your gracious help.	sospites ope gentem.

A. The first stanza stresses the importance of the purity of the singers. This might be included in our check-list as an aspect of the importance of correct ritual, a vital element in Roman religion.

B. In line 5 of the Catullus the address to the deity is introduced by *O*.

C. The deity is addressed, in the vocative case, in lines 5 and 17.

D. The name is followed by a description in apposition, 'Latonian goddess, great offspring of greatest Jupiter', sometimes including a participle, as in *Odes* 3. 21. 1.

E. The parentage of the deity is celebrated.

F. The name of the deity is followed by an adjective clause, 'Latonian goddess, *whom* . . .'.

G. The birthplace and the birth-myth of the deity are alluded to in lines 7–8.

H. In lines 9–12 and 17–20 the spheres of operation of the deity are listed.

I. In lines 13–16 titles of the deity are given. In some prayers the titles and the spheres of operation are joined by *sive . . . sive*, 'whether . . . or' as in *Odes* 1. 2. 33–41.

J. The prayer itself comes in lines 21–4.

K. The second-person pronoun occurs in lines 13, 15, 17, and 21.

L. In lines 21–2 a catch-all phrase is added, as though to make sure that the deity be not offended by being wrongly addressed. Some form of the word *quodcumque*, 'whatever', is standard, as here *quocumque . . . nomine*, 'by whatever name'.

M. The prayer is commonly supported by reference to previous services provided by the deity to the worshipper, as here in line 22, or by the worshipper to the deity.

N. In line 15 of the Horace *mihi salve* is like the Greek *chaire moi*, which is used at the beginning of prayers to hail the presence of the god or at the end to call down the blessing of the god on the worshipper.

In addition to these standard features, deities are commonly invited to leave their shrines and come to the suppliant (O) as at 1. 30; and their retinue is sometimes listed (P) as at 1. 2. 34 and 1. 30. Not in this prayer, but in many others, there occurs a request to convey some unpleasantness far away to some other people, as in 'Raine, Raine, goe to Spain'. This motif is richly exemplified in Nisbet and Hubbard's commentary on 1. 21. 13.

Odes 1. 32 is a kletic hymn. Horace tells us that in the first word, and there are several straightforward prayer features in the poem. The request follows in line 3 and the address in line 4. A participle in apposition (see D above) follows in line 5 and an adjective clause (F) in line 6. A further address is introduced by *O* in lines 13 and 14 (B), and the correct performance of the rite is referred to in the last line with *rite*, 'duly' (A).

These markers are unmistakable, but we learn with some surprise in line 4 that the god who is addressed is no ordinary god, but a musical instrument. To some extent therefore this is not a hymn but a parody of a hymn and some of its features are not quite straightforward. In the first three lines Horace invokes not his own services to the lyre or the lyre's services to him (see M), but instead humorously reminds the 'deity' that they have played together. *Tecum*, 'with you' is religious (K), but references to leisure and shade remind the deity that their relationship is unusually intimate and convivial. Given this mass of sacramental elements, the modestly understated hint of immortality in lines 2–3 is part of the fun. Line 5 speaks of the first tuning of the lyre exactly where we might expect the birth-myth of the deity, including the place of birth, Lesbos (G). The relative clause that follows describes spheres of operation (F), not of the deity, but of Alcaeus, but since the god was sounding in his hands and the standard *sive* is heard '*or whether* he had tied up . . .' we can take the hint. There follows a list of gods about whom Alcaeus sang and in this context these are enough to remind us that in prayers there sometimes occurs, as in 1. 30, a list of similar gods in the retinue of the deity (P).

This brings us to *cumque* in line 15 which after all these sacral touches suggests the frequent catch-all *quodcumque*, 'whatever' (L), 'grant thy blessing to me whenever I duly call upon you'. After three addresses to the deity, *decus . . . testudo . . . lenimen*, this strange, isolated *cumque* could surely be taken as activating our expectations of the catch-all phrase, 'when I call upon you by whatever name'. The best alternative to this suggestion appears to be the brilliant conjecture for *mihi cumque*, suggested *en passant* by Lachmann on Lucretius 5. 311, *medicumque*, 'a sweet lightener and healer of my labours'. This does not convince. Poets do pray that the labour of writing should be *eased* (*lenimen* is literally that which soothes), but such labour, in the case of Horace, would scarcely need *healing*.

It would be possible to dismiss this as yet another poem about poetry. This would be a great loss. In addition to the delicate sacral parody already discussed there is a vivid restatement of a vital part of Horace's assessment of his own achievement. As we saw on 1. 26. 10 he prides himself on having naturalized Greek lyric poetry in Latin. In lines 3–4 of the present ode he demonstrates the blend in words, *Latinum, barbite, carmen Lesbio*, where the four words alternate between the two languages. This is followed by a brilliant profile of the work of Alcaeus, which conveys Horace's love of his poetry and his keen sense of its vitality. By calling him a citizen, Horace alludes to the fact that Alcaeus spent much of his life fighting against Melanchros, Myrsilus, and Pittacus, three successive tyrants of Lesbos, and wrote poems about civil war, *stasiotika*. The mention of his storm-tossed ship is an allusion to his famous poem on this same subject quoted on 1. 14. The Mediterranean is a non-tidal sea, so if the shore is wet, *udo*, as in line 7, it is wet because of stormy weather (hence the translation 'spray-soaked'). The third stanza summarizes Alcaeus' subject-matter, drinking-songs, songs of love both heterosexual and homosexual, and songs in praise of the Muses. All of these are represented in this first book of Horace's *Odes*. For instance a song of wine and war inspired the beginning of 1. 37. Songs in praise of Muses appear at 1. 26 and surely here in 1. 32. Homosexual love appears in 1. 4, perhaps in 1. 9, in 1. 29, and 1. 38. The boy whom Alcaeus is said to love is described in melting terms rendered more eloquent by a delicious sound-effect. Lycus has black eyes and black hair. In the hodden grey of translation, this comes as a flat repetition but the Latin turns the words in the ear. The eyes being plural are *nigris*; the hair being singular is *nigro*. But that is only part of it. *Nígris* has a long first syllable and the word-accent falls on it; *nigróque* has a short first syllable and the word-accent falls upon the following *-o-*. The repetition of a word in different scansion, as Nisbet and Hubbard say, 'was a licence of Greek poetry which in Hellenistic and Latin times became an affectation'. Here the Greek poetic licence is an affectation for a purpose. The great musician Milton strikes similar chords:

> Not that fair field of Enna
> Where Proserpin, *gathering flowers*,
> herself a fairer *flower*, by gloomy Dis
> was *gathered*.

> (*Paradise Lost*, iv. 268–71)

An even closer parallel is cited by L. P. Wilkinson (1972) from lines of Mary Coleridge:

> Over the blue sea goes the wind complaining
> And the blue sea turns purple as he goes.

Horace's poem now ends with a triple invocation of the god in three of his manifestations. The second of these is as the lyre which was welcome at the banquets of the gods. The Latin for lyre here is *testudo*, which is literally 'the tortoise'. The allusion is to the story in the Homeric *Hymn to Hermes* 41–51, where Hermes invented the lyre by scooping out the marrow of a tortoise and stringing the shell with seven strings of sheep-gut (see on 1. 10 above). *Testudo* is commonly

---

2ˇ Asclp.

XXXIII

jↄↄ

ALBI, ne doleas plus nimio memor
immitis Glycerae neu miserabilis
decantes elegos, cur tibi iunior
    laesa praeniteat fide,

insignem tenui fronte Lycorida   5
Cyri torret amor, Cyrus in asperam
declinat Pholoen; sed prius Apulis
    iungentur capreae lupis,

used simply to refer to the lyre without any thought of tortoises, but Latin speakers were more aware of the literal meaning of words than we are. In this ode, some of them would have smiled at the portentous paradox which transformed the carapace of a reptile into an object welcome at the table of the gods. Horace plays the same surreal game at 3. 11. 3 and 4. 3. 17.

In 3. 21, the ode to the Wine-Jar, we see a blatant and outrageous parody of the prayer form. In 1. 32 the parody is subtler but it still lends lightness to the poem, a lightness also present in the modest tone of the first stanza and the cheerful delights of the third. Some commentators hold that the poem is the answer to itself. It is what Horace prayed for. This would unnecessarily narrow down its range. The dramatic setting seems rather to be that Horace is beginning to compose a poem about which we know nothing and before he starts he prays for divine assistance with the act of composition. That prayer becomes this poem. The tone is cheerful and humorous, but then Horace and his Muse were on cheerful and affectionate terms. Bacchus and the Muses, Venus and Cupid, were no pasteboard figures for Alcaeus and Horace but the divine forms of what made their lives worth living. Similarly, in the last stanza Phoebus Apollo is not only a sublime marble statue, but is also the sudden miracle of order which arrives on the pen of the poet as he flails around in the chaos of possibilities. When Horace speaks of the labour involved in composing these original and densely allusive poems in metres which no other Classical Latin poet ever mastered, and tells us that a divine power sweetened and eased that labour, he means it.

XXXIII

Do not grieve, Albius, remembering too well
your cruel, sweet Glycera and do not keep chanting
your piteous elegies wondering why she has broken faith
    and a younger man now outshines you.

Love for Cyrus scorches the beautiful,   5
narrow-browed Lycoris; Cyrus leans lovingly
over hard-hearted Pholoe, but sooner will she-goats
    mate with Apulian wolves

quam turpi Pholoe peccet adultero.
sic visum Veneri, cui placet imparis   10
formas atque animos sub iuga aenea
    saevo mittere cum ioco.

ipsum me melior cum peteret Venus,
grata detinuit compede Myrtale — (*my·tle*)
libertina, fretis acrior Hadriae   15
    curvantis Calabros sinus.

Albius is almost certainly the rich and handsome but melancholy friend about fifteen years younger than himself to whom Horace offers humorous advice in *Epistles* 1. 5. He is also almost certainly the Albius Tibullus who laments the faithlessness of his Delia in the fifth and sixth elegies of his first book, published in 27–26 BC while Horace was writing these odes.

This poem has a paradox in each stanza. Glycera is the Greek for 'sweet' but she is said to be cruel (in an attempt to bring this out the translation adds the word 'sweet'). Cyrus leans lovingly over Pholoe but she is said to be rough (*aspera*, 'hard-hearted' in the translation). Pholoe is also the name of a Greek mountain whose rugged rocks (*aspera . . . saxa*) Lucan later refers to in *Pharsalia* 6. 388, and Tibullus gives the name to a proud, unyielding woman in 1. 8. 69. Myrtale was savage and detained Horace with a fetter which he says was 'pleasing'. Yokes are made of wood, but the yoke of Venus is of bronze. This is not just word-play for fun. Horace is trying to persuade his friend, the learned elegiac poet with a penchant for Greek etymologies (see Cairns, 1979: 64–86), to stop moping over a woman. So he exposes the absurdity of love and he goes on to argue, like an elegiac poet, from examples: 'A loves B who loves C who refuses him.' Lycoris is strikingly good-looking with the low hairline which Romans approved, but is unloved; Pholoe is hard-hearted and finds Cyrus hateful, but Cyrus loves her. The closest precedent for this carousel of love is a poem by Moschus:

> Pan loved his neighbour Echo, but Echo loved
> the leaping Satyros, and Satyros was mad for Lyde.
> So Echo scorched Pan just as much as Satyros scorched Echo
> and Lyde poor Satyros, while Eros laughed at the entanglements,
> each hating their lover and loving the one who hated them,
> suffering the same as they inflicted. This is the lesson I read
> to all those who love: love those who love you
> so that, if you love, you will be loved.

than Pholoe soil herself with a foul adulterer.
Such is the decree of Venus, who decides in cruel jest   10
to join unequal minds and bodies
     under her yoke of bronze.

I myself once, when a better love was offered me,
was shackled in the delicious fetters of Myrtale,
a freedwoman wilder than the Adriatic Sea   15
     which scoops out the bays of Calabria.

The comparison with Horace shows his greater restraint, subtlety, and truth. The advice offered by Moschus would not be of use to any lover. Horace describes the same experience but draws no moral. Rather, like many a sensitive teacher, counsellor, or friend, he claims to have been through it all himself. He knows about the cruel jests of Venus. He remembers his servitude and the wildness of his mistress like a stormy sea hollowing out the bays of Calabria. He also remembers how delicious it was.

Horace uses this tactic elsewhere. In *Odes* 1. 24, for instance, a much deeper and more serious poem, similar arguments occur in a different order. 'No mourning is enough for this bereavement. Many know grief, but no grief is greater than yours. Patience will lighten it.' Horace claims to share the suffering in order to give himself the right to advise restraint. This is a tactic of friendship.

The centre-point of a Horatian ode is often a point of emphasis. Here Pholoe's revulsion for the unmentionable Cyrus forms the climax of the triad, Lycoris, Cyrus, and Pholoe, and is so strong that it cannot be contained in the first half of the poem but spills over into the second without any sense-break at the end of the stanza. And she spits it out with a plethora of the letter -p-, seven in less than three lines from *sed prius* to *adultero* (in Latin -ph- is pronounced as two sounds).

After this flood of human feeling comes the bald statement of the will of the god, *sic visum Veneri*, like Virgil's *dis aliter visum*, 'the gods decided differently' when a just man dies at the fall of Troy in *Aeneid* 2. 428. This is Venus' decree and *placet* in the same line 10 is also official language. The Romans would visualize more sharply than we do what would happen to unequal yoke-fellows. If you yoke an ox to an ass, the ass can't pull equal weight and falls in the mud (so Plautus, *Aulularia* 230).

What does Horace mean by 'a better love' in line 13? More attractive sexually, intellectually, morally, temperamentally? Who shall say? But in

1. 27. 14–24 Horace teases a young man by pretending to believe that his lovers are always free Roman women, and then pretends to be shocked when he hears the truth. In our poem Horace is tied to a freed-woman, a woman who had been a slave, when a better love is on offer. Why are we told in line 15 that she is a freedwoman if not to suggest to us that the better love is higher socially? Horace is gently mocking himself as he mocked the boy in 1. 27, putting himself in a bad light. This also is a tactic of friendship.

The ending raises a point of method. Myrtale was more savage than, literally, 'the waves of the Adriatic curving the Calabrian bays'. To Reckford in 1959 this suggested 'not so much the conventional "storm of love" as the very easily imagined sexual attractions of Myrtale'. It reminded Commager in 1962 of Myrtale's charms and 'emphasizes the physical immediacy of the comparison'. For Boyle in 1973 'what it suggests is the sexual vigour of Myrtale and the power of her voluptuousness'. Connor in 1987 finds that 'the last line has a fulsome [*sic*], rich sound which speaks of the sexual delights and sensuality of Myrtale'. These are views from America and Australia. My Scottish opinion is that they are all wrong.

Curvare means to curve. For us curves can be sexually suggestive, but never in Latin does verb, noun, or adjective from this root occur with a sexual connotation. *Sinus* is more complex. Its first meaning is 'the curve of drapery'. A second is 'the part of the body where drapery curved, the breast, the lap'. It also means 'a bay, a gulf'. When a word is used its full spread of meaning does not operate, only that part which is activated by the context. We hear Milton saying that Lycidas must not float upon his

---

XXXIV

PARCVS deorum cultor et infrequens
insanientis dum sapientiae
    consultus erro, nunc retrorsum
      vela dare atque iterare cursus

cogor relictos: namque Diespiter,   5
igni corusco nubila dividens
    plerumque, per purum tonantis
      egit equos volucremque currum,

watery bier unwept, and if we wish to remain sane we exclude extraneous associations. This is an acute example of a basic principle. As we listen or read, the mind is collecting, sorting, rejecting, and applying. So in the headline of today's newspaper: 'Saddam keeps US guessing', we know that keeping can involve retaining, defending, supporting, but we do not activate that knowledge any more than at 1. 32. 14 we think of the *testudo* formation of linked shields used by Roman soldiers at sieges. Literary critics, on the other hand, tend to the pansemantic fallacy, whereby any part of a word's range of meaning can be pulled into relevance. For example, in Ovid *opus* occasionally refers to the work of sexual intercourse. It takes a Kennedy to sense a sexual subtext when Ovid looks back at his great epic and says, *iamque opus exegi*, 'I have now accomplished a task'. There are few sentences which do not respond to this familiar actress–bishop syndrome. Take that one. A syndrome is a running-together.

So here only literary scholars would think about the sinuosities of the 'curvaceous' Myrtale. (The word 'curvaceous' is originally US, 1936 according to the *Shorter Oxford Dictionary* but the pansemantic fallacy is by no means confined to the USA.) Horace is not here thinking of Myrtale's figure but of her anger. He is setting the amatory sufferings of Albius against the elemental savagery of the sea driven by the south wind (the supreme arbiter of the Adriatic in Horace's second ode) as it scoops out the Bay of Tarentum under the arch of the foot of Italy not 70 miles from Horace's boyhood home at Venusia. Without preaching he is gently reminding his friend of the brevity and unimportance of his suffering in love, suffering which Horace, too, has known.

XXXIV

I used to worship the gods grudgingly
and not often, a wanderer, expert
   in a crazy wisdom, but now I am forced
     to sail back and once again go over

the course I had left behind. For Jupiter   5
who usually parts the clouds with the fire
   of his lightning has driven his thundering horses
     and flying chariot through a cloudless sky,

quo bruta tellus et vaga flumina,
quo Styx et invisi horrida Taenari   10
sedes Atlanteusque finis
concutitur. valet ima summis

mutare et insignem attenuat deus,
obscura promens; hinc apicem rapax
fortuna cum stridore acuto   15
sustulit, hic posuisse gaudet.

Epicurean philosophy had a profound influence in Rome. Virgil and Horace both studied it in their youth and both of them knew and admired Lucretius' poem *De Rerum Natura*, 'On the Nature of Things', in which he expounded Epicurean doctrine in the sublimest poetry ever written in Latin. The mainspring of this philosophy is the search for a way of life which will provide rational pleasure unruffled by such passions as fear and ambition. While human beings believe in avenging gods, they will be racked by guilt and fear of divine punishment, so Epicurus taught that the gods lived in idle bliss and took no interest in human affairs. The mysteries of our world are not to be explained as the work of gods, but are the result of the movement of an infinite number of imperceptibly small atoms. Lightning, for instance, is not a missile hurled by Jupiter, but a product of the action of winds in clouds causing concentrations and collisions of the atoms of fire.

This is where Horace starts *Odes* 1. 34. Lucretius has argued that lightning is caused by events in clouds. But if it occurs when there are no clouds, the Epicurean case collapses and we are driven back to the divine explanation. This is not the only Lucretian element in the poem. In the first stanza Horace says he was once *sapientiae consultus*, an expert in wisdom. Lucretius never calls Epicureanism *philosophia*, but he does refer to it at 5. 9–10 as 'that reasoned way of life which is now called wisdom', *vitae rationem . . . eam quae nunc appellatur sapientia*. Now Horace in an oxymoron speaks of Epicureanism as 'a crazy wisdom', *insanientis . . . sapientiae*. So too when he describes his Epicurean days as a wandering (*erro* in line 3 of the Latin), he is remembering how often Lucretius uses that metaphor of non-Epicureans, at 2. 82 and 3. 1052 for instance and in the proem to the second book:

> sed nil dulcius est bene quam munita tenere
> edita doctrina sapientum templa serena,

shaking the dull earth and restless rivers,
the Styx and the fearsome halls of hateful Taenarus,   10
   and the Atlantean limits
     of the world. God has the power

to exchange high and low, to humble the great
and bring forward the obscure. With a shrill cry
   rapacious Fortune snatches the crown from one head   15
     and delights to lay it on another.

despicere unde queas alios passimque videre
errare atque viam palantis quaerere vitae.

But nothing is sweeter than to hold the lofty regions
firmly fortified by the doctrine of the wise (*sapientum*),
from where you can look down at others and see them
wandering about and going astray as they search for the path of life.

                 (Lucretius, 2. 6–10)

Lucretius is everywhere in this ode. *Plerumque*, 'for the most part', is
an odd word to use in this argument. Horace's point collapses if light-
ning *usually* comes from a clouded sky. It is valid only if lightning *always*
comes in a clouded sky. The word belongs to daily speech. It occurs once
in Virgil and never in Catullus, Propertius, or Tibullus, but Lucretius
uses it twenty-one times, three of these when he is discussing lightning
(5. 1131–2, 6. 208 and 421). Lightning divides the clouds in line 6 of this
ode and several times in Lucretius, at 6. 283 for instance, and at 6. 203
where the burning winds tear apart the cloud and blaze out in dazzling
light, *divulsa fulserunt nube corusci. Per purum* in line 7 of the ode is used
also by Lucretius at 4. 327 of a cloudless sky.

In the third stanza the shaking of sky, earth, rivers, and sea, involves
also the Underworld. Even this is a dig at Lucretius. In the proem to his
third book he claims that he could see the whole universe as atoms mov-
ing through the void, and there was nowhere any trace of an
Underworld. This was not because the earth was obstructing his view
because he could see all the atoms moving through the void under his
feet. To the countercheck quarrelsome Horace has responded with the
lie direct. There *is* a river Styx. There *is* a hateful place down there,
Hades, which Horace here calls Taenarus. And it *is* inhabited, there *are*
dwelling-places, *sedes*. Horace knows because he felt it shake, and *con-
cutere* is a favourite Lucretian word for such phenomena. In line 11

Atlanteus may also recall Lucretius. There is no surviving use of this word before this except at Lucretius 5. 35, where also it refers to the western limits of our world. Here it may also suggest that Horace believes there *is* an Atlas who holds the sky above his head at the western end of the Mediterranean.

And what of the powerful and irrefutable commonplace in lines 12–14? At 5. 831–3 Lucretius describes how Nature changes all things, *omnia commutat Natura*. While one thing decays, another emerges from neglect, *e contemptibus exit*. This awareness of the impermanence of human achievements runs through the whole of the history of civilization at the end of Lucretius' fifth book. His final summary of the development of technology and the arts is expressed in similar terms:

> sic unum quicquid paulatim protrahit aetas
> in medium ratioque in luminis erigit oras;
> namque alid ex alio clarescere corde videbant,
> artibus ad summum donec venere cacumen.

> So *time* gradually draws forward everything into public view
> and *reason* lifts it into the shores of light. For [early man]
> saw in his mind one thing becoming clear from another
> until by his arts they had reached the highest pinnacle.

(Lucretius, 5. 1454–7)

Nature, time, and reason are the agents in Epicurean thinking. In Horace these are quietly changed into God, a proposition which Lucretius has been assaulting for nearly 700 lines, and Fortune, to which Lucretius and Epicurus allot only a very limited scope.

Some of these resemblances are more impressive than others but there can be no doubt that throughout this ode Horace is having fun with Epicureanism. This is confirmed by the middle of the poem where Horace asserts a literal non-Epicurean belief in Jupiter and the mythology of the Olympian gods. Similarly the end declares the power of God over human affairs and the sudden, drastic changes which rapacious Fortune delights to bring to human beings.

Commentators are baffled. They do not find in Horace's other odes in this collection or in any of his later writings any renunciation of his rather loose Epicurean sympathies. They know also that the refutation of Epicureanism is based on a lie. Lightning does not occur in a clear sky. Nor do they believe that a man as sceptical and sophisticated as Horace has shown himself to be in the *Satires* and the *Odes* could possibly be serious in explaining thunder as the rattle of horses' hooves and the rumble of chariot-wheels. The obvious rebound from Epicureanism would be to Stoicism and some scholars have found it in the description of Fortune at the end of the ode. For the Stoics, Fate was part of the divine continuum which contained Jupiter, Reason (the Greek *Logos*), *Aether*, and Fate. If Fortuna in the ode were the same as Fate, we should see Jupiter and Fortuna merging in the last three stanzas as parts of the Stoic conception of the divine. Against this interpretation there is the naïve anthropomorphism of the explanation of thunder and the awkwardness of the characterization of Fortuna. This is emphatically not the Stoic *Fatum*, an aspect of the will of God or identical to it, a realization of the divine reason which governs the universe, and with which the wise man lives in perfect harmony, but a capricious, squawking bird who delights in cruelty, both in humiliating the great and elevating the low, the latter surely not out of divine grace or reason but rather for the gleeful certainty of humiliation to come.

Fully aware of these and other difficulties, Nisbet and Hubbard take the view that the poem begins with self-mockery and moves through the mock sublime to the true sublimity at the end, which is the serious point of the ode. The lightning in a clear sky is a symbol of the sudden inexplicable violence of the action of Fortune in human life. This view does not quite enable us to see how the poem hangs together. Lightning in a clear sky is one thing, and it is there in the poem for its anti-Epicurean purpose. Why does Horace move from that theme to a Jupiter rumbling across the sky in his chariot? And why at the end does this sublime god work through the agency of squawking gull or eagle?

Syndikus cuts the knot. Observing that gods play a large part in the *Odes* but a tiny part in the *Satires* and the *Epistles*, he concludes that the divine is part of the furniture of lyric poetry, and that this poem has to be understood allegorically as a programmatic statement about Horace's lyric writing. Just as 1. 14 informs us that this collection will include political poems and 1. 16 lets us know that it will contain love poems, so 1. 34 announces that gods will appear in the *Odes* of Horace. 'It has not so much to do with the empirical "I" of the author as with the literary form' (Syndikus, 307). Horace never wavers in his agnostic, sceptical philosophy, but 'no ancient literary form allows its rules to be broken and lyric poetry demands gods'. Syndikus sees that this is no empty tradition, but a source of drama, sublime beauty, and allegory, and a means of expressing in poetry the spectacular growth and glory of Rome in terms of the favour and protection of the Olympian gods. Like the Nisbet and Hubbard interpretation, this is helpful, but does not bring us to an understanding of the details of the poem or of its argument. If this is meant as a programmatic statement about Horace's poetry, the riddle is too difficult to read.

Perhaps we can make progress by remembering from the *Satires* that Horace is deeply suspicious of the technical and the doctrinaire in philosophy. His interests lie in ethics, in the search for the good life, not in physics. On 1. 28 we quoted his account of the interests of Iccius from *Epistles* 1. 12, but there was no indication that Horace devoted himself to these lofty studies. So here, we may be wrong to find a renunciation of Epicureanism. What he is rejecting is Epicurean theology and physics, in particular astronomical physics. It would be entirely in his nature to make fun of the speculative explanations adduced by Epicurus and Lucretius while retaining respect for other aspects of their teaching, notably the high estimate they put upon friendship, peace of mind, and pleasure rationally assessed.

When Horace turns to Jupiter and Olympian mythology he speaks in naïvely fundamentalist terms which he would not have expected any readers who knew him to accept. Even at the start, instead of the normal word Jupiter, he uses the archaic *Diespiter*, with its not irrelevant etymological hint that the god is father of the day, of the sky, *diei Pater*. Fun is on the agenda. But again it would be wrong to read this as a solemn rejection of all belief in the Olympian gods. Syndikus's explanation that they appear in Horace's lyric poetry because lyric poetry demands them, is not the most likely solution. We have often seen and will continue to see that Horace frequently talks as though he had a sense of the divine acting in his life. When he says he is visited by Apollo or Bacchus or Venus, he is not saying simply that he is writing poetry or drinking wine or desiring his beloved. These bald descriptive terms denote the experiences but do nothing to convey them. Horace has recourse to religious language to tell us that at such times he has a sense of something extra, of an element which is beyond understanding and human power, almost beyond belief. He writes of gods because he has a sense of the presence of gods. He does not normally use such terms in the *Satires* and the *Epistles* because in those poems he is not talking at this level about such experiences.

So then, in the middle of this largely humorous ode he refers to his deep and genuine sense of the presence of the Olympian gods, but expresses this not seriously and systematically, but in this crudely literal and anthropomorphic way, at which his friends will have smiled. Aristius Fuscus, for example, whom we met in 1. 22 and *Satires* 1.9 there cited, would have known to take this with a pinch of salt.

What then would he have thought Horace was meaning to convey? The end of the ode gives some answer to that question. There, as we read about the sudden unpredictable exercise of divine power as God and rapacious Fortune elevate the humble and humiliate the great, we are with a Horace who is not Epicurean or Stoic, but a human being observing the sudden, drastic, and inscrutable events which overtake human beings from an incomprehensible source. In all this we can be guided by the first book of the *Epistles*. There Horace warns us that he is not the member of any philosophical school (1. 14–19) and that he is incurably inconsistent, changing his views from day to day. This makes him not a very good philosopher, but does not lessen his powers as a poet. On the contrary, it enables him to speak as a Stoic and as an Epicurean, as an atheist and as a polytheist, and even as a detached observer of life, strong within himself and determined not to be cast down by disasters or elated by success. Such, at any rate, is the view he presents with full earnestness and full poetic power in his testament of friendship in the great ode 3. 29. Another characteristic of his thought is that he is never overimpressed by dogmatic solutions. We find it difficult to arrive at a clear and convincing understanding of this ode, because the argument is not meant to be clear. Horace is not trying to produce a coherent series of philosophical propositions. Perhaps it helps to think of this ode as an introduction to the hymn to Fortune which follows it. Horace's Epicurean friends might raise their eyebrows at a hymn addressed to this non-Epicurean deity. So he has fun with Epicurean theology, restates the fundamentalist view of the Olympian gods, knowing that he will not be taken literally and seriously, and then ends with a view of life which is much more practical and in accordance with daily experience. Jupiter has merged into Fortuna at line 15 and the ground is cleared for the hymn to Fortuna which follows as 1. 35.

alcaics

O DIVA, gratum quae regis Antium,
praesens vel imo tollere de gradu
    mortale corpus vel superbos
        vertere funeribus triumphos,

te pauper ambit sollicita prece   5
ruris colonus, te dominam aequoris
    quicumque Bithyna lacessit
        Carpathium pelagus carina.

te Dacus asper, te profugi Scythae,
urbesque gentesque et Latium ferox   10
    regumque matres barbarorum et
        purpurei metuunt tyranni,

iniurioso ne pede proruas
stantem columnam, neu populus frequens
    ad arma cessantis, ad arma   15
        concitet imperiumque frangat.

te semper anteit serva Necessitas,
clavos trabalis et cuneos manu
    gestans aena, nec severus
        uncus abest liquidumque plumbum.   20

te Spes et albo rara Fides colit
velata panno, nec comitem abnegat,
    utcumque mutata potentis
        veste domos inimica linquis.

at vulgus infidum et meretrix retro   25
periura cedit, diffugiunt cadis
    cum faece siccatis amici
        ferre iugum pariter dolosi.

serves iturum Caesarem in ultimos
orbis Britannos et iuvenum recens   30
    examen Eois timendum
        partibus Oceanoque rubro.

Fortune (NC.
    is non egoists in power
    means prayers.
  - relative - but unbroken his
      - new to Olympic -

XXXV

Goddess, who rule over lovely Antium,
whose present power can raise mortal man
    from the lowest level or turn
        his proud triumphs into funerals,

the poor farmer appeals to you with anxious prayer,   5
the sailor vexing the Carpathian Sea
    on his Bithynian ship prays to you
        as mistress of the ocean.

The rough Dacian and Scythians famous in retreat,
the cities and peoples and fierce Latium,   10
    the mothers of barbarian kings
        and tyrants clad in purple,

all are afraid that your violent foot may kick over
the standing column, that the mob may gather
    to whip the laggards to war, to war,   15
        and shatter all authority.

Always before you goes your slave Necessity,
beam-nails and wedges in her bronze hand,
    and never without her cruel hook
        and molten lead.   20

Hope attends you, and Loyalty, rare upon this earth,
her hand swathed in white, who do not desert their friend
    when you change your coat and turn against
        the great and leave their homes.

Meanwhile the faithless mob and lying prostitute   25
fall away, and, when the jars are drained
    to the dregs, false friends disappear,
        not to be trusted to share the yoke.

Preserve Caesar as he prepares to go
to remotest Britain, and preserve the new swarm   30
    of young to spread fear in the regions
        of the East and the Red Sea.

eheu, cicatricum et sceleris pudet
fratrumque. quid nos dura refugimus
    aetas? quid intactum nefasti   35
        liquimus? unde manum iuventus

metu deorum continuit? quibus
pepercit aris? o utinam nova
    incude diffingas retusum in
        Massagetas Arabasque ferrum!   40

The divine takes many forms. We left the last ode with Fortuna por-
trayed as an inscrutable and irresistible force, a bird screeching,
swooping, and enjoying the rapid changes she inflicted upon human
beings, and never a hint that she could be accessible to human prayer. *En
passant* we glimpsed two philosophical gods, the divine Reason with
which Stoics aspired to live in harmony, and the idle deities of the
Epicureans living in unflawed serenity. Now in 1. 35 Fortuna has
become a cult god, the recipient of prayer, as worshipped in many
shrines in Rome and in Italy, notably at Praeneste and at Antium.

The prayer has many of the features of the kletic hymn as laid out in
the commentary on 1. 32. It starts with an address in the vocative case,
introduced by *O*. The place of worship is given in an adjective clause.
Praesens meaning 'present and effectual' is a participial form and also a
sacral term which has come into Christian prayer in 'a very present help
in time of trouble'. Spheres of operation of the deity are given as alter-
natives, and *vel . . . vel*, 'either . . . or', may hint at the sacral formula *sive
. . . sive*. Her first power, the power to raise the humble, chimes with her
cult in Rome, which was founded by Servius Tullius, the king who began
life as a slave, and was patronized largely by slaves and poor people
(*Corpus Inscriptionum Latinarum* I². 977–980). The second stanza adds
information about other places where she is worshipped, namely the
countryside and the sea. In Rome she was a goddess with agricultural
connections (so Columella, 10. 316), and on coins (Sydenham, 179) she
was often depicted carrying a rudder and a cornucopia. The poem con-
tinues with more examples of her spheres of operation and four stanzas
beginning with the second person of the pronoun (*te* in lines 5, 9, 17, and
21, compare 1. 10. 5, 9, 13, and 17). In 17–24 there is a detailed list and
description of the god's retinue. The two stanzas 21–8 contain one of the
most difficult passages in Horace. The translation follows an ancient
solution which takes *at* as a gently adversative adverb, meaning some-

Shame on our scars, our crimes,
our brothers! Our brutal age has shrunk
    from nothing. We have left no impiety   35
      untouched. Our young men have never

stayed their hand for fear of the gods
but have polluted every altar. If only
    you would reforge our blunted swords
      for use against Massagetes and Arabs.   40

thing more like 'while' than 'but'. So, when Fortune turns against the
great man, Hope and Faith leave his house, being loyal to Fortune, *while*
false friends and scheming prostitutes fall away when the wine is all
drunk. After this retinue comes the prayer proper in lines 29–32 and
38–40.

So much for resemblances between this hymn and others. But in
poetry differences are more interesting than resemblances. In the address
to the god there is no parentage, no birthplace, no birth-myth, no name
(only *O diva*), and no catch-all formula, 'by whatever name you prefer to
be called'. There are several possible reasons for this. Fortuna is a late
arrival on the Olympian scene, not equipped with the usual family con-
nections. She is also a native Italian god and Italian gods have no rela-
tives (the one exception is Fortuna of Praeneste, the first daughter of
Jupiter, *Diovo fileia primogenia* in *CIL* I². 60, but this ode is concerned
not with Praeneste but with Antium). All these absences present
Fortuna as a somewhat sinister, faceless, characterless deity, more of a
power than a person.

The sinister or malevolent aspect is repeatedly invoked in what fol-
lows. In the first stanza the expected opposite of raising would be lower-
ing but Fortuna does not lower. She kills. Even the raising of a human
being is expressed in demeaning terms. The human being is *mortale cor-
pus*, 'a mortal body'. Farmers address 'anxious' prayers to her (5). Sailors
are 'vexing' the sea (7). In the third stanza she is not worshipped but
'feared' and by what seems to be the whole world. In line 13 her foot is
iniurioso, 'destructive'. Her attendants in 17–21 are not personal deities
but insentient abstractions. Necessity, for example, is a slave to suit the
servile connections of Fortuna (see on line 2), and she is laden with fear-
some tools. Some of the beam-nails among the 12 tons of Roman nails
found at Inchtuthil are as long as half a yard and Necessity uses such
nails of adamantine steel to dire effect in 3. 24. 7. In the prayer we might

have expected the familiar motif, 'If ever you have visited us in the past'
or 'if ever we have worshipped you in the past'. Instead the poem con-
cludes with a string of impassioned exclamations striding across line-
endings and the end of the penultimate stanza. Instead of conditional
clauses alluding to the past, Horace describes the horrors of the Civil
War in a mounting series of rhetorical questions of which the last,
briefest, and almost unspeakable horror is the desecration of altars.
The normal form is abandoned because the pressure of Horace's emo-
tion has driven him to rhetorical questions, but we are still in the prayer
formula and still dealing with visitations of the god, as is confirmed in
the last words of the poem. These are clearly a version of the 'Raine
goe to Spain' motif, noted at the end of the scheme in our discussion of
1. 32.

Why does Horace choose to write this hymn to Fortuna? If we were
not told, we could guess, but we are told. The shrine of Fortuna at
Antium functioned as an oracle (1. 23. 13) and according to Appian, 3.
24. 97 the oracle had supported Octavian in the Perusine War in 41–40
BC and had profited from it. Benefactions continued and pseudo-Acro
tells us that the temple was very famous and 'had also been enriched by
gifts from many leading men', *multorum etiam principum donis ornatum*.
Presumably the shrine profited also from Augustus' policy of refurbish-
ment of the temples as pursued in Rome in the early 20s. The reference
to a fresh swarm of warriors about to cause terror to the East and the Red
Sea, would then chime with the allusion in 1. 29 to the expedition of
Aelius Gallus against the Shebans in 26–25 BC. Line 30, in turn, fits Dio
Cassius' account in 53. 22 and 25 of attacks on Britain planned by
Augustus in each of these years. The Massagetae of line 40 on the other
hand, a tribe living east of the Caspian Sea, are a panegyrical exaggera-
tion, like the Chinese in 1. 29. 9.

On this conjecture the ode would then celebrate the benefactions of
Octavian to this famous shrine, perhaps describing some of them. The
iconography of lines 13 and 17–20, for example, may have corre-
sponded to what would be seen at the temple, perhaps a sculptured
frieze with Necessity's right hand done in bronze. The god and her ret-
inue would be led by her slave Necessity carrying her instruments of tor-
ture or execution, nails as used in crucifixions, wedges as used to pierce
the breast of Prometheus in Aeschylus, *Prometheus Unbound* (translated
as *cunei* by Cicero at *Tusculan Disputations* 2. 23), the hook as used to
drag the bodies of executed criminals to the Tiber, and molten lead as
used to force Andromache from the altar in Euripides, *Andromache* 267,

like the pitch in Lucretius' list of such devices at 3. 1017. This stanza
has often been censured. Nisbet and Hubbard quote a note from the
end of Lessing's *Laocoon*, chapter 10: 'the passage is one of the coldest
in Horace . . . The passage is unpleasing . . . because the attributes . . .
are peculiarly addressed to the eyes; and if we attempt to acquire by the
ear conceptions that would naturally be conveyed through the eyes, a
greater effort is required, while the ideas themselves are incapable of the
same distinctness.' There is no need for this. The Romans were more
adept than we are at reading the iconography of gods and would have
found the picture of the slave Necessity and her tools of torture cir-
cumstantial and impressive. On the other hand, it has to be admitted
that this is not the usual interpretation of the stanza. Almost all mod-
ern commentators except Pöschl see the equipment rather as tools of
the building trade, imagining a Necessity whose hand is made of bronze
carrying heavy-duty nails to secure beams, clamps (*cunei*) to tie blocks
in the same course, dowels (*unci*) to tie blocks in different courses, and
lead to melt for holding both in place. The emphasis is then not upon
the cruelty of Necessity but upon its fixity. This fits the beam-nails very
well, since they are proverbial in this sense. Cicero, for instance, in
Verrines 5. 53 speaks of fixing a kindness in mind as though by a beam-
nail, *ut hoc beneficium, quaemadmodum dicitur, trabali clavo figeret*.
Nevertheless this interpretation cannot stand for the simple reason that
there are no examples in Latin of *cuneus* or *uncus* meaning masonry
clamps or dowels. On either interpretation, however, throughout this
stanza Necessity is associated with metals put to figurative use. The
final stanza, where Fortuna is asked to busy herself at her anvil, contin-
ues the image.

A further small point refers vividly to a ritual scene presumably dis-
played at Antium which therefore lends particularity and point. *Fides*,
'Faith, Trust, Loyalty . . .' is veiled in a piece of white cloth, *albo . . .
panno*, and commentators are surely right to refer to the description of
the priests of Fides in Livy 1. 21. 4, who sacrificed with their hand
swathed, *involuta*, in white to indicate the sanctity of Faith, and also of
its holy seat in the right hand.

We now look back at 1. 34. These two poems are both in the same
metre and the goddess named at the end of the first is referred to with-
out a name at the beginning of the second, which attributes to her the
same function in different words. On our supposition, Horace decided
to write a prayer for Octavian to commemorate his benefactions to the
temple of Fortuna at Antium. He has a problem, since Fortuna is a god

of the disadvantaged. She is also a god who has dubious associations with the prestigious Olympian pantheon. Horace's friends knew about his scepticism and sophistication. In consideration of this, 1. 34 could be read as a skilful manœuvre to disarm criticism. It starts with clever mockery of Epicurean dogma, erects a naïve theology, and even as we smile Horace ends by restating the theistic position in terms that no human being could ever deny. We are now ready to move to Fortuna of Antium.

Commentators point to the relevance of Pindar, *Olympian* 12. After three or four details in the first stanza, this is difficult to see. But the poem deserves to be read for itself, for the conceit which acclaims disaster for the good that can come of it, and for Pindar's profligate mixture of metaphors; for instance, where the Fame of this runner's feet would have lost its leaves at the beginning of the third section. Here the verb *phullorroein* means 'shed leaves' of a tree, and 'moult' of a bird. This makes poetic sense since the Olympic victor would be crowned with olive leaves and sometimes even showered with leaves (for *phyllobolia*, see Borthwick):

4ᵇ Ἀσ(φ)

XXXVI

Eᴛ ture et fidibus iuvat
placare et vituli sanguine debito
   custodes Numidae deos,
qui nunc Hesperia sospes ab ultima

   caris multa sodalibus,   5
nulli plura tamen dividit oscula
   quam dulci Lamiae, memor
actae non alio rege puertiae

   mutataeque simul togae.
Cressa ne careat pulchra dies nota,   10
   neu promptae modus amphorae,
neu morem in Salium sit requies pedum,

I pray, O Saviour Fortune, daughter of Zeus the Liberator,
keep watch over Himera's broad kingdom,
for you steer the swift ships on the sea
and on land you govern the instant decisions of war
and the counsel-bearing assemblies of men. Yet their hopes
plough seas of lies and folly, many times tossed high
and sometimes plunged into the depths.

No creature on the earth has yet received a clear token
from the gods of events to come,
but man's sight of the future is blinded
and many unexpected things befall him.
Some who have met foul seas have known
the opposite of pleasure, others in a moment
have exchanged anguish for deep delight.

Son of Philanor, the fame of your feet,
like the cock fighting in its own yard,
would have shed its leaves, unsung, if civil strife,
that sets man against man, had not taken you from Cnossos,
your fatherland. But now, Ergoteles, you are crowned at Olympia,
twice at the Pythian games and twice at the Isthmos,
and in your own fields you exalt the hot springs of the nymphs.

XXXVI

With incense and with the lyre
and with the blood of a calf to pay my vow, I delight
   to propitiate the guardian gods
of Numida, now safely home from the furthest West

   and sharing out so many kisses   5
to his dear friends, but to none
   more than his beloved Lamia, remembering
his boyhood when none but Lamia was king,

   and the time when they both put on the toga.
Now we must not fail to mark this glorious day with chalk,   10
   and the jar we bring out must know no limit,
and feet no rest from dancing like the priests of Mars,

neu multi Damalis meri
Bassum Threicia vincat amystide,
   neu desint epulis rosae   15
neu vivax apium| neu breve lilium.

       omnes in Damalin putris
deponent oculos, nec Damalis novo
       divelletur adultero
lascivis hederis ambitiosior.   20

Here as in 1. 16, 21, and 22, Horace sometimes writes with an eye on Catullus:

> Verani, omnibus e meis amicis
> antistans mihi milibus trecentis,
> venistine domum ad tuos Penates
> fratresque unanimos anumque matrem?
> venisti. O mihi nuntii beati!   5
> Visam te incolumem audiamque Hiberum
> narrantem loca, facta, nationes,
> ut mos est tuus, applicansque collum
> iucundum os oculosque suaviabor.
> O quantum est hominum beatiorum,   10
> quid me laetius beatiusve?
>
>   (Catullus, *Poem* 9)

> Veranius, worth more to me than any
> three hundred thousand of my friends,
> have you come home to your Penates,
> to your brothers and your old mother?
> You have indeed. Great news this for me.   5
> I'll see you safe and hear you talking
> about Spanish places, manners, tribes,
> as is your way, and lay my neck against yours
> to kiss your lovely mouth and eyes.
> Of all the men who have ever been blest,   10
> was ever a man happier or more blest than me?

This reads more like an outburst then a poem. Catullus is not afraid of offending these 300,000 of his friends because four of the noughts could be dispensed with and the remaining thirty would all know Veranius themselves. In line 3 although Catullus finds the news difficult to believe, he immediately imagines the scene in Veranius' home, with

nor must Damalis, that great drinker,
down a deeper Thracian draught than Bassus,
    nor must there be any shortage of roses at the feast   15
or long-living celery or soon-dying lilies.

All will fix their melting eyes
  on Damalis, but Damalis will not be torn
    from the arms of her new lover
but will wind more clingingly than ivy.   20

the delighted Penates, the gods of home, with the brothers who are all of one mind together, and with Veranius and his old mother. There is no beating about the bush. She is old, so there was all the more doubt whether he would get home in time. By line 5 Catullus does believe the news and answers his own question *venistine? . . . venisti*. The realization leaves him capable only of an exclamation. But in the next line he begins to imagine what will happen when he goes round to see Veranius. Veranius will be talking. Wiseman (pp. 266–9) has gathered three possible references to a person or persons of that name, and concludes that if all three are to be combined into a single character, he might have been called Lucius Veranius Flaccus, and have had 'linguistic interests ranging into religious and constitutional antiquarianism at one end and the controversies of oratorical style at the other'. We may never know, but such a composite agrees temptingly with the Veranius of lines 7–8, 'narrating places, deeds, tribes, as is your way'. This would then be an affectionately sly dig at a friend who enjoyed talking. Catullus then imagines their passionate reunion, and the poem ends as it began with Catullus' expression of his own excitement. Catullus had produced a vivid, personal poem in colloquial language, full of affection and fun, giving an impression of spontaneity, an imagined stream of consciousness.

Horace, too, is welcoming the return of a friend from the West (probably also from Spain, where he may have served under Augustus in the campaigns of 27–25 BC). In both poems there are kisses. Catullus, too, has in 107. 6 and 68. 148 the notion of a calendar marked with white to celebrate a glorious day. But again, differences are more illuminating than resemblances. Numida is an unknown. Horace gives no indication that he loves him and his poem is not addressed to him, as Catullus 9 was to Veranius. The obvious explanation is that Numida is not as important as Lamia, presumably the distinguished Lamia addressed in 1. 26, who perhaps suggested to Horace that he might write a poem to celebrate his friend's return from the wars. Numida may even have been serving under Lamia's father, whom Augustus left in charge of Hispania Citerior in 24 BC. If then the poem is written for Lamia, not for Numida, we can understand why it is without an expression of personal affection, without the family scene so economically suggested by Catullus, without the sly hints of his friend's character, and without the impression of spontaneity and the stream of consciousness.

Apart from a brilliant exposition by Syndikus, by and large this poem has not had a good press. It has a striking start with three elements each longer in the Latin than the one before it and each introduced by *et*, *et ture et fidibus . . . et vituli sanguine debito*, the familiar ascending tricolon with anaphora. Scholars assure us that allusion to sacrifice is a stock feature of poems of greeting, but it is much more important to remember that sacrifice itself was a stock feature of Roman life. Romans actually did make vows for the safe return of friends going on journeys, and they did pay their vows when they returned. The blood of sacrifice is not simply a card to play in a poetic game. It is something Romans frequently saw. A pleasing demonstration of this is the story cited from Seneca, *De Beneficiis* 3. 27. 1, of one Rufus who had prayed at dinner that Caesar might not return safely from a journey he was about to make and added that bulls and calves were all making the same prayer, *optaverat ne Caesar salvus rediret . . . et adiecerat idem omnes et tauros et vitulos optare*.

The spotlight is on the important figure Lamia, and Horace wields it skilfully. We deduce that the vow of the second line was Lamia's vow and that Lamia is the principal comrade of line 5 and the host of the symposium. In line 7 his name arrives with an imposing enjambement. This is a convenient technical term, but what it means is something important for the movement of the poem. It opens with a long sentence, and the adjective clause beginning in line 4 demands a long breath, sustained till the name of Lamia arrives at long last in line 7 and forces the speaker to pause in mid-line. A similar expressive enjambement is noted on 1. 26. 5 (cf. 31. 15 and 37. 12). It is followed by a vivid reference to the basis for the affection between Lamia and Numida, introduced by the key word *memor* in line 7, which has to be read closely with lines 8 and 9. Memories of childhood are not only appealing, they also perform a mild panegyrical function. Lamia was the senior partner in the boyhood relationship and is the more important person in later life. By referring to his loyalty to Numida, Horace incorporates into his poem a testimonial to the character of Lamia. This long opening sentence ends with a nostalgic reminder of the ceremonial family occasion when on the same day the two 15-year-old boys put on the toga of manhood, *toga vir-ilis*, and again the metre lends weight to the sentiment. Every ode of Horace with the exception of 4. 5 where the manuscripts appear to be in error, has a number of lines which is divisible by four and many of the metres are four-line units like the Alcaic of 1. 35 and the Sapphic of 1. 32. This establishes in the mind of the reader an expectation that all the odes will fall into four-line stanzas and in this book that is how they are printed. Immediately we see, and should hear, that this long opening sentence not only fills two stanzas but at the mention of the boyhood of Lamia and Numida, swells into a third stanza with line 9. In the Catullus emotion is declared, in the Horace it is suggested.

In the rest of this poem Horace suggests the emotions of Numida's return by the abundance of the provision to celebrate it, item after item of visible object and action, linked by repeated anaphora of *neu*, 'nor . . . nor . . .', with all these negatives forbidding economy caught up in the celebration of love which begins with *omnes* . . . 'all' eyes on Damalis. An amphora is taken out of the cellar and there is vigorous dancing, heavy drinking, and a Thracian contest to find who could drink most in one draught. For this occasion Horace has waived his dislike of Thracian drinking which we met in 1. 27. 2. We are perhaps to guess that Bassus is a mutual friend of Numida and Lamia who on this great occasion is to forget his normal temperance and is not to be outdone even by the courtesan Damalis, who is in fine form because of the return of her beloved Numida.

Some scholars have been dissatisfied by the separate allusions to wine at lines 11 and 13–14 and the separate mentions of Damalis, and have emended the manuscripts by putting lines 13–14 after lines 15–16. This is not fair to Horace. In his convivial poems he arranges selections from the same repertoire of motifs. In the first of these, for instance, at 1. 4, we saw dance, garlands of greenery and flowers, sacrifice, death, the *carpe diem* motif 'enjoy the hour', death again, wine, and love. Flowers, death, and love are a familiar and expected nexus in these poems, but death is not invited to the joyous welcome-home dinner for Numida. Invited or not, he is waiting outside, and we are quietly reminded of him by the mention of roses in line 15, the all-too-swiftly passing blooms of the lovely rose, *nimium brevis flores amoenae* . . . *rosae* as Horace calls them at 2. 3. 14. If we sense death with the rose in line 15, we hear him in line 16. Celery leaves were used by Romans in dinner garlands because they would stay fresh for long evenings, and a garland which combined celery with lilies which soon drooped in the heat, would readily act as a *memento mori* to impressionable diners and drinkers. The metre again gives edge to the sense. Line 16 can be divided into two halves exactly equal in word lengths and in patterns of word accent, *neu vívax ápium | neu bréve lílium.* I have not found any other line in this Glyconic metre in Horace which falls into this pattern. It therefore seems that the sound of the verse is drawing our attention to this contrast between length of life and brevity of life, thus subtly carrying the mind along the familiar route from wine by way of flowers and death to love. The emendation suggested above moves less eloquently from flowers and death to wine, and from wine directly to love. The text is right as it stands and the poetry works.

The convivial poem ends in love and again the sound reinforces the dynamic of the thought. Where all fix their *melting* eyes on Damalis, but Damalis cannot be torn away from her *new* lover, the Latin modulates in grammatical case from *Damalin putris* ending line 17 to *Damalis novo* ending line 18. (For such polyptoton, see on 1. 24. 9–10 and 1. 32. 11–12.)

Throughout, the poet has conveyed his delight not by asserting it, but by an abundance of concrete, perceptible phenomena. In the last line, however, he rises to his first conspicuous metaphor, and joins in his last contest with Catullus. In 61. 31–5 the god of marriage is being addressed:

Mca..

XXXVII

Nvnc est bibendum, nunc pede libero
pulsanda tellus, nunc Saliaribus
    ornare pulvinar deorum
      tempus erat dapibus, sodales.

antehac nefas depromere Caecubum   5
cellis avitis, dum Capitolio
    regina dementis ruinas
      funus et imperio parabat

ac dominam domum voca
coniugis cupidam novi,
mentem amore revinciens,
ut tenax hedera huc et huc
     arborem implicat errans.

Call home the mistress of the house
longing for her new husband,
and bind her mind with love
as the tenacious ivy wanders
     everywhere entwining the tree.

Horace accepts the metaphor and the difference between the two versions is typical of the differences between the two poets. The word *ambitiosior* is ambivalent. Literally it means 'more winding' (*ambire* means 'to go round'). Metaphorically it means 'to be insistent, demanding, to solicit' (as candidates went round canvassing for votes). When the translator has solved the problem of translating *ambitiosior*, he turns back to *lascivis*, a word which is nowadays untranslatable, although earlier ages came near it with 'wanton'. The senses of these three words which make up the last line, and the distant echo of the Catullus passage, reverberate in the mind and the reverberation is the deeper because this last line of the poem is the only Glyconic in the odes which consists of only three words. The ivy is spreading.

Praistr vicion → suspect for deceit Cleopatric

XXXVII

Now we must drink, now we must
beat the earth with unfettered feet, now,
    my friends, is the time to load the couches
      of the gods with Salian feasts.

Before this it was a sin to take the Caecuban   5
down from its ancient racks, while the mad queen
    with her contaminated flock of men
      diseased by vice, was preparing

contaminato cum grege turpium
morbo virorum, quidlibet impotens   10
   sperare fortunaque dulci
     ebria. sed minuit furorem

vix una sospes navis ab ignibus,
mentemque lymphatam Mareotico
   redegit in veros timores   15
     Caesar ab Italia volantem

remis adurgens accipiter velut
mollis columbas aut leporem citus
   venator in campis nivalis
     Haemoniae, daret ut catenis   20

fatale monstrum; quae generosius
perire quaerens nec muliebriter
   expavit ensem nec latentis
     classe cita reparavit oras;

ausa et iacentem visere regiam   25
vultu sereno, fortis et asperas
   tractare serpentis, ut atrum
     corpore combiberet venenum,

deliberata morte ferocior,
saevis Liburnis scilicet invidens   30
   privata deduci superbo
     non humilis mulier triumpho.

The battle of Actium on 2 September 31 BC made Octavian master of the Mediterranean world but Antony and Cleopatra escaped. In due course Octavian followed them to Alexandria where they both committed suicide, Cleopatra on 10 August 30 BC, a few days after the death of Antony. Why does Horace start his poem to celebrate her death by translating the first words of a poem written nearly 700 years before by Alcaeus (fragment 332)?

> Now we must get drunk, we must drink
> with some vigour since Myrsilus is dead . . .

The simple answer is that Myrsilus was a hated tyrant killed in battle and that Horace is suggesting that Cleopatra was like him. The foot is free in

the ruin of the Capitol and the destruction
of our power, crazed with hope   10
   unlimited and drunk
      with sweet fortune. But her madness

decreased when scarce a ship escaped the flames
and her mind, which had been deranged by Mareotic wine,
   was made to face real fears   15
      as she flew from Italy, and Caesar

pressed on the oars (like a hawk
after gentle doves or a swift hunter
   after a hare on the snowy plains
      of Thrace) to put in chains   20

this monster sent by fate. But she looked
for a nobler death and did not have a woman's fear
   of the sword, nor did she make
      for secret shores with her swift fleet.

Daring to gaze with face serene upon her ruined palace,   25
and brave enough to take deadly serpents
   in her hand, and let her body
      drink their black poison,

fiercer she was in the death she chose, as though
she did not wish to cease to be a queen, taken to Rome   30
   on the galleys of savage Liburnians
      to be a humble woman in a proud triumph.

the first line, *pede libero*, because it is thumping the ground. It is free also
because it has escaped the threat of enslavement to an Egyptian queen.

But in Horace simple answers are rarely enough. The first three words
and the theme are Greek, but Horace instantly modulates and speaks as
a Roman. Even the rhetorical structure is Roman, with its ascending tri-
colon and anaphora of 'now ... now ... now' (compare 1. 36. 1–3).
Then, if we take the hint from *Saliaribus* in the second line, the dancing
is in the Roman style of the priests of Mars, which we have just wit-
nessed at a symposium in 1. 36. 12. It is entirely appropriate that the god
of war, the father of Romulus who founded Rome, should be involved in
the celebration of this triumph of Roman arms. These same priests were

famous for their lavish feasts and in lines 3–4 they are associated with the Roman practice of *lectisternium*, whereby images of the gods were laid on couches outside their temples with rich fare set before them as part of the *supplicatio*, the festival of thanksgiving for victory. Augustus himself records the frequency of such *supplicationes* in his *Res Gestae* 4: 'On account of successes won by myself or by commanders acting under my auspices by land and by sea, the Senate decreed 55 thanksgivings to the immortal gods. The number of days on which thanksgivings were offered in accordance with the decree of the Senate was 890.' There is little doubt that the death of Cleopatra would have been celebrated in this way in Rome. This ode is celebrating not only the death of an enemy, but the splendid celebrations of the event.

In the years before Actium a cunning and unscrupulous propaganda war had been fought between Antony and Octavian. Octavian's victory at Actium now started such a wave of myth-making that the truth was obliterated for ever. We cannot assess the justice of Horace's allusions in this ode but it may be revealing to compare his version of events with the versions in other writers, notably the historians Plutarch, writing more than a hundred years after the events and Dio, nearly three hundred.

In the second stanza Cleopatra is referred to simply as the queen, *regina*, and this is in harmony with Octavian's propaganda in exploiting the Roman detestation of royal rule. Even the antonomasia, the reference by allusion rather than by name, acts here as a calculated sneer, just as the pirate Sextus Pompeius is called 'the Neptunian leader', *dux Neptunius*, and Antony simply the enemy, *hostis*, in *Epode* 9. In *Odes* 1. 37 Antony himself is not even mentioned and that too is a part of Octavian's strategy before and after Actium, for example in the *Res Gestae*, in order to give the impression that this was no civil war but a war against a foreign enemy. Similarly in *Epode* 9 which celebrated the battle, 'Antony is simply ignored and Cleopatra is too abominable to be named' (Nisbet, 1984). In lines 7–8 the queen is said to have planned to destroy the Capitol and break the power of Rome. For the latter there is firm evidence in the Donations of Alexandria of 34 BC whereby her son Caesarion was officially declared to be the son of Julius Caesar, and at the same time Egypt, Cyprus, and all Roman territories in Asia were donated to Caesarion, Cleopatra, and her three children by Antony. The suggestion that she wanted to destroy the Capitol may well be a slight exaggeration. Her own most powerful oath, according to Dio 50. 5, was the words, 'as surely as I shall sit in judgement on the Capitol'. This looks like a dramatized version, if not a propaganda lie, but it may well be that Horace has given this slightly different account for poetic reasons. 'The ode's second half answers the first in contrapuntal detail' according to Commager, citing the *supplicatio* at the beginning answered by the triumph at the end; the queen, *regina*, in line 7, answered in line 31 by her refusal to become a *privata*; her madness in the first half contrasted with her serenity in line 26; and even the eunuchs of lines 9–10, answered by Cleopatra's unwomanly courage in line 22. It may then be that the ruins of the Capitol are invented by Horace to be answered by the ruins of Cleopatra's palace in line 25, and that he invents also the destruction of her palace to answer the ruins of the Capitol. As for the madness attributed to her in lines 7, 12, and 14, and the uncontrollable passion of line 10, *impotens*, Horace only slightly exaggerates the ancient accounts, which agree in presenting a woman determined by whatever means to retain her power, and capable of passion, cruelty, and megalomaniacal extravagance.

The literal sense of the opening of the next stanza in the Latin, lines 7–8 in the translation, is 'with the contaminated flock of men disgusting with disease', *contaminato cum grege turpium morbo virorum*, and the word *morbo*, 'disease' often refers to sexual perversion. This phrase with the letter -r- five times in the last four words surely encourages us to read the last word *virorum*, 'men' as a sarcastic allusion to the eunuchs who were conspicuous in the court of the Ptolemies in Alexandria, but the general import of the phrase is to suggest sexual licence, including the royal marriages between brother and sister such as Cleopatra's with her brother Ptolemy VII, and her other liaisons including those with Julius Caesar and now with Antony. Sexual licence is a frequent target in Augustan propaganda, as we saw for example at the end of *Odes* 1. 12. Here, in line 12 Cleopatra is said to be drunk with sweet fortune, and this is clearly a metaphor, but Mareotic was a sweet wine (Athenaeus, 33 D–E), so when we are told that she was crazed with it, this strengthens the insinuation that she was drunk not only with sweet fortune but also with sweet Mareotic. This accords with the contemporary view as represented by Propertius in 3. 11. 55, where he makes her drunken tongue say that Rome did not have to fear her so much while it had such a citizen as Octavian. The same slur was made against Antony and drove him to write a rebuttal, unfortunately lost, 'On His Own Drunkenness', *De Ebrietate Sua*. Horace by suggestion in 12 and statement in 14 is joining in the hue and cry against the notorious profligacy of the entertainments enjoyed by Antony at the court of Cleopatra.

The central section of the poem deals with Cleopatra's flight from Actium and the point of attack changes. Cleopatra ceases to be a madwoman and becomes a frightened fugitive. In line 13 when Horace says that scarcely a single ship was saved from the fire, again he seems to be massaging the tradition in order to heighten the panegyric. According to Plutarch, *Antony* 68. 1 and Dio, 50. 33, Cleopatra escaped with sixty ships and Antony with some others, and the flame-throwers were nothing like so destructive as Horace suggests. Most of Antony's fleet, 300 out of 500 according to Dio, surrendered intact. The turning-point came, according to the tradition, when Cleopatra panicked prematurely and made off for Egypt, sailing through the battle lines with her sixty ships, at which Antony gave up the fight and sailed after her. This critical moment caught the romantic imagination of the ancient writers and Horace seems to have hinted at it in line 15. Octavian brought her back to the real fears, *redegit in veros timores*, of flight and the struggle for survival instead of the imagined fears which had led her to abandon the fight at Actium. To say in line 16 that she was flying from Italy is slightly inaccurate, because the battle was fought on the north-west coast of Greece opposite Italy, but Horace allows himself this slight inaccuracy, presumably in order to heighten the pathos by reminding his audience of the threat to their homeland.

Now, as the dramatic first word in the Latin of the central two lines of the poem, we have 'Caesar', and his immense power is graphically presented by the statement that pressing on with oars he can pursue a fugitive who is flying, *volantem*. There is a kernel of truth in this exaggeration in that Octavian's ships were being rowed in battle order, when Cleopatra sailed through them under canvas. The simile that follows is epic in tone (Homer, *Iliad* 22. 139–42). Octavian is compared first to a hawk pursuing doves. The flying in the narrative corresponds to the flying in the simile by a transfusion of terms which is common in similes in Latin epic poetry (West, 1968: 48–9). The elevation of style continues in the second comparison to a huntsman and a hare. We noted the epic flavour of double comparisons on 1. 23. 9–10. Horace keeps up this epic tone by setting the hunting scene in Haemonia, which in Latin poetry is another name for Thessaly. The great warrior who learned his hunting on the slopes of Mount Pelion in Thessaly was Achilles (and here the epic flavour is perhaps enriched by a dash of Pindar) who, according to Pindar, *Nemean* 3. 50, could catch deer without dogs or traps by the speed of his running. We now come to five words in the Latin which do not sit easily in their context, 'in order to put chains on the monster', *daret ut catenis fatale monstrum*. It is very difficult to read this passage, either aloud or silently, without seeing the fatal picture of a huntsman struggling to put chains around a monstrous hare. The translation offered tries to avoid this disaster by setting the simile in brackets but these were not available to the Latin poet. It seems that in straining to make the episode as impressive as possible, Horace has run into a problem which he has not been able to solve. In addition to what we have noticed, Augustus did not pursue Cleopatra personally and the eleven months between Actium and the death of Cleopatra are dramatically telescoped. All in all, then, Horace has made full use of the motifs of Octavian's propaganda, and has at several points even gone beyond it to heighten the case against Cleopatra.

The third section moves to a totally different mode—the madwoman who became a fugitive now becomes a proud heroine. Cleopatra was looking for a nobler death, more befitting her royal ancestry and nobler than the helpless death after vain flight which awaits doves and hares, and which would have awaited her if she had been led in triumph in Rome. In having no womanly fear of the sword she annuls the fear she had shown at Actium. The sword is a reminder of the despairing resistance she tried to organize with Antony when they had reached Alexandria, and it also calls to mind what is said to have happened after she had locked herself in a tomb with all her treasure. When Antony came to the tomb, dying slowly after his attempt to kill himself, she could not open the doors for him but with the aid of her handmaidens pulled up his bleeding body on ropes to take him in by a window. After his death, Octavian's agents arrived and Gallus engaged her in conversation while Proculeius climbed a ladder and entered by the same window through which she had pulled Antony. She immediately reached for a dagger to stab herself but Proculeius took it from her. If Horace is alluding to this melodramatic incident, he is doing so in terms which confer the greatest possible credit on Cleopatra. Another well-known incident reflects less well upon her. When Antony had arrived at Alexandria he found that Cleopatra was engaged in dragging a fleet of ships nearly 40 miles across the neck of land that separates the Mediterranean from the Red Sea (the line of the present Suez Canal) in order to sail away to the south and live in peace far from Octavian's armies. This foolish plan was given up when the ships which had reached the Red Sea were burned by the Arabs of Nabataea on the eastern shore (Plutarch, *Antony* 69; Dio, 51. 7). Horace seems to be denying this story, again presumably to present Cleopatra in a nobler light.

He has also drawn a veil over reports of some even more questionable behaviour, her dealings with Octavian, her attempt to prevent the Alexandrians from resisting him, and her betrayal of Antony in the final battle (Plutarch, *Antony* 72. 1, 76. 3; Dio, 51. 6, 9, and 10).

In line 25 he praises her courage (or endurance, *ausa* can indicate either) in daring to look at the ruins of her palace with serenity on her features. There is no other record of such damage being done or Cleopatra seeing it. The famous story of her death by the bite of an asp is the version of her death as approved by Octavian—an effigy of Cleopatra was carried in his triumph with one asp or two clinging to her body (Plutarch, *Antony* 85–6; Propertius, 3. 11. 53). Horace tells it with masterly economy and immediacy. The serpents are *asperas*, which means 'fierce, deadly', but since she is said to be handling them and the literal meaning of the word is 'rough', he is quietly suggesting the horror of the feel of them. Readers of Horace were not to know that asps are smooth to the touch. When in lines 27–8 her intention is to drink the black poison with her body, there is a similar spread of suggestion. *Atrum* means 'black', but it also means 'deadly'. One version of the suicide is that she applied a serpent to each of her breasts. If this were known to Horace's readers, they would savour the paradox that breasts were drinking, and drinking poison, and drinking what was black. In the first part of the ode Horace went to great lengths to damage the character of Cleopatra, but from *quae generosius* in the middle of line 21, he veers to the opposite tack and does everything in his power to present her in a creditable or sympathetic light.

Horace was a court poet and that is no disadvantage. Some of the world's greatest music, art, and literature has been created for patrons, particularly when the client has believed in the value of his patron's achievements. In the first twenty-one lines of this poem Horace is celebrating the death of a woman who was the enemy of his patron, and by statement, insinuation, and inaccuracy, he has exploited current propaganda to do everything in his power to demolish her character. Why does he then change his approach and do everything in his power to present her in a creditable light? There may be many reasons. Pöschl and others find here evidence for a generous and typically Roman streak in Horace whereby he admires an enemy who suffers death bravely. On this analysis the poem starts with rejoicing over a fallen foe, like the fragment of Alcaeus, but nothing like so brutal, and moves at the end towards a grudging admiration and compassion for a brave woman in appalling adversity. It is thus a truly humane document for its realization of the inner drama of Cleopatra, her *Seelendrama*, and for the human, ethical, and philosophical–tragical aspects of the experiences it describes.

I incline to a different assessment, observing that everything in this ode is played for melodramatic effect and seeing no trace of any particularized understanding of Cleopatra's predicament. How would this poem have looked from Octavian's point of view? He would have welcomed the attack upon Cleopatra's character. Wyke shows that the main points in that attack were used by Augustus before Actium and exploit deep-seated Roman prejudices, against female rulers, for example, and against Orientals, their cowardice and their luxurious living. But Octavian's propaganda after Actium made no play with Cleopatra. Wyke concludes that this is because the image of Cleopatra in defeat was potentially subversive. I think rather that Octavian and his advisers realized that little was to be gained by gloating over the death of a woman. He knew that even Romans were capable of pity and that Antony had been loved and admired. Clemency and civilization were to be planks in the new settlement and the public humiliation of Cleopatra would have been no way to demonstrate the magnanimity of the new regime. Certainly he arranged that the bodies of Antony and Cleopatra should be embalmed and buried in the same tomb. 'The tale of Cleopatra's barbaric death was a godsend to Octavian's propaganda', write Nisbet and Hubbard (410), and Horace certainly gives it centre stage. It is no bad thing in panegyric to exaggerate the pride and ferocity of a patron's enemies after they are dead.

The mention of the Liburnians is a last glance at the myth of the battle of Actium, according to which the huge galleys of Antony and Cleopatra, so heavily armoured that they could not be rammed and so high in the water that they were floating artillery towers, were outmanœuvred by Octavian's smaller, swifter, and more expertly sailed ships, notably a contingent of Liburnian galleys. The ode then ends with a demonstration of the concentrated firepower of the Latin language, seven words each of which is connected by positive or negative charge to each of the others, *privata deduci superbo non humilis mulier triumpho*. A literal translation—I adjust the Loeb by Bennett—(scorning, in sooth, the thought) 'of being taken unqueened to a proud triumph—no humble woman she.' Taking the order of the Latin, we read that the queen is now *privata*, a private person in counterpoint with *regina* in line 7. *Deduci . . . triumpho* strictly means 'carried to a triumph' but must also suggest *duci triumpho*, 'be led in triumph'. *Superbo . . . triumpho* is spread in a hyperbaton to give it a fortissimo and this gap between the adjective *superbo* and the noun *triumpho* is filled by 'no humble woman'. This is not only an allusion to Cleopatra's pride. Romans would know how women were humiliated in triumphs. It must have seemed impossible to Horace to match the power of Cleopatra's own two Greek words, *ou thriambeusomai*, 'I shall never be triumphed over' but he has done so in a

XXXVIII

PERSICOS odi, puer, apparatus,
displicent nexae philyra coronae;
mitte sectari, rosa quo locorum
sera moretur.

simplici myrto nihil allabores   5
sedulus curo: neque te ministrum
dedecet myrtus neque me sub arta
vite bibentem.

'Now it was like all instruments, now like a lonely pipe.' After the patriotic fanfare of 1. 37 Horace ends his book with two short stanzas telling his slave boy that he does not want elaborate provisions as he drinks.

Horace loves the simple life. The first poem in the book implies this in his rejection of politics and of wealth. In 1. 17 his enjoyment of his country estate is a message of gratitude to his patron and an assurance that he will not be forever begging for more and 1. 20 adds to that a deft statement of his own independence. In 1. 31 he joins in the spectacular national celebrations with a little celebration of his own, making clear that his own wishes are modest. To follow the great Cleopatra ode with a poem which, according to Nisbet and Hubbard, 'L. Müller, with remarkable precision, numbered among Horace's three least important productions' shows how Horace values the simple life and how shrewdly and humorously he will protect his independence, well aware, of course, that the simple life is part of Augustan ideology (see Powell). His patrons have a poet, but they do not have a man.

Commentators have not been satisfied with this explanation. Pasquali and many modern scholars see it as a programme poem stating Horace's

different idiom. At such passages translators collapse and one cannot but
envy and admire the freedom and brilliance of James Michie:

> Was she to grace a haughty triumph,
>   dethroned, paraded by
> rude Liburnians? Not Cleopatra!

---

style 17

XXXVIII

I hate Persian luxuries, my boy.
Garlands woven with lime-tree bark give me no pleasure.
There's no need for you to seek out
    the last rose where it lingers.

I am anxious that you should not labour over   5
the simple myrtle. Myrtle is not unbecoming to you
as my cupbearer, or to me as I drink
    in the dense shade of the vine.

commitment to the poetry of wine and love. Fraenkel sees it as a defence
of simplicity of literary style. Popular as the movement is to see poems
as being about poetry, the first interpretation falls short because it fails
to do justice to the humanity and savourable particularity of the poem
and puts in their place a boring generality. The same objection applies to
Fraenkel's interpretation, which is further weakened by the fact that
Horace's style is anything but simple. But my own view also is that there
is more to the poem than meets the eye.

The clue is Ganymede, the lovely Trojan boy caught up by the eagle
to be Jupiter's cupbearer and lover. This combination of employments
was not unusual in Greece or in Rome (see *Odes* 1. 29. 7–8 and the score
of references in the index under 'Ganymede' in Dover's *Greek
Homosexuality* or the frequent play with the idea in the twelfth book of
the *Palatine Anthology* (168, 175, 180, 194, 199, 220, 221, 230, 254) or
nearly a score of instances in Martial, for example 9. 93, where the poet
asks the boy pouring his wine for ten kisses on the grounds that there are
ten letters in the name of the emperor Domitianus).

But the hint, though delicate, is clear in the second stanza of the text.
Myrtle is the badge of Venus. Apart from this passage it is mentioned six

times in the odes and often with an amatory implication, as at 1. 4. 9, 1. 25. 18, 2. 7. 25, and perhaps at 2. 15. 4–6 and 3. 4. 19. Here the emphasis is audible as *myrto* in 5 is picked up by *myrtus* in 7—'do no added work (*nihil allabores*) on the simple myrtle. Myrtle looks not bad on you as you my cupbearer or on me as I drink beneath the vine.' From this we know that Horace is alone with the boy, that Horace and the boy are each wearing a garland of Venus' plant and that Horace finds that it suits the boy as it is—he does not need to go and work at it to make it more elaborate. After all these statements how can we not hear the quiet compliment, the hint of consideration and of gentle bibulous and amatory impatience? Looking back over the ode from this point we now see the garlands in the second line are unpleasing partly because they are woven and the boy would have to weave them. We catch also the flavour of the command in line 3. *Sectari* means not simply 'search for' but rather 'search strenuously for' and *mitte* implies that the boy has been doing so and Horace wants him not to bother—'Give up hunting for the last rose.' The singular *rosa* suggests that he is so conscientious that he would go to all this trouble for Horace for *one* rose. My translation of line 6 goes against the usual view. Nisbet and Hubbard rightly point out that *sedulus* 'refers to the officiousness of an over-zealous servant' and they therefore attach it to the verb *allabores*. But the line-break gives *sedulus* a nudge towards *curo* and without *sedulus*, the verb *curo* sounds thin. The Latin has better balance if *nihil allabores* has *sedulus curo* as a counterweight: 'I care conscientiously that you should not do any more work on that myrtle' (to overinterpret: 'as though I were your busy slave and you my master'). To allaborate the point, we look back at *apparatus*, a compound of *parare*, in the first line and become aware that it carries just a hint that these Persian luxuries have to be pre*pared*. Again Horace is letting it be known that he wants the boy to stop all that and come and drink with him.

There is one other reason for seeing adumbrations of homosexual love in this poem. It is Horace's ambition often expressed and often implied to emulate the poetry of Alcaeus in Latin verse and Horace's stereotype of Alcaeus' poetry includes poems addressed to his boy lover. This was made explicit in 1. 32. 9–12, where after allusion to Alcaeus' poems about his part in civil war and about storms at sea, drinking-poems and love poems, Horace tells us that Alcaeus used to sing of 'Lycus with his jet-black eyes and jet-black hair'. Homosexual love is part of the tradition which Horace is consciously revitalizing and it appears quite often in his poetry, in this book in 4, 9, and 29. It is also, for example, the subject of a vivid programme poem which is also a love poem at 4. 1, quoted in the comments on 1. 9. It is not at all unHoratian if Horace has chosen to remind us with a smile of his poetic affiliations in this last little poem of his first book.

Commentators array dozens of earlier Greek and Latin poems in which masters give instructions to their slaves to prepare for drinking sessions, often giving them long shopping lists. The best fruit culled from these parallels is that they show the greater economy of Horace, since there are only three items on his shopping list and two of them are scored out. The parallels could be made to work harder. In the other poems it is usually clear that there are going to be guests at the party. The implication in 1. 38 is that there are to be no guests, that Horace and his slave boy are the only wearers of garlands. Further, in the other poems the slaves are there to receive orders. There is no suggestion of any other personal relationship between master and slave to compare with the near half-dozen which flicker in this short poem to give it a light, affectionate tone which is totally foreign to the 'models'.

'Down the swift Hebrus to the Lesbian shore' writes Milton, demonstrating that the important thing about poetry is that it should work, not that we should know how it works. It may nevertheless sometimes be useful to pause, as we did at the end of 1. 37, and look closely at technicalities. In 1. 38 the first stanza consists of three negative propositions, three things the poet does not want, and the tricolon, as so often in Latin, ascends to a third element longer than the two which have gone before. Often each of the three cola begins with the same word or words but such rhetorical tooling would not give Horace the simple, intimate tone he needs in this poem, so he rather masks the parallelism. It is difficult not to translate with anaphora: 'I hate Persian luxuries, I dislike garlands of lime-tree bark' but such point is false to the tone. It is part of the texture and therefore of the essence that 'I hate', *odi* comes second in its line and 'they displease', *displicent* comes first. The second stanza also consists of three propositions, this time three positive wishes of the poet, but the last two merge into one so that there is enough balance to gratify our expectations and again enough variety to enrich the music. At the same time the last two propositions are so subtly welded to the verse structure that we almost hear the relationship between the cup-bearing slave and the wine-drinking master, as *neque te ministrum* at the end of one line is echoed by *neque me sub arta* at the end of the next.

Syndikus, whose commentary is excellent in this area, points out also that the ode has a strong concentric movement. The negative command in lines 3–4, expressed without a negative word, is balanced by the prohibition in lines 5–6, expressed with the negative *nihil*, 'nothing'. Horace would not have counted, but Syndikus might have added that each of these cola consists of sixteen syllables. Such statistics can be death to poetry but not if they lead us to appreciate more of the music and logic of the verse. Here, for instance, the command and the prohibition sit exactly in the same position in the verses, but yet again mathematical symmetry is avoided because the quantities of *sēdŭlŭs cūrō* are teasingly and pleasingly varied from the quantities of *sēră mŏrētŭr*. And does it give pleasure to hear how the Persianisms with which the first stanza begins are answered at the beginning of the second stanza by the simplicity Horace prefers? Is one right also to see and savour the lingering of the late rose at the dying fall of the first stanza, *rosa quo locorum sera moretur*, as answered in the last words of the second by the drinking under the vine, *neque me sub arta vite bibentem*?

Appendix: A Conspectus of Metres Used in the Odes of Book 1

See section on the Sound in the Introduction. (Syllables marked ‾ are long, ◡ short, ~ either long or short.)

1. First Asclepiad: (a series of Asclepiadic lines):
   ‒‒ ‒◡◡‒ | ‒◡◡‒ ◡~
   All of the Asclepiadic metres are based upon the choriambic foot ‒◡◡‒.

2. Sapphic: (three Sapphic lines followed by an Adonius):
   ‒◡‒‒‒ | ◡◡‒◡‒~ (three times)
   ‒◡◡‒~

3. Fourth Asclepiad: (Glyconics alternating with Asclepiads):
   ‒‒ ‒◡◡‒ ◡~
   ‒‒ ‒◡◡‒ | ‒◡◡‒ ◡~

4. Third Archilochean: (the only use of this metre in the odes):
   ‒◡◡‒◡◡‒◡◡ ‒◡◡ | ‒◡‒◡‒‒
   ‒‒◡‒ ‒‒◡‒ ◡‒‒

5. Third Asclepiad: (two Asclepiads followed by a Pherecretean and a Glyconic):
   ‒‒ ‒◡◡‒ | ‒◡◡‒ ◡~ (twice)
   ‒‒ ‒◡◡‒ ‒
   ‒‒ ‒◡◡‒ ◡~

6. Second Asclepiad: (three Asclepiads followed by a Glyconic):
   ‒‒ ‒◡◡‒ | ‒◡◡‒ ◡~ (3 times)
   ‒‒ ‒◡◡‒ ◡~

7. First Archilochean: (Dactylic Hexameter alternating with Dactylic Tetrameter) (six dactyls alternating with four dactyls):
   ‒◡◡‒◡◡‒◡◡‒◡◡‒◡◡ ‒~
   ‒◡◡‒◡◡‒◡◡ ‒~

8. Greater Sapphic: (Aristophaneus alternating with Greater Sapphic):
   ‒◡◡‒◡‒~
   ‒◡‒‒‒ | ◡◡‒ | ‒◡◡‒◡‒~

9. Alcaic:
   ~‒◡‒‒ | ‒◡◡‒◡~ (twice)
   ~‒◡‒‒‒◡‒~
   ‒◡◡‒◡◡‒◡‒~

10. Sapphic as 2.

11. Fifth Asclepiad:
    ‒‒ ‒∪∪‒ | ‒∪∪‒ | ‒∪∪‒ ∪∼

12. Sapphic as 2.
13. Fourth Asclepiad as 3.
14. Third Asclepiad as 5.
15. Second Asclepiad as 6.
16 and 17.   Alcaic as 9.
18. Fifth Asclepiad as 11.
19. Fourth Asclepiad as 3.
20. Sapphic as 2.
21. Third Asclepiad as 5.
22. Sapphic as 2.
23. Third Asclepiad as 5.
24. Second Asclepiad as 6.
25. Sapphic as 2.
26 and 27.   Alcaic as 9.
28. First Archilochean as 7.
29. Alcaic as 9.
30. Sapphic as 2.
31. Alcaic as 9.
32. Sapphic as 2.
33. Second Asclepiad as 6.
34 and 35.   Alcaic as 9.
36. Fourth Asclepiad as 3.
37. Alcaic as 9.
38. Sapphic as 2.

List of Works Cited

Allen, W. S., *Vox Latina* (Cambridge, 1970).

Badian, E., *Philologus*, 129 (1985), 82–98.

Bennett, C. E., *Horace: The Odes and Epodes* (London, 1919).

Bentley, R., *Q. Horatius Flaccus*[3] (Amsterdam, 1728).

Borthwick, E. K., *Classical Quarterly*, 26 (1976), 198–200.

Boyle, A. J., *Ramus*, 2 (1973), 174.

Bradshaw, A., *Horace in Sabinis* (Collection Latomus, ccvi: Studies in Latin Literature and Roman History, v, ed. C. Deroux), 160–86.

Brown, R. D., *Lucretius on Love and Sex: A Commentary on De Rerum Natura 4.1030–1287* (Leiden, 1987).

—— *Phoenix*, 45 (1991), 326–40.

Cairns, F. J., *Liverpool Classical Monthly*, 1 (1976), 71–7, with discussion, 78–84.

—— *Tibullus: A Hellenistic Poet at Rome* (Cambridge, 1979), chapter 4.

—— *Author and Audience in Latin Literature*, ed. T. Woodman and J. Powell (Cambridge, 1992) 84–109.

Campbell, D. A., *Greek Lyric with an English Translation*, 4 vols. (Cambridge, Mass., 1982–92).

Carter, J. M., *The Battle of Actium* (London, 1970), 229–30.

Commager, S., *The Odes of Horace* (New Haven, Conn., 1962).

Connor, P., *Horace's Lyric Poetry: The Force of Humour* (Berwick, Victoria, 1987).

D'Arms, J. H., *Romans on the Bay of Naples* (Cambridge, Mass., 1970), 56–7, 173–4.

Dover, K. J., *Greek Homosexuality* (London, 1978).

Edmunds, L., *From a Sabine Jar* (Chapel Hill, NC, 1992), 54–7.

Fowler, H. W., *Modern English Usage*, revised E. Gowers (Oxford, 1965).

Fraenkel, E., *Horace* (Oxford, 1957).

Gigante M., *Filodemo in Italia* (Florence, 1990).

—— *Studi Italiani di Filologia Classica*, 7 (1989), 3–6.

Goar, R. J., *Classical Journal*, 68 (1972), 116–18.

Goold, G. P., *Catullus* (London, 1983), 19–27.

Griffin, J., *Journal of Roman Studies*, 66 (1976), 87–105, revised version in his *Latin Poets and Roman Life* (London, 1985), 1–31.

Jenkyns, R., *Three Classical Poets* (London, 1982), 32.

—— *Latomus*, 41 (1982), 146–51.

Jocelyn, H. D., *Classical Philology*, 77 (1982), 330–5.

Kennedy, D. F., *The Arts of Love* (Cambridge, 1993), 60.

Kenney, E. J., *Gnomon*, 34 (1962), 313.

Kiessling, A., *Q. Horatius Flaccus*: Oden² (1890), revised by R. Heinze (1960)¹⁰.

Kissel, W., *Horaz 1936–1975*: *Eine Gesamtbibliographie* in *Aufstieg und Niedergang der Römischen Welt*, 2. 31. 3 (Berlin, 1981).

Kukula, R. C. W., *Wiener Studien*, 34 (1912), 237–43.

Kumaniecki, C. F., *Eos*, 42 (1947), 5–23.

Lyne, R. O. A. M., *The Latin Love Poets* (Oxford, 1980), 196–201.

McKay, A. G., and Shepherd, D. M., *Roman Lyric Poetry*: *Catullus and Horace* (London, 1969).

Macleod, C., *Greece and Rome*, 26 (1979), 31, reprinted in his *Collected Essays* (Oxford, 1983), 229.

MacMullen, R., *Historia*, 31 (1982), 484–502.

Martindale, C., *Redeeming the Text* (Cambridge, 1993), 8.

Mette, H. J., *Museum Helveticum*, 18 (1961), 136–9.

Michie, J., *The Odes of Horace* (London, 1963).

Moritz, L. A., *Classical Quarterly*, 18 (1968), 116–31.

Nietzsche, F. W., *Werke*: *Taschenausgabe* (Leipzig, 1906), x. 343.

Nisbet, R. G. M., 'Horace's *Epodes* and History', in A. J. Woodman and D. West (eds.), *Poetry and Politics in the Age of Augustus* (Cambridge, 1984), 12.

—— and Hubbard, M., *Horace*: Odes *Book 1* (Oxford, 1970).

Page, T. E., *Q. Horatii Flacci Carminum Libri IV Epodon Liber* (Basingstoke, 1895).

Pasquali, G., *Orazio lirico* (Florence, 1920), reprint by A. La Penna (1964).

Perret, J., *Horace*, trans. B. Humez (New York, 1964), 94.

Pöschl, V., *Horazische Lyrik* (Heidelberg, 1970), 110–16.

Postgate, J. P., *Classical Quarterly*, 16 (1922), 33.

Powell, A., 'The *Aeneid* and the Embarrassments of Augustus', in Powell (ed.), *Roman Poetry and Propaganda* (London, 1992), 160.

Quinn, K., *Horace*: *The Odes* (London, 1980).

Romano, E., *Q. Orazio Flacco*: *Le opere*, i. *Le Odi* (Rome, 1991).

Reckford, K., *Classical Journal*, 55 (1959), 25–33.

Sydenham, E. A., *The Coinage of the Roman Republic* (London, 1952).

Syndikus, H. P., *Die Lyrik des Horaz*, i (Darmstadt, 1972).

Traill, D. A., *Classical Journal*, 78 (1982), 131–7.

West, D., *Reading Horace* (Edinburgh, 1967).

—— *Journal of Roman Studies*, 59 (1969), 48–9.

—— *Proceedings of the Virgil Society*, 21 (1993), 1–16.

Wickham, E. C., *Quinti Horati Flacci Opera Omnia*[3], i (Oxford, 1896).

Wilkinson, L. P., *Horace and his Lyric Poetry* (Cambridge, 1945), 4.

—— *Golden Latin Artistry* (Cambridge, 1970), 72.

Will, E. L., *Classical Philology*, 77 (1982), 240–5.

Wiseman, T. P., *Catullus and his World* (Cambridge, 1985), 266–9.

Woodman, A. J., *Classical Philology* (1980), 60–7.

Wright, J. R. G., *Mnemosyne*, 27 (1964), 44–52.

Wyke, M., 'Augustan Cleopatras: Female Power and Poetic Authority', in A. Powell (ed.), *Roman Poetry and Propaganda* (London, 1992), 128.

Brief Notes on Ancient Authors

The references are to page numbers, given only where the authors are discussed.

AESCHYLUS (525/4–456 BC): Greek tragedian.

AFRANIUS (b. *c*.150 BC): Latin comedian.

ALCAEUS OF MITYLENE (7th–6th century BC): Greek lyric poet. 6, 42–3, 48–9, 67–9, 154, 182, 188, 192

ANACREON (b. *c*.570 BC): Greek lyric poet. 108

APPIAN (early 2nd century BC): Author of Roman history in Greek.

ATHENAEUS (early 2nd century BC): Author of *Deipnosophistae*, 'The Learned Banqueters', a polymathic dialogue at a symposium.

AUGUSTUS (63 BC–AD 14): *Res Gestae* is the official account of his achievements.

BACCHYLIDES (b. *c*.518 BC): Greek choral lyric poet.

CALLIMACHUS (*c*.305–240 BC): Greek poet and scholar at the Alexandrian Library of the Ptolemies. 28, 33, 122, 149–50

CATULLUS (84?–54? BC): Lyric poet. 28, 64, 78, 80, 100–2, 104, 107, 152–3, 176–8, 180–1

CICERO (106–43 BC): Author of speeches, letters, and philosophical dialogues.

DIO CASSIUS (consul AD 205 and 229): Author of Roman history in Greek.

EURIPIDES (*c*.485–*c*.406 BC): Greek tragedian.

GALLUS (69–26 BC): Creator of Roman elegy. Only fragments survive.

GELLIUS (AD *c*.130–*c*.180): Author of *Noctes Atticae*, 'Attic Nights', learned essays on mainly literary questions.

HESIOD (*c*.680–50 BC): Greek didactic poet. 87

HOMER (before 700 BC): Greek epic poet. 29–30, 34, 46–7, 74–5, 138

HYGINUS (end of 1st century BC): Polymath and librarian of Palatine Library.

LUCRETIUS (98?–55? BC): Didactic poet of Epicureanism. 24, 85, 122–3, 132, 162–4, 166

MELEAGER (*c*.100 BC): Greek epigrammatist and anthologist. 69

MOSCHUS (*c.*150 BC): Greek pastoral poet. 158–9

NONNUS (5th? century AD): Greek epic poet.

OVID (43 BC–AD 17): Latin poet. 105, 121

PALATINE ANTHOLOGY: A collection of Greek epigrams written from 4th century BC onwards, compiled around AD 980. 22, 69, 98–9, 119, 135, 143

PHILODEMUS (110–*c.*38 BC): Greek epigrammatist and philosopher. 51, 98–9

PINDAR (518–438 BC): Greek choral lyric poet. 6, 32, 56–7, 174–5

PLAUTUS (before 251 BC–at least 184 BC): Latin comedian.

PLINY THE ELDER (AD 23/4–79): Encyclopaedist.

PLUTARCH (before AD 50–after 120): Greek biographer and essayist.

POSIDIPPUS (*c.*270 BC): Greek epigrammatist. 143

PROPERTIUS (47?–after 16 BC): Writer of elegies produced 28–16 BC. 105, 117, 138, 148, 185

SAPPHO (7th–6th century BC): Greek lyric poet. 5, 64, 142

SIMONIDES (*c.*556–468 BC.) Greek lyric and elegiac poet.

STATIUS (AD 45–96): Epic poet.

STESICHORUS (*c.*630–*c.*554 BC): Greek lyric poet.

STRABO (64/3 BC–AD 21 or later): Greek geographer and historian.

SUETONIUS (after 70?–after 122): Biographer.

THEON (2nd century AD): Greek rhetorician.

TIBULLUS (55?–19 BC): Writer of two books of elegies produced in 26–25 BC. 105, 117, 156–8

VARRO (116–27 BC): Polymath.

VIRGIL (70–19 BC): Writer of *Eclogues* in 39 and *Georgics* in 29. The *Aeneid* was edited after his death in 19 BC. 12–13, 92, 109–10, 112–4, 118–9, 146–8, 159

Select Index of Names

Index of Topics

203